THE ENDLESS FALL

True Stories From an early Skydiver

by Mike Swain

eShore

Pittsburgh, PA

ISBN 1-58501-054-5

Trade Paperback
©Copyright 2000 Mike Swain
All rights reserved
First printing - 2000
Library of Congress # 99-67089

Request for information should be addressed to:

CeShore Publishing Co.
The Sterling Building
440 Friday Road
Pittsburgh, PA 15209
www.ceshore.com

CeShore Publishing Co. is an imprint of SterlingHouse Publisher, Inc.

Cover design: Michelle S. Vennare - SterlingHouse Publisher, Inc.
Typesetting: Lucy Matyjaszczyk
Photographer: Mike Swain
in collaboration with John Cloud and Dick Dickinson

Printed in Canada

Dedication

This book is dedicated to my friends who have died prematurely. They were all skydivers and jump pilots who helped make sport parachuting the safe and modern sport that it is today. May they have blue skies forever!

PHIL TODD, 52 - airplane crash 09/12/65
RON ZIMMERMAN, 31 - airplane crash 10/16/66
PAUL DUNCAN, 33 - skydiving accident 06/21/68
LEO "Iron Man" KRISKE, 45 - killed in action 8/25/68
BILLY REVIS, 24 - airplane crash 02/21/75
TONY PATTERSON, 32 - skydiving accident 05/29/76
JOHN CONWAY, 33 - skydiving accident 11/20/77
JACK SPAHR, 37 - skydiving accident 05/12/79
PAUL HEALY, 47 - heart attack 11/21/80
JIM ELMAKER, 46 - blood cancer 11/07/81
JIM SHOCKLEY, 39 - suicide 10/08/84
WAYNE FULLER, 41 - airplane crash 10/17/87
JOE SMITH, 52 - heart attack/airplane crash 5/13/90
CHARLIE HILLARD, 54 - airplane crash 4/16/96
BAYLISS FAIELLA, 54 - cancer 8/17/98
STEVE SNYDER, 64 - airplane crash 6/19/99

To my good buddy
Jack La Londe

I certainly enjoyed
jumping with the
infamous Delray
Aerial Circus many
years ago. I hope
all the guys are
alive & well.

Mike

Acknowledgements

My warmest thanks to all the individuals
who helped make this book possible.

Especially:

ROSEMARY, my wife
POLLY, my sister
& TONY, my brother

CONTENTS

CHAPTER 1: It's A Good Day To Die 1

CHAPTER 2: Fear 5

CHAPTER 3: Duffy 9

CHAPTER 4: Bob 15

CHAPTER 5: Malfunctions 19

CHAPTER 6: The First Malfunction 27

CHAPTER 7: John 31

CHAPTER 8: Landings 35

CHAPTER 9: Demos 41

CHAPTER 10: Jim 51

CHAPTER 11: Jumping Blind 55

CHAPTER 12: Billy 59

CHAPTER 13: The Student Who Almost Died 65

CHAPTER 14: The First Night Jump 71

CHAPTER 15: Paul 79

CHAPTER 16: Don 83

CHAPTER 17: The Watermelon 89

CHAPTER 18: Going Low 93

CHAPTER 19: Big Paul 101

CHAPTER 20: Photography 103

CHAPTER 21: Dave 109

CHAPTER 22: Bruce 113

CHAPTER 23: The Altitude Record 121

CHAPTER 24: Bill 129

CHAPTER 25: Chuteless 141

CHAPTER 26: Rose 146

CHAPTER 27: The Wedding 149

CHAPTER 28: Neil and The Great Swamp Jump 153

CHAPTER 29: The Maltese Cross 163

CHAPTER 30: Wide Angle 171

CHAPTER 31: Not Yet 175

GLOSSARY 176

Chapter One
IT'S A GOOD DAY TO DIE

— July 1967 —

I turned off the highway onto the short dirt road leading to Buchan Air field near Englewood, Florida. It was a hot summer day. I was driving my '66 candy-apple-red Corvette convertible. I geared down without braking and let the back end break loose into the turn, fishtailing as I powered out of the skid. I kind of liked the dramatic entrance haloed with a cloud of dust and tried to improve on it each time. I was looking forward to a day of skydiving but, as usual, I was late. The jump plane, a blue, red, and white Cessna 182, was already taxiing toward the end of the runway with the first load of the day. I roared down the short dirt road toward the packing area but on the spur of the moment skidded off onto the grass in a wide "S" turn and pulled up to a stop opposite the jump plane that was now about to take off. Two friends of mine were in the back of the plane bedecked in jump gear: olive grey mains on their backs, front-mounted reserves, gloves, altimeters, goggles, and helmets. A static-line student, sweating out his second or third jump, was sitting on the floor next to the pilot.

The Cessna and my Corvette sat side by side, aimed down the runway. Sitting almost under the wing tip, I looked over at John Clement, the pilot, and with the clutch in, revved the powerful 300-hp 327 engine ... wahaaa! ... wahaaa! ... like a car in a James Dean movie. The student's eyes were really big. John looked over at me, smiled, shook his head to himself as he always did when I pulled some damn fool stunt, and hit the throttle. I popped the clutch and the plane and Corvette started down the runway neck and neck. We flashed by the packing area where everyone stood mouths agape, never before having seen a car race a plane. The plane quickly outdistanced me and took off into the cloudless blue sky. I slowed down and pulled off the runway back onto the dirt road leading back toward the packing area and skidded to a stop in my normal parking place under the pine tree.

I felt great! I was full of youth, health, and adventure. The Sioux Indians used to greet each other before battle with the saying, "It's a good day to die!" That attitude was how skydiving was to me. It was a glorious battlefield and you had to be ready and willing to die for the privilege of being one of the few chosen combatants. Death came swiftly to anyone momentarily careless or unlucky. Like soldiers in battle, jumpers made close friends — at times, closer than family. But you paid a price. Occasionally those friends were killed without warning. As a result, we all had a fatalistic view of life and a macabre sense of humor. Our standard joke to wide-eyed newcomers was that we had a club life insurance policy: "If a jumper 'bounces,' we drag his body to the nearest highway and throw it in front of a truck so his wife can collect his life insurance." This was one of our more subtle jokes, but non-jumpers didn't seem to appreciate the humor. The other variation of this was that we'd put the body back in the plane because if he didn't go back up and jump again right away, he'd always be scared.

But death didn't scare us as much as the possibility of a bad injury; that is, an injury bad enough to keep us from jumping. We expected to be hurt; that was part of the game. We could ignore pain and we could conquer fear, but not to be able to jump would be worse than death. Why? Let me try to explain.

On a normal weekend, a hard-core jumper would make three or four jumps if he had the money. The average jump was made from an altitude of 7,500 feet, which allowed about 30 seconds of freefall before the ripcord was pulled at 2,000 feet to deploy the parachute. That means a gung-ho jumper would get in about two minutes of freefall time on an average weekend. This jumper would have had more vivid, memorable experiences in those two minutes than he would have in the rest of the week's 10,078 minutes. Compared with the adventure of skydiving, a normal life at home and at work became almost meaningless. Skydiving was 3-D Technicolor with Surround-sound; the rest of life was silent black-and-white. I used to think of skydiving as "reality" and all the rest a dream. My job simply became a necessary evil to pay for jumping. The majority of my life became just a waiting period until I could jump again.

When you jump out of a plane, the tremendous adrenaline rush speeds up the brain to the point that you are thinking and reacting in fractions of a second. A skydiver seeing movies of himself shot and projected in slow motion is usually not aware that it is slow motion. To him it looks like normal speed because that is how he experienced it and how he remembers it. Footage shot at normal speed looks fast and jerky, like old silent movies. That adrenaline rush was addictive. We became hooked on the action, the danger, and the excitement. The more you did it, the more you *wanted* to do it, and the more you *needed* to do it.

While the adrenaline slows your sense of time and speeds up your reactions, it also immunizes you to pain. Many times without realizing it, I would rip off half a fingernail or get badly cut in freefall, only to discover the wound back on the ground. I would be repacking my chute when, to my surprise, I would find myself dripping blood all over my gear.

But skydiving at this time, in the 1960s, was much more than just jumping out of a plane. It was a way of life. You lived, talked, ate, and dreamed skydiving. I got into a bad habit of classifying people into just two categories: jumpers or non-jumpers. And I had no use at all for non-jumpers. I missed most family functions because I was at the drop zone every weekend and holiday. But the reason I was at the DZ was because anything else to me was a monumental waste of time. I don't know what my family thought of me because Easter, Thanksgiving, or Christmas day found me skydiving at Zephyrhills, DeLand, or Indiantown, instead of at family gatherings. If I had to be around non-jumpers, I was bored to tears. On the other hand, non-jumpers found the life-and-death exploits of skydivers fascinating — up to a point. And that point was when they foolishly wanted to talk about something other than skydiving. The wives and girlfriends of skydivers became sick to death of jump stories, and most parties polarized into the men talking jumping and the women trying to talk about something else — *anything* else! Ultimately skydivers were boring as hell because they talked about only one thing: jumping.

This macho attitude applied to all the other activities we did, whether it was driving a car or hang-gliding. If it wasn't dangerous, if it wasn't on the edge, it wasn't worth doing. I hated to watch football because I felt a little jealous of the players. They were getting the glory and the money for something that really wasn't so dangerous in comparison to skydiving. I had nothing but disdain for the armchair quarterbacks gathered around the TV who had never put themselves at risk in their lives. How many people, including professional athletes, had ever put their life on the line for *any* reason, much less a sport?

Putting your life on the line was what it was all about. That's what we did every time we got in the plane. If you didn't pull the ripcord when skydiving, you died. It was that simple. You died even if you had planned to pull the ripcord but simply lost track of altitude. It is a very unforgiving sport. I used to tell first-time jump students that if they weren't prepared to die that day, they should go home and take up bowling. I truly felt it was very important to have the proper mental attitude to take up this sport. In my opinion, the student jumper should fully understand that he was exposing himself to death or injury, and that a decision to learn skydiving should be made only after careful consideration. For myself, I felt that when your time was up, it was up, unless, of course, you were just stupid, careless, or suicidal. If it was your prescribed time to die, it didn't matter whether you were in freefall, walking across a street, or home in bed. But given a choice, "I'd rather it be in freefall," most of us declared. It was the old cowboy philosophy of dying with your boots on. It could be called macho or fatalistic but, as "neat" as it sounded to us, it actually worked only as a philosophy. There was nothing "neat" in watching a friend "bounce," or seeing a body with the bone structure of tapioca pudding.

In the skydiving world, if you died in an accident, it seemed you not only lost your life, you also lost some of your reputation as a good skydiver. As trivial as that sounds, the potential loss of face may have kept many of us alive. A "good" skydiver was supposed to be able to take it right to the edge but not fall off; to "push the envelope," in the parlance of fighter pilots. If he failed, then maybe he wasn't such a good skydiver after all. It didn't matter if the accident wasn't his fault, or simply bad luck. In some mysterious unspoken way, ability

3

and skill were supposed to transcend luck or fate. So this concept was a philosophy of life, not death. We didn't have a "death wish" as much as a "life wish." To us, close brushes with death actually enhanced life, made us appreciate and savor it even more. Action and danger were the spices added to the otherwise bland diet of existence. In other words, skydiving was so much fun, it was worth risking your life for. So much for philosophy.

Chapter Two

FEAR

Let's get one thing straight. Height can kill you. Your body is smart. It knows this. I have my doubts about anybody who looks down from a height, *any* height, and is not scared. Self-preservation is one of the brain's primary axioms and rightly so. Just falling off a curb has killed people. Fear is healthy; it keeps you alive.

Skydiving is not natural in either form or function, so overriding the body's natural safeguards is, for the most part, what a student jumper must achieve. *And*, if fear cannot be totally mastered, at least it can be subverted and used for a more constructive purpose than pure panic. Fear is as natural an emotional response as pain is a physical one. They work hand in hand to keep a being healthy and alive. Pain is there to remind you not to go too far. Bend an arm and it will hurt, for example. Bend it further and the pain increases. Bend it too far and it will break. That is the danger that the pain is trying to signal. The brain, in the meantime, will store this information for future reference. You will be careful after that not to bend your arm too far. If some bully says, "I'm going to bend your arm!", you will experience fear. If he jumps forward to grab your arm, that "fear" will cause a physical reaction. Your body will secrete adrenaline into your system to give you instant strength to flee or resist.

The brain also has some fear instincts hard-wired into it that are not dependent on any learning experience. Fear of height is one of these. Fear itself is nothing to be ashamed of, or even to be avoided, since it will give you strength in an emergency. Panic, however, is counterproductive and dangerous in a situation that demands immediate action. Panic is something a skydiver must learn to control when he needs to override the body's natural tendency to freeze.

For the first few jumps, getting out of an airplane in flight is not only dangerous, it's frightening! The problem is that most people have never experienced anything like this. Most people have never been in an open airplane. When they fly, it's either in a big commercial airliner where the only view of the ground is through a tiny plexiglass window in air-conditioned comfort or in a small private plane safely enclosed and belted in. Not only have they never thought of getting out of a perfectly good airplane, they have never had that cold icicle of primal fear deep in their gut where breath becomes short, sweat beads on the forehead, and palms get slippery with moisture. Normal people do not put their life on the line — not on purpose, and certainly not for a sport.

Before going to the trouble of training potential students, I always liked to take them up in the jump plane as observers to give them a preview of what to expect. When we began our jump run and popped open the in-flight jump door, I watched their reaction as the ice-cold ninety-mile-an-hour slipstream slapped them in the face and took their breath away. Later, safely on the ground, I listened to their reactions to having watched the jumpers get out of the open door, only to fall away, going from full size to ant size in a few seconds, then continue to fall for twenty-five more seconds against the unmoving background of the earth. This told a lot about the person. It tended to separate the "I always wanted to make one jump" people from the "Let's go do it" people. There's nothing worse than taking days of your time and experience to train students, only to have one of them refuse to get out of the plane. When that happens, it's embarrassing and disappointing for both the jumpmaster and the student.

Along with an altimeter and stopwatch, we used to carry a sheath knife strapped to the top of the front-mounted reserve. This was to cut lines in an emergency, one of the leftovers from the paratrooper days. Once, one of our students froze in jump position while standing outside the plane on the step. He had a death-grip on the strut and, with a determined shake of his head, refused either to jump or get back in the plane. There was an equal danger of the plane stalling from lack of air speed if the student stayed out there too long or if, in trying to get back in the plane, the student fouled his gear on the wheel or tail. In either case, everyone in the plane stood a good chance of being killed. The jumpmaster had to take some kind of action. In this case, the jumpmaster decided simply to reach out with one leg and kick the student free of the strut. Instead of dislodging him, the kick galvanized the student into action. Holding on with one hand, he pulled out the reserve knife and threatened his way back into the plane. The next day we removed the knives from all the student reserves.

As a jumpmaster, I always had the attitude that if anyone didn't want to jump, it was no disgrace to get back in the plane and land with it. But if this *did* happen, usually they never wanted to attempt to jump again.

One time, one of my students changed his mind on the step, so I yelled to him over the engine noise to get back into the plane. He turned to get back in, slipped and fell off, inadvertently making a perfect jump. Amazingly, he continued in the sport to become a good skydiver.

One of the funniest student stories happened at an airport in Bartow, Florida where Bob Overstreet and Chuck Henderson had just started a new jump club . My good friend Duffy Nathan knew them, so we decided to drive up there and make a few jumps. They told us that they had recently talked a pilot into flying for them who owned his own Cessna 182. This pilot had never flown jumpers before and, for some reason, when he arrived and removed his door, they immediately loaded the plane with a static-line student and three jumpers. No one went over to brief the pilot on "how to fly jumpers" and he innocently took off with his first jump load with no special instructions. Wouldn't you know it — the student froze on the step. Nothing the jumpmaster could do would dislodge him. Not knowing any better, the pilot lost air speed and suddenly the plane stalled out. The plane instantly rolled into a dive and flipped over on its back. Actually, this was good because when the student hit hard, flat on his back on the underside of the wing, the impact broke his death-grip on the strut. He slid down the entire length of the wing and sheared off the "gull-wing" tip. The static line pulled open his pack, and his parachute opened clear of the plane. He landed bruised and bewildered and never jumped again. The other jumpers managed to climb hand over hand out the door despite the G-forces of the spin, freefall clear of the plane and open their parachutes safely, although dangerously low. The pilot finally was able to pull out of the spin at tree-top height and flew away. The funny part was that he never came back for his door. They never heard from him again.

Chapter Three
DUFFY

D uffy Nathan was a real piece of work! I've never met anyone before or since who even came close. At the time I first met him, he was an ex-Navy man in his mid-thirties. He was of medium height, stocky but not fat; not muscled either. It was more like his extra bulk was made up of solid flesh rather than flab, and this tended to round off his figure. He had a military crew cut and a cocky attitude that bordered on rudeness. He could be a foul-mouthed, sloppy drunk that only the Navy could spawn, or he could charm the pants off anybody. He told me once with pride that a shipmate of his could swear for a solid five minutes without repeating the same word twice. Duffy came in a close second. Often he would make you laugh at the same time as he was chewing you out for some real or imaginary infraction. It was his colorful way of combining swear words in a new and unexpected way that was so funny. The more graphic it was, the funnier it became. When I finally had to introduce him to my parents, I steeled myself for some awful obscenity to pop out of his mouth at any moment. I was still holding my breath when he left and my parents exclaimed how lucky I was to have such a fine young man as a friend. After that I was totally at ease in Duffy's company in high or low society. I realized he could hold his own in either situation.

There was no doubt that Duffy was the "king" of our club, the Mission Valley Skydivers. He had been "burned" earlier by a disagreement between the officers of the old club who democratically voted him out of office. He simply withdrew his support and let the club fall apart. When he reorganized a new club, it had no meetings, no official rules and, most emphatically, no club officers. Duffy ruled despotically. He happened to be the ASO, the Area Safety Officer, which gave him a lot of authority. An ASO was an experienced jumper who was appointed by PCA, the Parachute Club of America (later changed to United States Parachute Association, USPA), to oversee the rules and regulations of this national organization within his particular geographic location. Being the ASO entitled Duffy to either approve or disapprove any sport parachuting activity in this region, which loosely covered a huge area from Tampa to Naples. The title carried real power since it was fully backed and authorized by the federal government through the FAA, the autonomous Federal Aviation Administration. He also was a licensed master parachute rigger who re-packed reserves (required by law, at that time, every 60 days) and repaired rigs. In addition, he owned the jump plane, all the student gear, and made all arrangements for jump pilots. Without him, there would be no skydiving in our area. However, as neat a guy as he was, he would never hesitate to use this power for his own personal benefit. If you crossed Duffy, you had better be prepared to make the long drive every weekend to the next nearest DZ in Zephyrhills or DeLand. If you didn't like his rules, that was tough — it was the only game in town.

Duffy was the only person I ever saw who could walk into a bar, go up to a good-looking lady sitting next to her date, put his arm around her, and exclaim in a loud voice, "Do you want to fuck?" I saw it but I didn't believe it. In a short time, instead of getting beat up and thrown out, he would become such great friends with these people that they'd buy him drinks all night. Later I took him aside and explained that he couldn't go around doing stuff like that in polite society. "Oh, don't worry about it," he explained. "Nine out of ten times I strike out ... but that tenth time is worth all the trouble!"

Duffy's mind worked in mysterious ways. There was the time he unexpectedly bought sweatshirts for a bunch of us. He handed them out one day after jumping when we had arrived at a bar for our customary after-jump drinking session. Each of them had a large capital letter silk-screened on the back. Duffy explained that the letters represented colleges. I got the one with the "F" because I had gone to Florida. I didn't have the heart to tell Duffy that it should have read, "U of F" to distinguish the University of Florida from Florida State University, FSU. The others — "C," "K," and "U" — he said, represented Colorado, Kentucky, and Utah. The other guys complained that none of them had gone to those schools.

"Never mind," Duffy said and parceled them out according to who had at least traveled through those particular states. Then he insisted we all put them on right then and there and line up at the bar for a toast. For some reason he insisted that we line up in the order of Florida, Utah, Colorado, and Kentucky. Shortly thereafter, we found ourselves thrown out of the bar and told not to come back until we were dressed more appropriately. We were all very puzzled. Didn't they like sweatshirts, or what? Duffy was laughing so hard, he couldn't explain. It was only then we realized what word we had unknowingly spelled with our backs turned to the other patrons of the bar.

With the passing of the "space race" at Cape Canaveral at the end of the moon-landing era, many engineers and technicians were out of work and looking for jobs in our area. It was not unusual to see a man with a PhD pumping gas. Since Duffy worked on space-related contracts as a draftsman for many years, he knew a lot of those guys and often invited them to our parties. At one party, Duffy and I were standing around drinking and talking to one of these refugees from the Cape. He happened to be a top-notch aeronautical engineer who was obviously super smart but had a tendency to remain serious and reflective even at a party. Duffy was feeding him drinks and telling jokes trying to get the guy to lighten up a little, but nothing helped. Finally, in desperation, Duffy brought up a topic that was more in the line of aviation and designed to give him a chuckle. The only problem was that the guy took it seriously and it laughingly became known in our circle as the "fly paradox."

"Have you ever considered how a fly takes off?" Duffy asked with a twinkle in his eye.

"What do you mean?" the engineer replied.

"Well, for example, does he take a few running steps before taking off or does he rev up his wings and take off like a helicopter?"

"He probably does both," he said, choosing a safe answer.

"Yeah," said Duffy like an angler about to set the hook, "but what if he's upside down on the ceiling? Does he take off and then flip over, or does he drop off and flip over before he starts flying?"

"Well, aeronautically speaking ... " the guy began.

I could see the guy was hooked.

"Or maybe the fly does a half-Immelmann," Duffy continued, waving his drink. "Or maybe just a half-barrel roll. I know! If he wanted to go in the opposite direction, he'd do half an outside loop!" Duffy demonstrated with a flat hand like a fighter pilot describing a dog fight.

The engineer's mouth was moving but no words were coming out. You could almost see the equations going through his head.

"Then there's taking off or landing on a wall," Duffy continued relentlessly. "The fly has to fly sideways in order to do that, right? How does he land at right angles to gravity?"

The engineer's eyes began to get a glazed-over look to them.

Duffy pulled me aside. "That ought to keep him occupied for the rest of the evening," he said with a grin. "Let's go get a new drink."

The engineer never saw us leave — he was lost in thought.

Halfway through the party, the engineer reappeared with somewhat of a crazed look. "It's the power curve!" he exclaimed to Duffy, a little louder than need be. "If we diagrammed the fly's energy resources against the energy requirements for flight, we'd find that the insect is flying way ahead of the power curve!"

"So tell it to us in English," Duffy said.

"Well," the engineer paused, trying his best to rephrase it. "What it means is the fly has so much excess energy that he doesn't care which way is up or down. He flies in whatever attitude he pleases."

"Oh, yeah?" Duffy snapped back. "When was the last time you saw one of those little fuckers flying around upside down?"

The rest of us couldn't suppress a grin, but the engineer's superior smile slowly faded into a frown. Later I saw him standing alone in a corner talking to himself, still trying to solve the conundrum of the fly paradox.

Duffy was good friends with Leo Kriske who, at the time, was the team captain of the Army skydiving team, the Golden Knights. The Knights practiced every year at Zephyrhills and whenever Duffy and I went there to skydive, we'd always party with the Knights after the jump day was over. If it turned out to be a weekend of bad weather, Leo and a few of the Knights would drive down to Sarasota and party with us at Duffy's house. At these impromptu parties, there was always something silly going on. One time Duffy insisted on all of us reading Dr. Seuss books out loud. Each one of these rough, tough military men — Leo was known as the "iron man" because he was so tough — would take turns reading these tongue-twisters while the rest of us laughed our heads off. With everybody half-smashed on scotch or bourbon, it really was funny. But with my stuttering problem, I was scared to death to take my turn. The Golden Knights would accept no excuses and, to my embarrassment, I had to read from their favorite book, *The Cat in the Hat*. To everybody's astonishment, including my own, I read a whole page flawlessly. Up to that point, to the Golden Knights I was just one of Duffy's friends, but because I didn't chicken out, I was accepted as one of their friends in my own right. Later that evening, I had to leave the party to play drums in a dance band. To my chagrin, Duffy, Leo, and the other Golden Knights all showed up, drunk and unruly, to heckle the band. Leo demanded that the band play his favorite tune "The Green Tambourine." The band leader didn't know the song, but scared to disappoint such a tough crowd, he faked his way through it. This was my first job with this particular band. Needless to say, it was also my last. Duffy thought it was all pretty funny.

Duffy had his own sense of morality but no matter how offensive he could be, it was hard to get too mad at him. He was always like a cute little boy who was naughty without really meaning to be bad. A few years after I got married, Rose, my wife, decided to throw a big birthday party for Duffy. She went to quite a bit of expense and trouble fixing a fine dinner, inviting friends, and buying a present. On the allotted day and time everyone arrived with gifts and cards — everyone but Duffy, that is. We stalled dinner as long as we could but finally had to go ahead without him. Our party, without the appearance of the main guest, fell flat, and soon everyone made their excuses and left. Our emotions had gone from annoyance to anger to concern to worry.

"Where could he be? What could have happened to him?" ran through our minds as we cleaned up the house and washed the dishes. By the time we finished, it was fairly late, we were tired and demoralized, and it was time to turn out the lights and go to bed.

"Ding-dong!" At this hour, the musical chime of our doorbell startled us.

"Bam! Bam! Bam!" The hammering on the front door was immediately followed by a loud "Come on, open up the Goddamed door!" It was Duffy.

I opened the door. Duffy was drunk or stoned, or both. He could barely stand upright. Now, knowing that he had been detained by drinking at some bar instead of dying in a car accident, our worry and concern changed back into anger. Considering the lateness of the hour and his extreme rudeness in standing up his own party, we had all the right to tell him to go to hell and leave us alone. But it didn't work out that way. He talked his way into the house and, against our wishes, plopped himself down on our couch. I was hoping he wasn't going to pass out; then we'd *never* get him to leave. He stayed for about two hours but it was the funniest two hours we've ever spent. We never stopped laughing the whole time except to rest our sides because they hurt so much. I wish I had a tape recording of it because I can't possibly re-create now what he regaled us with then. This was what made Duffy, Duffy. The more drunk he got, the faster his mind worked, and he was funnier than any nightclub comedian I've ever heard. I was amazed that he could get up and walk, but he finally left about 2 a.m., having converted us into his friends again. We collapsed into bed still laughing.

Duffy's ability to take the most ordinary thing and turn it into something funny was extraordinary. I stopped by his office one day and we were sitting there talking about nothing in particular when his phone rang. He answered it and I overheard the strangest conversation. It started with his saying, "Sure, I'd be glad to talk about tires." Although I was hearing only his side of it, I couldn't make head nor tail of it. It wasn't about business: I'd hear, "Well, I put radials on mine and I'm getting good mileage out of them." It wasn't a friend: Duffy was using no swear words. It wasn't about skydiving: I'd have recognized some jump terms and expressions. I couldn't figure it out so I resigned myself to waiting and asking him after he hung up. It went on and on until abruptly, he said, "No I'm not." Pause. "Well, you're the one who wanted to talk about tires!" He shrugged and hung up.

"Who was that!" I asked, more curious than ever.

"Wrong number," he replied.

"What? You talked for half an hour!" I said incredulously.

"Well, this lady asked if I could talk to her about tires, and I said yes. Which I proceeded to do," he said with a grin. "Then she got all pissed off that I wasn't the Goodyear Tire store and hung up on me!"

Duffy and I were always telling each other jokes. I think between the two of us, we knew every joke ever created by man. In fact, we knew so many, we would get into long joke-telling sessions and save time by skipping the body of the joke and just relate the punch line.

Duffy would say, "Who do you think I am, a stunt car driver?" And we'd break into gales of laughter.

I'd say, "I'm the guy in the refrigerator!"; more laughter.

Inevitably, someone overhearing us would try to horn in by telling us a punch line of their own. We'd purposely not laugh. The guy would look bewildered and Duffy would turn to me and say, "Pitiful, isn't it?"

"Yes," I'd reply, right on cue. "Doesn't know how to tell a joke!" And we'd break into laughter again.

The stories about Duffy were legendary. I wouldn't have believed them myself if I hadn't been there. Just mentioning the time he popped a smoke grenade in the men's room at the Crescent Club would bring gales of laughter from our group. With red smoke billowing out of the bathroom, the bar had to be evacuated and Duffy had almost gotten stuck crawling out of the tiny bathroom window. When the cops arrived, they found him hiding, wedged under a car, drunkenly oblivious to the fact that he would have been killed had the owner driven off.

Or the time he took the whole party outside his house to demonstrate the volume and shade of smoke emitted from a red smoke grenade. It was a breezy day and we all went quietly back inside for another drink when we saw the cloud of red smoke engulf and pass his neighbor's house. His neighbor had just finished painting his house white. I don't think the paint manufacturer could ever explain to Duffy's neighbor why their flat white paint had changed overnight to a pleasant shade of pink.

Chapter Four

BOB

Bob Malott was one of my heroes. He seemed like the ideal skydiver or, at least, what I thought a kydiver ought to be. He was handsome, well-spoken, one of the better skydivers in freefall, and had a friendly, happy personality. What impressed me most, however, was his gorgeous blonde wife, Sharon, who was wild about him.

When I joined the Mission Valley Skydivers, I had only ten jumps recorded in my logbook. At that time a jumper needed at least two hundred jumps to obtain the highest "expert" license through the Parachute Club of America (PCA). Very few jumpers in our club had made that number of jumps, and I held anyone with over fifty jumps in complete awe. Bob had over two hundred jumps and I thought he was completely unapproachable.

The skydivers always had a favorite bar in which all the jumpers re-gathered for R & R after a hard day of skydiving. At that time, it was Barney's Bar on the south Tamiami Trail in Sarasota. No matter how many "normal" customers were in the bar, the skydivers tended to take it over, moving tables at will, shouting drink orders, and even turning out the lights if we had movies or slides to show. We spent more money in there in one evening than Barney's took in all week, so the owner didn't mind at all. The customers usually didn't mind either, enthralled to watch such a rowdy crowd at play.

Soon after I joined the club, I happened to be the first to arrive at Barney's. Bob was the second and, without hesitation, came over, sat down next to me, and started talking as if I were an old friend. I was completely dumbfounded. I had no idea that he even knew that I was in the club. This impressed me deeply. It showed that no matter what the difference in experience, skydivers respected each other's courage. The simple fact that you jumped out of a plane set you apart from other people and made you special. I always made it a point after that, once I gained more jump experience, to talk to new jumpers and make them welcome.

The Parachute Club of America (PCA) was formed in 1956. I started jumping only eight years later, in 1964. When I joined PCA at that time, there were fewer than 3,000 members nationwide, so it was a really small and close fraternity. You could go to any strange town, call up the local jump club and instantly have a place to stay and sometimes a free meal with no questions asked other than, "How many jumps do you have?" I used to actually wear my "expert parachutist" wings and recognize other jumpers the same way. It was somewhat like being Masons with their secret recognition signals.

Bob and Duffy worked together and were good friends, but this didn't stop them from constantly competing with each other. Both were "camera hogs," and it used to crack me up to watch them when I took jump pictures of them. The instant I got within camera range of them in freefall, one or the other would do something to make themselves look good in the air and the other foolish. I had more photos of one guy right side up holding the other upside down, one facing the camera while turning the other away, or one simply putting a hand in the other's face. You never knew what crazy thing they were apt to do to each other in freefall.

It was general knowledge that during his two-hundred-some-odd jumps, Bob had, at one time or another, broken practically every major bone in his body. He always had on some kind of splint or brace or Ace bandage when he jumped. This became one of our unspoken laws: never let an injury stop you from jumping. Our guys were always skydiving with half-healed injuries covered with casts or bandages.

After a hard day of jumping, everyone arrived at our current favorite bar straight off the drop zone, dirty and disheveled. Bob, however, somehow arrived clean and fresh, looking like a million bucks. I never knew how he managed this magical transformation until I happened to stay at the DZ a little longer than usual one day. Bob went to the back of his station wagon, an imitation "woody," and got out a jug of water, soap, and a washcloth. I was surprised to see Bob give himself a French bath before donning clean clothes.

"Gee," I said to myself, "that's a good idea; arrive at the bar all fresh and clean." Then after an instant's reflection I thought, "Nah — too much trouble!" I continued to arrive at the bar like the others — dirty and grungy.

Bob and Duffy liked to organize party trips. They would plan a trip, make arrangements for transportation and hotel rooms, and sign up friends. They'd charge everyone enough per person to cover costs and give themselves a free trip.

One time they planned an excursion to the island of Bimini. Bob made all the hotel arrangements while Duffy supplied a DC-3. It became a legendary trip which fueled bar stories for years to come. It started out in spectacular fashion. We were scheduled to leave from the Sarasota/Bradenton Airport exactly at 8:00 a.m. Friday morning on a four-day group vacation. Everybody showed up early with loads of baggage, jump gear, scuba gear, and party ingredients. At that time, the airport terminal was just a small two-story building serviced by only by two airlines, Eastern and Delta. There was no computerized ticketing, mechanized baggage handlers, airport fences, security gates, or satellite airline ramps like the modern airport of today. The aircraft pulled right up to the building, and the passengers boarded by walking out through the rear doors of the terminal.

By 8:30 a.m. our DC-3 hadn't appeared, so Duffy went and made a call to see what happened. He came back shortly to report that the plane had a mechanical problem. It would be a little late, he said, so we should all relax and take it easy. A relatively quiet collective groan went up from our group. They were either subdued by the early hour or hung over as usual.

One of our group, I believe it was Dave Hester, wandered upstairs to the little airport bar. Normally it wasn't open at this hour, but the bartender happened to be there cleaning up, getting ready to open later that afternoon. Dave talked the bartender into making him a drink and then asked casually, "Say, if I were to go bring up a friend or two, would you give me a free drink?"

"Hell, I'll give you a free drink for *every* person you get in here who orders a drink," replied the bored bartender as he wiped the bar. How many people, he thought, would be drinking before 9 a.m.?

One whistle and a wave of Dave's arm was all it took. We packed the place like it was happy hour on a Friday afternoon. We all cheered when the bartender kept his promise and gave Dave a whole bar tray of free drinks for himself. By the time our DC-3 arrived a little after noon, we were all half-stewed and ready to travel, especially Dave.

Our overworked bartender looked as if he were in shock when we finally stumbled out of his bar to board our private DC-3, dwarfed by the larger airliners parked nearby. It was a perfect start to an exciting trip.

The short trip to Bimini was the most memorable of flights. Half-drunk though I was, I remember with clarity the constant bizarre activity going on all around me. The normal "stay in your seat unless you are visiting the bathroom" rule of commercial airlines didn't apply to us.

One guy, rather inebriated, had stretched out his parachute in the isleway in order to pack it in flight. I was glad I didn't have to jump *that* pack job!

I couldn't figure out what the devil one group of four guys were doing once the parachute was out of the way. They were laughing, drinks in hand, marching up to the front of the airplane then back toward the tail while making wisecracks to everyone along the way. When they passed me the next time, I asked them what was going on. "Add up our combined weight and then think about what the pilot is doing right now," one of them responded. I had to laugh when I envisioned a puzzled pilot frantically "trimming" the flight angle every few minutes because of the mysteriously shifting weight load. It struck me funny because it was so technically ingenious — something I would have never thought of.

Other people were mixing drinks and passing them over the seat tops, tossing objects back and forth, or, in the case of one guy, making out with his girlfriend in the last row. I sat in my seat in fuzzy contentment, just happy to be there to observe all the craziness.

When we arrived in Bimini, the tower instructed our pilot not to pull up to the small terminal but rather to park way out on the tarmac to receive the custom inspectors before disembarking. We sat out there in a closed aircraft in the tropical heat for about ten minutes. Finally two Bahamian customs inspectors arrived with the rolling aircraft steps and stood aside, waiting while their one-man ground crew positioned it in front of our door toward the rear of the plane. The inspectors were two very formal black men clutching clipboards and dressed - incongruously, considering the heat - in white shirts, coats, and ties. They looked very official and intimidating standing at the bottom of the stairs waiting for some-one to emerge as if we were some kind of spaceship just landing from Mars rather than visitors bringing lots of tourist dollars.

Inside the plane there were a few moments of confusion as to who was to go out and what the proper procedure was. Finally, we pushed Bob out the door as the trip organizer and, as such, our representative. Bob stood momentarily at the top of the flight stairs as his eyes adjusted to the harsh tropical sun. He adjusted his shirt to see that the collar was straight and solemnly descended the metal staircase toward the waiting officials. We all watched from the plane's porthole windows in anticipation of seeing Bob's considerable diplomatic prowess in action. Bob reached the bottom of the stairs, took two steps out onto the tarmac, and, before anyone could say a word, fell flat on his face on the hot asphalt, passing out right at the feet of the two startled officials. And that was just the start of our trip! As usual, it got better.

Chapter Five

MALFUNCTIONS

S urviving a malfunction was about as close to death as anyone would want to come. Before the advent of ram-airs, the modern square para chutes, the average drop zone would experience about one malfunction every two or three months. At the big skydiving meets, however, you could expect to see four to five malfunctions a day. I was never sure if this was because we were seeing a lot more jumps in a shorter period of time and the ratio was normal, or if the jumpers were packing their chutes more hurriedly. But whatever the cause, there was a lot more action going on at a meet and everyone went around in a continual state of excitement.

Watching a malfunction is exciting, but it's no fun. It's not a game. It's a life-and-death struggle taking place right before your eyes; many times it would be a personal friend who was trying to stay alive.

One of the most horrifying sights is to watch a low-altitude malfunction where every detail is visible but the chances of survival are slim. One such accident took place directly over the packing area at Zephyrhills during one of the Thanksgiving meets. Two parachutists, Charlie McGurr and Carl Doughtery, were making their final turns to land in the packing area when they crossed paths, wrapped lines, and plummeted toward earth. They were only about 200 feet up so they had no opportunity to recover and were far too low to cut away. They were in full view of everyone in the packing area, all of whom stood frozen in horror. It was obvious that these guys had no chance whatsoever. The immediate emotional response to the sight was not excitement but a sickness in the pit of the stomach. It was one of those times that you want to look away but you can't. By sheer dumb luck they impacted on the corrugated metal top of the packing shed, leaving distinct impressions of their bodies visible from underneath. Luckily, there was just enough spring and give in the roof to save them. Charlie walked away with just sprains and bruises. Carl was not quite so lucky. He had a broken kneecap, a fractured arm, and a few broken ribs, but nothing life-threatening. They were very, very lucky and the incident put the fear of God into everybody who saw it. Shortly after that, there was a "no-pull" down to tree-top level where the jumper finally got out his reserve. For the rest of the meet, everyone was spooked and intently watched the openings of every load.

But what killed most jumpers usually was not some catastrophic failure in their equipment or gross error in their judgment but rather a series of minor things: for example, an altimeter in error by 500 feet; going low because of taking pictures; or a pilot chute hesitation. Any one of these things are minor in themselves, but together, they add up to a dangerously low opening. Combine this with illness or lack of experience, and you might have a fatality.

Here's an example of a combination of factors: We were jumping at Sun City not long after I had experienced my first malfunction. I was taking 16mm movies of Duffy in freefall. All went well, and we opened at a normal altitude of 2,500 feet. I wanted to get some air-to-air movies of parachutes in flight, so I had brought along a spare film magazine. I reached up and, by feel, opened the door on the rear of my helmet camera. I took out the exposed magazine and, being careful not to drop it, switched it with a fresh one. All this took a little time so I was down to about 1,800 feet before I was ready to shoot again. I looked around for a subject but no one was close to me. Then, looking up, I saw Duffy's red-and-yellow parachute above me. I fixed my eyesight on him and switched on my camera. Duffy must have seen me and realized I was taking movies of him because, ever the actor, he immediately began to spiral his canopy.

I was getting great movies and I kept the bull's-eye glued to his canopy which was getting closer and closer as he lost altitude. I was moving my head in circles keeping him exactly centered in the lens of my helmet camera when, to my surprise, he disappeared behind my own canopy over my head. I was looking at my own parachute. An instant later, a shape that looked suspiciously like Duffy plummeted into the top of my canopy. I was puzzled for a moment. Then I realized what had happened: Duffy had dropped into the top of my parachute and was completely shrouded in the material. I could see the exact shape of his body with his arms frantically pushing, trying to find a way out of the folds of nylon surrounding him. Since I no longer had a colorful parachute to film, my first reaction was to turn off the camera to conserve film. It never occurred to me to document this life-and-death struggle. My next reaction was a mild, "Oh, my gosh, Duffy's in trouble." Then the true facts of the situation sank in: Duffy's canopy was still open and was holding us both up; *my* canopy was the one that had collapsed; *I* was the one in trouble.

"Oh, my God! I'm the one in trouble!" a voice cried out in my head, and I immediately cut away without another thought for poor Duffy.

Now, here's the point to this story. It was my eighty-second jump and I had a background of only one malfunction, and that happened to be one that occurred at terminal velocity of 120 mph. I had no experience whatsoever with cutting away from a fully opened chute, even if it wasn't my own in this case. This time I would be cutting away from what amounted to a dead standstill in mid-air, and, since my chest-mounted reserve had no pilot chute, I had the mistaken idea that I needed to build up some falling speed for my reserve canopy to grab air and deploy. We had already used a lot of altitude taking movies, and I had no idea of how high I was at the moment. Despite all this, when I cut away, I slowly counted to five before I pulled the reserve ripcord. Needless to say, I opened very, very low.

The people on the ground who watched the whole thing thought we were too low to cut away to begin with. And when I went back into freefall, they thought I had "bought the farm."

I opened so low, I hit the ground after only a couple of swings under my tiny reserve canopy. I thought Duffy would be mad as hell at me for abandoning him. But once he landed, Duffy was full of praise. He said proudly that I had reacted perfectly, except for the delay in opening my reserve. The axiom is to save yourself; this will give the other guy a chance to do the same. The entanglement had been his fault in the first place and his first reaction had been to cut away himself. He had even reached up to his "Capewells" before pausing to think, he said. If he had cut away, wrapped as he was in my chute, it probably would have killed us both. Once I had cut away and my weight was gone, however, he easily threw off my jettisoned canopy and made an uneventful landing under his own chute.

That's how close the difference was between life and death, and that's why we had to rely on each other's abilities and reactions. At times it boiled down to milliseconds. A skydiver's instincts and training had better be correct; his own life as well as others' depended on it. There was never a pat scenario that a jumper could trust to get himself out of trouble every time. Each malfunction was a totally different and unique experience. However, with each malfunction, I gained more confidence in my ability to suppress panic and react calmly in an appropriate manner. That was the secret of survival: to be able to think under stress.

For example, one time I accidently routed my chest strap through my ripcord. I found out about my little error when I reached for my ripcord in freefall and couldn't pull it. For some reason this situation didn't scare me; I just found it amusing as I continued falling toward earth at 120 mph. I very deliberately unhooked the chest strap, pulled the ripcord free of it and re-connected the snap. When I went to retrieve the ripcord handle now out of its pocket and dangling free, I found I had trapped a finger of my glove in the chest strap snap. This really tickled me and I started laughing out loud as I continued falling. I undid the chest strap for the second time, freed my glove, reconnected the snap, caught the dangling ripcord and pulled it. I opened very low, still laughing like a maniac.

There were several classifications of malfunctions. One was "high-speed." This was when you had not yet deployed a chute or if the pack had opened, the canopy, for whatever reason, had not yet come out of its container. My first malfunction was a "high-speed" type since my backpack had not opened at all. With this type of malfunction, the jumper has only a matter of seconds to react before impacting with the ground. And impacting with the ground at terminal velocity must be why it's called "terminal." It is definitely something to be avoided.

Almost 500 jumps later, I had another high-speed malfunction. We were jumping at Bartow that day and it was my first jump in over a month. My front-mount reserve was out of date so I asked Warren Kauffman, one of the Tampa Skydivers, if I could borrow one of his. He was a licensed parachute rigger and agreed to take mine home with him to repack the following week. When he gave me his reserve, he jokingly said, "Now don't open this one, OK?" I was jumping with my good friend Dan Haggerty but as I flew in to hook up, my left shoulder dislocated from an old skydiving injury. In pain, I waved off and pulled my ripcord. My Para-Commander came out of the pack in a big wad. It was obviously a major malfunction. I paused only long enough to get my arm back into joint and made a textbook cutaway. As I went back into freefall on my back, I reached in with my right hand and pulled the ripcord of the borrowed reserve. Nothing happened. The ripcord didn't budge.

"Oh, shit!" I thought. I was in big trouble now. Adrenaline flooded my system and when I pulled the ripcord again, this time with both hands, I could have bent a steel bar. To my relief, the ripcord pulled free, the reserve deployed with a tremendous opening shock, and I floated to earth under the small canopy. Luckily I landed on the grass just off the concrete runway, otherwise I'd have killed myself. Even so, the impact with the ground knocked me senseless — but I was happy to be alive.

Much later, I had a couple of "bag-locks" with my ram-air parachute, the Sled. These were back-to-back malfunctions, one right after another at two different drop zones. The first one caught me totally off guard and, although I handled it fine, it taught me a lesson: a good jumper must be prepared for a malfunction on every jump. This malfunction was caused by a worn grommet on my container which had pulled off and kept the Sled in the bag. The next jump taught me another lesson. I had ignored the worn grommet and thought by packing a little differently, I could avoid the problem. I was wrong — another malfunction. But this time, I was prepared for it and felt very good about how I reacted. This one taught me to respect my gear and always keep it in perfect condition.

Another category of malfunctions is the "slow speed." This is when a canopy has already been deployed and, since you are no longer in freefall, there is a lot more time available to study the problem and figure out the best way to handle it. This could be a canopy malfunction causing a spin, or an entanglement with another parachutist.

I had a canopy entanglement once which was pretty funny. It happened at one of the big skydiving meets at Zephyrhills. These events were attended by jumpers from all over the country and many from overseas. Over a long weekend, there was constant aviation activity involving a whole fleet of large aircraft. All day long, DC-3s, Lockheed Loadstars, or Twin Beeches would be taking off, flying on jump run, or coming in for a landing. There were dozens of colorful canopies filling the sky every minute of the day, and the atmosphere was charged with excitement. This was not an "accuracy" meet, so most of the jumpers ignored the target and landed wherever they pleased. Anyone on the ground had to be constantly alert for jumpers flying in for a landing. This was "big star" stuff with judges watching from the ground with high-powered binoculars. Since they needed to see the formations as they built, it was more important to avoid all clouds than to land near the target. As a result, jumpers were constantly landing all over the big airport. Ground crews with open-bed trucks made frequent runs, out and back, to return errant jumpers to the target area. Many jumpers flew in to where the cars were parked to land alongside their car. One guy landed on the back of a station wagon and broke the rear window. Hoop, the drop zone manager at that time, immediately outlawed the parking area as a landing site, a rule which many jumpers ignored; Hoop couldn't be everywhere at once, they figured. Others, to avoid any walking, simply landed in the packing area right on top of their own packing mat which was spread out on the grass. It was as if a circus and a carnival had collided head-on. There was something weird or funny or interesting going on every second. I wished that I could slow down the passing of time so I could take it all in and not miss anything.

There were no trees out in the middle of the airport and it was always hot and dusty. There were a couple of food and drink vendors operating out of little trailers who did a brisk business. I practically lived off grape-flavored ice cones. I must have had ten to twelve a day, and I doubt if I would have survived without them. At night, there was always a loud rock band and lots of free beer. Most of us stayed right on the airport, camping out in tents, trailers, or campers.

Among all of this carnival-like atmosphere, I left my wife, Rose, with friends in the packing area and went off to jump. I was on a ten-man team with a few of the guys from the Delray Aerial Circus. The formation we were attempting was a round circle of jumpers which we called a "star"; in this case, it was a ten-man star. After jumping from the aircraft, a star was built one man at a time as each man flew in to hook up. By flying in between two jumpers already in the formation with linked hands, a jumper would connect on their wrists, break their grasp, and enter the formation. In this manner, the formation grew larger and larger as the diameter of the circle expanded. A star was usually built from the heaviest men to the lightest. The heavier men fell faster and provided a more stable base while the lighter guys could fly in fast with no danger of upsetting the formation or going low.

Dave Jebb, one of the Delray Aerial Circus, was a little heavier than the rest of us so he went "base." He and I were good friends even though I was one of the last in the formation and usually never sat near him in the plane. On large formations, break-off altitude was usually set higher than normal at 3,500 to 4,000 feet, to give everybody time to split apart. At break-off, everyone made a 180-degree turn while still in freefall and tracked away for several hundred yards before pulling their ripcords in order to get good separation between canopies.

This particular jump went well. We built the formation, held it for the required five seconds and broke off to open. For some reason, Dave and I opened very close together facing each other about twenty yards apart at exactly the same altitude. I was jumping a PC while Dave had a ram-air. Since Dave's "square" was much more maneuverable than my "round," it was up to him to take evasive action. However, as often happened, Dave had a slight line twist which momentarily prevented him from steering. He slammed into me going about twenty miles per hour, and our canopies began wrapping up around each other.

It was the strangest thing; there was nothing I could do. I was revolving around Dave's lines and I had absolutely no leverage to stop it. So I just had to wait until the lines wrapped as tight as they could go and I had stopped moving. As it turned out, I ended up standing on top of Dave's shoulders. I looked up and saw that, even though our lines were wrapped tightly together, both of our chutes were still open side by side. We were probably dropping a lot faster than normal, but the chutes were stable and holding us up so I knew I had time to solve the problem, hopefully without cutting away.

Looking down, I saw that Dave was badly cut across the forehead where his head had slammed into my jump boot during our collision. He was bleeding, and I was concerned that he was fully conscious. "Dave, are you OK?" I shouted.

He looked up. "Yeah," he responded. "Should I cut away?"

"No, hold on a minute and I'll try to clear it." With that, I grabbed the lines over my head and began the long unwinding process. I really wasn't sure what was going to happen once we got the lines untangled. My previous experience with canopy entanglements made me very nervous about the whole thing. Finally, the last twist of the lines came undone and I raised up off Dave's shoulders, up to the rear of his canopy, pushed off of it, made a turn, and flew away. I looked back and saw that Dave was flying normally, too.

"Whew!" I was really shaken up.

My landing was uneventful, way out in the northeast quadrant of the airport about half a mile from the target area. When the truck rumbled up to pick me up, there was Dave, bleeding but smiling, happy to have survived. I climbed into the back of the open truck beside him and nodded to a couple of other jumpers who were strangers. Dave and I just sat there quietly holding our canopies wrapped in our arms, bouncing along in the truck as it made frequent turns and stops in the open field to pick up other jumpers. We were white and shaken, a little benumbed by the entanglement. As we were heading back to the target area, I couldn't help but notice the open stares of a cute French girl sitting near us. I looked back with an expression of, "What?"

"You guys," she said in faltering English, "ah, do you guys jump laike zat all ze time?" she asked incredulously, referring to our entanglement.

"Oh, sure," I replied.

Dave and I couldn't help but break out in laughter. Little did we know that, in a few years, canopy relative work (CRW) would beome a whole new skydiving activity.

I got off the truck, shook hands with Dave, and hurried back to the packing area. I was concerned that Rose would be frantically worried about my safety after witnessing such a hair-raising spectacle overhead. As I approached my group of friends, I half-expected her to rush out, throw her arms around me, and tearfully exclaim in a loud voice, "Oh, thank God, you're all right!"

Instead, Rose looked up from a borrowed recliner chair and asked in a half-bored, half-sleepy voice, "Oh, have you jumped yet?"

Chapter Six
THE FIRST MALFUNCTION

S trangely enough, my first malfunction was not over our usual drop zone in Englewood, south of where I lived in Sarasota, Florida. It was north at a temporary DZ we were using in Sun City. There was a little grass landing strip on raw land just across the road from this new retirement community located halfway between Sarasota and Tampa, just west of Route 301. The airstrip was unusual because it ran parallel to the road with nothing in between except about ten feet of grass. The north side of the road was nothing but new homes with manicured lawns. The south side, where we jumped, was nothing but cow pastures and raw land consisting of nothing but palmettos and scrub oak. Unlike other drop zones at the time, which had no amenities at all, if the Florida sun got too hot, we could walk across the street to civilization and buy a cold drink at the Standard Oil station any time we felt like it. Of course none of us ever thought of bringing an ice chest with drinks and food. That would have been too much like normal people with their little picnics. We were supermen who could brass it out all day in the heat and make up for it later with lots of cold beer! Further back off the road was a new restaurant built especially for the development. At first we ate there occasionally after jumping, but it seemed a little incongruous for our wild group to be there among all the retirees. It tended to put a damper on our normally boisterous inclinations. We finally gravitated to a little seafood restaurant about five miles back toward Sarasota, probably because it had a liquor bar for our after-jump partying.

It was my first visit to this new location, and to reach it I drove north out of Sarasota on Route 41. It was a perfect Florida day and in my exuberance to get to the drop zone, I must have been driving my Corvette a little faster than normal. A few minutes after I arrived at the DZ, a guy named Red Morris who was jumping with us at that time arrived in his big Cadillac convertible.

"Jeeze, Mike!" he said. "How fast were you going? I was behind you for a while but when I hit 100 miles per hour, you were still pulling away from me!"

The date was September 30, 1966. I was a tall skinny kid of twenty-five who looked about nineteen. It was a little after noon when I went up for a jump with two friends, Jim Shockley and Dave Hester. It was my fifty-sixth jump. I was taking 35mm photos in freefall with a hand-held camera from an altitude of 7,200 feet. At that altitude we had about 30 seconds of freefall. We got so in-

volved in taking pictures that we inadvertently broke off below our normal opening altitude of 2,500 feet. I tracked away, looked above and waved off, thereby
warning any jumpers near me that I was about to pull.

I was already fairly low when I reached into my chest with my right hand
and pulled the ripcord. Nothing happened. The ripcord was out of its pocket on
the harness and in my fist but the cable that ran through a tubular metal housing
over the shoulder to the pins holding the backpack closed hadn't budged! I was
still falling toward earth at 120 miles per hour. This had never happened before.
It wasn't supposed to happen. Maybe I just thought I had pulled it. I very deliberately pulled the ripcord again, very hard. Again nothing happened! Instantly
the situation became very clear to me. I was about to make a very big, nasty
indentation in the ground. I had lost track of altitude. I must be passing through
one thousand feet. I had no time to check my altimeter or calculate the number of
seconds until impact. I didn't know that I had less than six seconds left to live.
All I knew was that I had to get that chute open damned soon!

Adrenaline flooded my body like white heat. Without consciously thinking, my left hand let go of the camera and came in to join my right in a frantic
two-handed power pull. The ripcord didn't budge. It felt like jerking a chain
bolted to a brick wall. Nothing happened except now, with both hands pulled in
to my chest, I went head down and picked up even more speed. I didn't feel my
camera on its wrist strap whipping around in the slipstream bruising my chest and
arm. I could see the housing development in a blur rushing up at me.

It finally dawned on me. After three fruitless pulls on my main ripcord,
this was a case where I certainly ought to pull my reserve.

I had been taught to pull either main or reserve only in a stable position.
I was falling head down almost on my back, but intuitively I knew this was no
time for the niceties of the sport. Everything seemed to be in super slow motion.
I saw my hand slowly reaching for the reserve ripcord at my belly. It took an
eternity for my hand to pull the short ripcord toward the right and free of the pack.
I saw the pack open and the lines snake out upward through my legs, popping
loose from side to side from the rubber band stows inside the container. I was
fascinated. As if in a dream I saw the white canopy blossom open against the
cobalt-blue sky like a flower in time-lapse photography. Then suddenly everything went back into normal speed as the tremendous opening shock hit me and
flipped me upright. Holy smoke! That practically knocked my boots off ... but I
was alive!

In actuality, all this took less than a second. I had gone from maybe 300
feet per second to something like 18 to 20 feet per second in less than one hundred
vertical feet. I looked up in wonder at my 24-foot "twill." Compared to my main,
it looked awfully small — just four feet less in diameter made a big difference!
Later on I found out that the "twill" was obsolete and had been replaced by safer
canopies using ripstop nylon. As the name "ripstop" implies, a tear would travel
only a short distance in the material. The old twill, on the other hand, had a nasty

reputation of having a small rip turn into a catastrophic failure. But, believe me, at this point, I wasn't complaining. I was very thankful to have it.

I was oscillating very badly and was surprised to see how close I was to the ground. I was coming down very fast and it looked as if I was going to land on top of the Standard Oil station, in the middle of traffic on the highway, or in the high-tension power lines. Yep! I was going to die. It was just a question of how. I felt a little sad about my imminent demise. I didn't feel at all like the man in the joke who jumped off the top of the Empire State building. As he fell past the twentieth floor, one of his friends at a window heard him say, "So far, so good!" I wasn't nearly so optimistic. I was still a long way from getting down alive.

Our reserve canopies had no steering slots or steering lines like our mains, so I had no way to control where I might land. I had read stories about paratroopers in the war who side-slipped their canopies by pulling lines to spill air out of one side of the parachute. I did this two or three times, but the amplitude of the oscillations increased so dramatically that I thought the canopy might invert and collapse. I scared myself so badly that I gave that up and resigned myself to landing wherever I happened to come down, Standard Oil or not.

As luck would have it, I landed with a bone-crunching thud at the rear of the filling station in a little plot of grass. I should have been knocked unconscious, but wasn't. I had automatically done an Olympic-quality parachute landing fall, known as a PLF. Once I regained my senses and took a damage inventory, I realized my early parachute training had saved me from any major injury.

As I gathered up the little parachute in my arms and started walking back, all the jumpers rushed over to ask what had possessed me to open so low. Estimates of my opening altitude ranged from 800 to 400 feet. I was exonerated when one of the heavier, stronger jumpers put my backpack on the ground, stood on top of it, and pulled the ripcord with all his strength in both hands. It wouldn't open. Upon examination, we discovered that my backpack did not have a neat little metal device called a "stiffener." The top pin on the ripcord had hung up on the edge of the metal tubing. The more pressure applied, the more the ripcord bent at right angles instead of sliding through the housing.

Suffice it to say that the next day, I had a stiffener installed on my backpack at the end of the ripcord housing where it ought to have been in the first place. This is how we learned safety — by trial and error. But in this case, unlike a lot of others, I was alive to profit from it personally. From that time on, I felt no apprehension about the possibilities of a malfunction. Now I knew that my reserve really worked and, most importantly, I knew that I could function in an emergency. This was good because, as it turned out, I needed all the help I could get.

Chapter Seven

JOHN

John Clement was one of the best pilots I've ever had the pleasure of knowing. In over ten years of flying for us, he never missed a day, and we never had the slightest safety incident due to pilot error or aircraft maintenance. John was a little older than most of us, but he was trim and fit and didn't show his age. He was the epitome of the soft-spoken, pipe-smoking, square-jawed, keen-eyed flyer and I always picture him as I most often saw him, at the controls of his plane, tanned and relaxed with his lips in a half-smile under his tinted aviation glasses. Most of the guys took him for granted. To them, he just represented a bus ride to altitude. But a few of us who had experienced near crashes, plane malfunctions, no-shows, and aborted takeoffs with other pilots thought very highly of him. We called him our "skydiver driver" but as much as he pretended to be annoyed at us for our crazy antics, he enjoyed the weekends being around what he called "the wild bunch."

John and I had a deep respect for each other and got along very well. More often than not, I got stuck with the thankless job of keeping the manifest straight and collecting jump money at the end of the day. He knew that I constantly looked out for his interest by making sure that everyone paid what was due. John was very trusting and never questioned the day's total, so I was always very careful with the money.

John appreciated my skydiving abilities but he was always looking askance at me, not knowing what crazy stunt I was going to pull next. The only time I ever saw John really get mad was the time I brought my big, authentic boomerang to the airstrip. This, of course, prompted Duffy to tell his joke about the kid who got a new boomerang for his birthday.

"He nearly went crazy trying to throw away his old one!" Duffy exclaimed.

When I walked out past John's plane parked on the side of the runway, John said, "Hey, Mike, don't throw that thing around my airplane, OK?"

"Aw, John," I replied, "trust me! I know exactly what I'm doing. This is not a toy, it's a professional model!"

With that, I launched the boomerang with an expert throw, cocked slightly at an angle and parallel to the ground. It was a perfect throw and the projectile at first dipped, skimming the ground, and then swooped up and away in a long graceful curving path. The day was beautiful. There was an eight- to ten-knot breeze, though not enough to affect the flight characteristics of the boomerang, and the polished wood reflected a glint of the morning sun with every revolution. All activity stopped on the drop zone as heads turned in unison following the slow arced flight against the blue of the cloudless sky. Whit, whit, whit, whit ... like a miniature helicopter, the sound of the curved throwing stick faded as the device followed the outer limits of its trajectory about sixty yards away. It was great. I felt in perfect control. I couldn't have made a better throw. Whit, whit, whit, whit ... it was returning to me as if on an elastic leash.

I lifted my arm in a heroic pose, ready to catch the stick as it completed its epic flight from the opposite direction. It passed unceremoniously over my head about a foot over my upraised hand and I spun around in disbelief. I watched helplessly in horror as the boomerang ricocheted off the top of the left wing with a sickening "CLANG"!

Everyone immediately went back to what they had been doing -- packing parachutes, conversing, whatever — anything to avoid looking at John. I was left standing there all alone. I had screwed up again. John never "said" anything, but his stance — legs spread, arms folded across his chest, and a little tightening around his eyes — said it all. After that, every time I saw John stand back to admire his plane, he'd give his head a little shake and I knew he was thinking about that damned dent in his wing.

When I was recuperating from one of my more traumatic skydiving accidents, on a very long nine-month disability, the guys, out of pity, would stop off at my parents' house, gather me up, and take me along to the DZ. I could barely walk due to back injuries, swollen knees, and swollen ankles. I was able to move around only with crutches and, due to the intense pain, very slowly at that. Watching other people jump was no fun for me and I was going crazy with nothing to do. In between flights, John would walk over and try to cheer me up, but I was not in a very good mood. While John took up another load, I idly watched someone's kid, a little boy about the age of ten, who was running around the DZ playing a solo game of cowboys and Indians. I assumed he was an Indian because he had a bow and a few arrows. Out of boredom I watched him shoot arrows at an improvised target when slowly an idea began to form in my mind.

We always had fireworks lying around just in case some unsuspecting person went across the runway to go behind the huge clump of palmettos which served as our latrine. Our "explosive of choice" was the powerful TNT bomb which, when tossed over into the palmetto bush with the appropriate timing, was guaranteed to flush (pardon the pun) out the intended victim whether he had finished or not.

I painfully hobbled over to Duffy's car and, sure enough, he had a few hidden away in his glove compartment. When I told the kid I had something special in mind that he had never seen before, he let me borrow his bow. He even had an old arrow with a broken point that he didn't mind losing. By the time the jumpers were down, I had the TNT bomb taped to the head of the arrow and all set to go. I was going to fire the bomb with burning fuse, high into the air for a spectacular explosion. This could be the start of a whole new sport: high explosive archery.

I was standing there balanced with a crutch under each arm, holding the bow and trying to figure out how to light the fuse on the arrow, when John landed the plane and walked over. He was very skeptical about my idea and wanted no part of it.

"Don't worry," I said. "I know exactly what I'm doing."

John looked at me askew. Here I could barely walk, and I was fooling around with explosives!

"All I need," I explained patiently, "is for you to light the fuse so I can fire the arrow before it explodes. Simple. What could go wrong?"

He could see that I was bound and determined to do this; he might as well help me so I didn't hurt myself. The other jumpers started gathering around, curious as to what the "cripple" was up to.

"OK," John said cautiously, "but you fire that thing the instant I light it!" He still didn't quite trust me for some reason.

I was standing in the narrow aisle between two parked cars so I could prop myself up. The slightest movement put me in extreme pain, so it was a very delicate ballet for me to aim the bow and still retain my balance on the crutches. I slowly drew back the bow and rested the string against my cheek.

"Light it, light it," I grunted out between clenched jaws.

John struck a match but it went out in the wind. He got another going and, with cupped hands, held it to the fuse on the bomb which was attached to the end of the arrow. The fuse wouldn't light. My arms were starting to quiver. All of a sudden the fuse caught hold in a shower of sparks.

"Shoot it, shoot it!" John shouted and backed away.

I stood poised for an instant, wobbling back and forth on the crutches, as I aimed the arrow into the sky. It was at that moment that I realized that the string had pulled off the notch on the back end of the arrow. There was no way I could shoot it.

Oh my God!

I frantically wobbled the arrow shaft back and forth, trying in vain to line up the notch to the string. The fuse was burning madly. Both arms were shaking from the strain of keeping the bow cocked. I gave up and in desperation released the string in the hopes it would miraculously mate with the notch and launch the arrow. No such luck! The string twanged ineffectively and the arrow slid off the bow and fell to our feet. John and I looked at each other in horror. Everyone else was diving for cover behind cars and trees but John and I were trapped between the cars. John hit the dirt. I dropped the bow and flailed at the crutches trying to backpeddle the hell out of there. I made one step, lost my footing and fell half over a car trunk, sliding off and landing behind the car in a convulsion of pain.

The explosion rocked the area with a clap of thunder, throwing up a cloud of smoke and debris. There was a sharp smell of sulphur in my nostrils and my ears rang with a constant buzzing.

"Whew, that was close," I sighed with relief. Then I remembered John.

I'll never forget the sight, as I looked over the lid of the trunk. One hand, then the other came up to grip the top of the rear fender. Then, between the hands, John's head slowly emerged. Drifting smoke framed the wild hair, the blackened cheeks, and the red eyes.

I could never get John to admit that it would have worked if only that damned notch hadn't gotten loose from the bowstring.

Chapter Eight
<u>LANDINGS</u>

Over the years, I've had many unusual parachute land ings. On my seventh jump, in error I landed going downwind. I hit ground so hard, face first, that my front-mounted reserve knocked all the breath out of me. Then, to add insult to injury, as I was dragged dazed along the ground, my reserve ripcord snagged on a root. The pack opened and the reserve canopy strung out behind me. What was worse, I had to pay to have the reserve re-packed. Since I was paying for jumps with my food money, the re-pack hurt me more than the landing.

On another windy day, I hit out in the middle of an open field and dragged right through the largest ant colony I had ever seen. I had dirt and ants all inside my clothes, my boots and my helmet — even in my underwear! I don't know who was madder — the ants or me. At least I learned how to jive-dance in one easy lesson.

Another time, I landed in the woods in the middle of a poison ivy patch. I was still in college, so I went to the school infirmary for relief of the itching. They gave me a white ointment for my face and arms and advised me to wear cotton gloves until the swelling and itching subsided; otherwise, they said, I'd spread the poison. Friends visiting my dorm room were startled at my appear-ance and I caused a minor sensation when I attended classes. With the gloved hands and white ointment all over my face, I looked like the ghost of Al Jolson.

We were always having to rescue jumpers who had landed in trees. Land-ing in trees was very dangerous. Hitting a branch or a tree trunk could be crip-pling or life threatening. But if the jumper snagged his chute in a high branch, just getting down could be one of the most dangerous situations a jumper could face. In a situation like that, we were taught not to do anything — just wait for help.

One of our student jumpers from Sarasota, a very nice young lady, went to Zephyrhills to jump and landed in a tree. The guys at the drop zone immedi-ately called a fire rescue crew with a ladder truck to get her down. But before they got there, she cut away from her parachute and fell about thirty feet. On the way down, she hit a large branch and impacted the ground on her back. Tragically, she was permanently paralyzed. This was an accident that shouldn't have happened. Why it resulted in paralysis instead of sprains or broken bones, which could have healed, was one of those strokes of bad luck that seem to afflict the innocent more often than not.

When I first joined the Mission Valley Skydivers, I landed in a tree late one afternoon. As my canopy caught in the branches of the tall pine tree, I thought, "Wow, this is the softest landing I've ever had!" That image was shattered when I flashed past the sturdy tree trunk as I swung backward at a high rate of speed. I realized that if I had landed a couple of feet to the right, I would have certainly been badly injured or even killed. As it was, I ended up hanging only five or six feet above the ground, so it was no problem to get out of my harness and drop to earth. But my student canopy was firmly lodged in the top of the tree. There seemed to be no way I could get it down so I walked back to the DZ to tell Duffy.

I must have expected to be able to go home and let Duffy solve the problem because I was somewhat shocked at his curt attitude.

"In a tree?!" he roared. "Get the axe out of my car and don't come back without my canopy!"

Somewhat hurt by his gruffness, and put out that I had to go chop down a whole tree all alone, I walked back out into the woods and got to work. I was out in the woods long after dark chopping on that damn tree. It was a hot Florida evening and by the time I was through, I was covered in sweat and mosquito bites. That experience alone taught me to stay away from trees. Besides, I wasn't too proud of myself for having to cut down a perfectly healthy tree.

The funniest story about a tree landing was told to me by the Williston Skydivers when I first started jumping in college. As I said earlier, the rule was to wait for help. But if no help came in a reasonable amount of time, then the second rule of tree landings was to pull your reserve ripcord and let your reserve parachute fall below. You could then slip out of your harness and use the lines and material of the reserve canopy to slide down to the ground.

The story they told was about a guy who did exactly that. But as he slid down the lines, his feet accidentally went inside the reserve canopy instead of on the outside. By the time he realized it, he was down to his armpits inside the chute and didn't have the strength to pull himself back out. Soon, as his strength failed, his whole body was inside the canopy with only his hands holding on to the edge of the skirt where the lines attach. Then when he finally had to let go, he was standing upright inside the parachute. His weight caused the material to stretch tight around him encasing him like a moth in a cocoon. He didn't have a knife to cut his way out so he thought that maybe he could squeeze through the hole at the top of the parachute which he was now standing over. So he wormed his way upside down but he could only get his head out through the tiny hole. That's the way the rescue party found him: his face turning purple from the blood rushing to his head, only inches from the ground. To his dismay, he never lived the story down.

At our drop zone in Englewood, Sarasota County was responsible for the upkeep and maintenance of Buchan Airport. One day county workmen removed a large tree that was near the shorter of the two runways. For a long time pilots had been complaining that the tree was a danger to aviation. The workers cut the tree down, chopped it up, and hauled it away. But that left a huge stump which still posed a threat.

The first step in removing the stump was to dig a big hole around it. The workmen piled up the dirt around the lip of the hole and managed to tip the stump halfway over. They must have run out of time since it was left that way over the weekend.

Enter the skydivers. Not knowing or particularly caring about the pit with the stump at the bottom, we began a day of skydiving. This particular day was very windy, which didn't bother us one bit. We always jumped no matter how windy, unless it was a hurricane. I take that back; once Dan Liddy and I jumped on a bad day right after a hurricane passed through. Anyway, suffice it to say that I was not surprised, after opening my parachute, to find myself backing up at a high rate of speed. When this happened, it was imperative to keep your parachute headed directly into the wind when you were about to land. This kept your speed across ground to a minimum. Any other angle off the wind line increased your landing speed drastically. However, in staying turned upwind, it was extremely difficult to see directly behind to know where you were landing as you were backing up. We had a perfect exit "spot" and we were all landing on the flat open area of the airfield, so I had no worries. Little did I know that the pit was directly behind me and that the fates were drawing me to it like a bee to honey. As luck would have it, my feet made contact with earth exactly at the highest point of the dirt pile. Thinking I was on flat ground, I automatically went into a PLF, a Parachute Landing Fall, which had saved me from injury on many a jump. As I fell backwards and my legs and back didn't immediately make contact with the ground, I was a little confused. I just kept falling. The other jumpers saw me disappear from view into the ground. I hit the stump backwards and head low. The upper part of the stump happened to be flat and tilted at such an angle that it matched perfectly the downward angle of my body. I landed flat on my back on top of the stump and was almost knocked unconscious. If I had hit any other way or at any other angle, I have no doubt that I'd have been badly hurt. As it was, I lay there on the stump for quite a while as I regained my breath and my senses, looking up at the circle of blue sky which was the only view available from the bottom of the pit. Nobody would believe my story that I had landed in the pit on purpose just to see how deep it was.

Of course, there were also the "good" landings. For a long time as I jumped at Englewood, I was fascinated by my aerial view of a home near the drop zone to the east where Route 775A joined 775 (redesignated Route 776 on modern maps). In the backyard of this home was a little lake. And in the lake was a little island — actually the tiny island was connected by a narrow land bridge, technically creating a peninsula. It was a feature that no one would ever see from the road, but from the air, it beckoned to me as a challenge to my ability to land my parachute in impossible places. Finally, one day during a skydive, I couldn't take it any more and I peeled off from the rest of the jumpers landing at the airstrip and made for the "island." I made a perfect standup landing in the middle of the island. Even so, it was so small, I had a difficult time keeping my canopy from falling into the lake. To my surprise, the elderly home owners, Mr. and Mrs. Carl Carlens, were delighted to have me land there. After we introduced ourselves, Carl said, "Next time, tell us beforehand, and we'll have a cold beer and lunch waiting for you."

He didn't have to wait too long. The next weekend I stopped before I turned into the drop zone and told Carl I'd be dropping in after a while. This time I had even less room to land on the island because they had set up a little table holding a plate of fried chicken and a can of beer. We became good friends, and several times I'd bring other jumpers over to meet them. The Carlens even held a party one night for the skydivers, and I brought a 16mm movie projector to show them freefall movies which I had filmed several thousand feet above their house. In much this way, the skydivers were friendly with many of the homeowners who lived around the airport. Bob Hibschman, who was one of the first to build a home with an aircraft hanger just off the airport, became one of our many supporters. I use to try to get Bob to bet me a beer that I couldn't land on his roof, but he thought I was crazy enough to try it.

The Mission Valley Skydivers became known as "windy day" jumpers. Once another club drove many miles to join us for a day of jumping. It was so windy that day that they all sat in their cars and fumed while we made jump after jump as if it were a normal day.

Then came the day that was too windy even for us. We sat on the ground all day waiting for the wind to die. Finally, I could see that John, our pilot, was getting bored and probably thinking he could just as well be at home watching a football game on TV. So, in a moment of bravado, I said loudly, "I didn't come down here just to sit on the ground."

Everyone looked up.

"John," I bragged, "if you're crazy enough to fly, I'm crazy enough to jump."

I guess I thought that John would turn me down but I was wrong.

"Come on," he said. "You can jump out as I fly home."

Maybe he thought I'd back down, but now, in front of everybody, I felt committed.

Since this was the first jump of the day and no one had yet determined where the "spot" was, I took up in the plane with me a wind drift indicator, known to us as a WDI, and, at 2,000 feet, threw it out over the packing area. The wind was from the south and I couldn't believe how far north the WDI went before it hit ground. It told me that the spot, my exit point, was a long, long way to the south.

Holy smoke! This was going to be the longest spot I had ever had. John came around on jump run, north to south. Since I was alone, I didn't need any altitude for freefall. As we came over the airport at only 3,000 feet, I could see everyone standing in the packing area. They must have been wondering if I was really going to jump or if this was just an elaborate joke that John and I cooked up. We kept flying due south until the road to Englewood curved to the east. Then we kept going out over the bay. I knew we had to be at least a mile and a half from the airport.

John and I shook hands. "Thanks, John," I said.

"Good luck!" he replied. "See you next weekend."

"I hope," I said as I climbed out of the plane and jumped. I opened at exactly 2,000 feet. I could barely see the airport to the north. The only time I had jumped this far south was the time we made a water jump into the bay right below me. *That was the time Mike Stahl had a malfunction and rode it into the water,* I thought.

I made a turn downwind to check the speed of the wind and took off like a rocket. I immediately turned back upwind, to the south, to minimize my movement over the ground. The wind was worse than I had thought. Even headed into the wind, I was backing up over ground faster than I had ever flown in a parachute in my life. I had only lost 500 feet of altitude and I was already halfway to the airport. If things didn't improve rapidly, I was in big trouble. They didn't and I was.

At 1,000 feet, I was still backing up. I started to get very, very worried. As I passed over the packing area where I was supposed to land, I looked down and saw a long black hearse stopped halfway down the airport road. That really gave me a fright.

Where in hell did that come from? I thought.

I had never seen a hearse around here before. This was a very bad omen as far as I was concerned. I squirmed around in my harness and tried to look behind me at where I was going. It was impossible to see much or make any rational plan of how or where I would land. Besides, I was traveling so fast that the landscape was changing too rapidly to know what to expect.

I tried to think of what was to the north. I was traveling parallel to Route 775 and I knew that I'd soon be past the golf course just across the road to the east. That meant that very soon I'd be over the highway and the accompanying power lines where they made a little jog to the west. I thought maybe I'd better turn toward the east and cross over the road to find a less dangerous landing area.

Just then, my feet brushed over something and it was so unexpected, I nearly had a heart attack. It was the top of one of the tall Australian pine trees in front of the trailer park. My feet had just touched the wispy top and I was surprised to find myself coming down in the middle of a perfect triangle of these tall green trees. As my chute came behind this natural windbreak, the wind was cut off and I made a soft stand-up landing without even trying. I was in a daze. I couldn't believe it. One moment, I was in fear of my life with no hope of reaching ground intact, and the next, I was deposited safely on the ground without a scratch. I was completely surrounded by the triangle of pines and when I looked up, I couldn't understand how there had been enough room for my Para-Commander to come down inside of them. Was I lucky, or what? This was probably the only place on the face of the planet that day where a parachutist could have landed without being dashed to pieces.

When the other jumpers came roaring up in their cars to find my body, they were surprised to find me alive and uninjured.

"Piece of cake!" I replied nonchalantly when they asked about the jump. Surreptitiously, however, I made the sign of the cross - and I'm not even religious.

Come to think of it, I never did find out why that hearse was parked on the airport road.

Chapter Nine
DEMOS

Exhibition jumps, what we called "demos," were animals unto them selves. On one hand, they were a skydiver's dream. The rewards were what a skydiver fantasized should be his compensation for *every* jump, but he could still hardly comprehend it. Someone actually paid him to do what he loved to do: skydive. And upon landing, he received a hero's welcome from adoring crowds who were awed by his bravery in the face of danger. Also there were often newspaper write-ups or television coverage showing the jumper in full glory.

On the downside, for some reason it seemed that the weather was always exceptionally bad on exhibition days. Not bad enough to call it off, mind you. Oh, no, it would always be marginal right up to jump time. Then the jumper would feel like a coward if he cancelled the exhibition or feel like a fool if he went ahead with it. In addition, the jump site was always too small and/or filled with hazards. Adding to the pressure was the fact that you got only one shot at the landing. If you made an error and missed the target, that was it; you didn't get a second chance to redeem yourself. One brutal reality about skydiving is that once you leave the plane, it's all downhill; you are going to end up on the ground one way or another within a very limited amount of time. And the manner or style in which you do reach the ground is very obviously a measure of your skill and experience.

My first demo was a disaster. As a joke it was billed as the highest high dive. Advertising flyers showed purposely misleading artwork depicting a man springing off a diving board into a swimming pool. My target was the large swimming pool in the recreation area of a trailer park east of Sarasota called Sun-N-Fun — what would now be called an RV park. It had a nice restaurant where I often ate lunch. That was how I got to know the owner, Dick Hysell, and got him interested in hiring me for an exhibition jump. Of course, when I sold the job, I exuded self-confidence, claiming that hitting the pool would be easy for an expert like myself who had 378 jumps. There were plenty of hazards in my proposed landing area: power lines, buildings, metal fences, concrete structures — you name it. But the pool was large enough that I thought I just might be able to land in it, given half a chance.

On exhibition day, I had no problem borrowing the jump plane from the drop zone. It was too windy to jump — at least for fun. But I had taken a down payment for the exhibition and turned "pro," so I felt obligated to come through for my client.

I made what I considered a very long "spot" upwind, but it turned out to be about half the distance I needed. Hanging helplessly under my parachute, the high winds propelled me backward past my proposed landing site and I left the pool about a mile in my wake. I hit ground along the highway between the road and the power lines and dragged a dozen yards.

Despite the fiasco, and against my protests, Dick good-naturedly paid me the second half of my contract. He knew I could have cancelled the jump and he figured, under the conditions, that I had earned every penny of my fee. In retrospect, it was probably a godsend that I had missed my target. If I had ended up anywhere near that pool, I'd have killed myself.

Duffy told me about one of his first demos before I had started jumping in Englewood. A bunch of the first skydivers in Sarasota made a jump into the Sarasota County Fair — at night — in high winds. Since this was before the development of the easier landing Para-Commander parachutes, they were still jumping the old military surplus chutes, which always came down very hard. One of the jumpers, I believe it was Bill Dondanville, hit so hard right by the Ferris wheel in the midway that he was knocked unconscious. Later they found him wandering aimlessly around the fair without knowing who or where he was.

Duffy was an expert at selling skydiving demos. Several times he arranged to do two in one day in different cities. On one occasion, he and Bob Branch from the Tampa Skydivers made a jump in St. Petersburg earlier in the day before flying to Sarasota for a second exhibition skydive. As part of Sarasota's "King Neptune Festival," they planned to land in the bay near the pier where Marina Jack's Restaurant is now.

It was March of 1965 and, at that time, I still had very few jumps, so I wasn't qualified to take part in the exhibition except as a member of the ground crew. Duffy told me that maybe I could help out on the Sarasota jump by being in the rescue boat at the bay front. I thought that this was a perfect chance for me to use my self-taught scuba diving skills.

So when Duffy and Bob parachuted into the bay, I was in the rescue boat decked out in my scuba gear with the little tiny tank. Duffy's parachute opened fine, but Bob's opened into what we called a "Mae West" — there were several shroud lines over the top of the canopy, dividing it almost in half like a giant bra. Bob struggled with it for a moment or two and then, without cutting away, pulled his reserve ripcord. Luckily, the reserve came out and opened without entangling with the main parachute, which then deflated and hung limply beneath him as he descended. Bob landed before Duffy, so we maneuvered our boat to help him out of the water first.

I jumped into the water to give a hand from below. As Bob was being pulled out by the other guy in the boat, I grabbed his foot underwater to help shove him up. The instant I touched his foot he disappeared. Bob was a big man and I thought that the guy in the boat must have been pretty strong in order to yank him out of the water that way. After we got to land, I found out what had really happened.

First, Duffy told about the events that had taken place earlier in St. Petersburg. On that jump, Bob drifted off target and landed unintentionally in Tampa Bay. Bob was deathly afraid of sharks, and when he was drifting out over the bay, he spotted some large dark aquatic creatures in the water below. An old man fishing in a small boat nearby was startled to hear a parachutist overhead screaming, "Shark! Shark! Come save me! Shark!"

The old fisherman couldn't see what the fuss was about. All he could see were a few porpoises playing nearby in the bay. Duffy said laughingly that Bob ended up in only waist-deep water anyway and simply waded in to shore.

So, on the next jump, when I grabbed his foot underwater, Bob said he thought a shark had gotten him for sure this time. He practically leaped into the boat, almost knocking over the guy helping him.

By the time Duffy sold another "double-header," I had a lot more jumps but it was Christmas and these were single skydiver "Santa" jumps; I still wasn't needed as a skydiver. But Duffy asked me if I wanted to go along for the plane ride. I had nothing better to do, so I agreed. One jump was in Gainesville and the other was in Ocala, both small towns north of Tampa near the middle of the state. John Clement, our regular pilot who flew for us in Englewood, flew in to meet us at the Sarasota Airport and we took off for Gainesville. As it turned out, it was lucky that I went along.

It was about a forty-five-minute flight to Gainesville. When we arrived over the downtown jump site, Duffy threw a crepe paper wind streamer to determine the direction and velocity of the wind. As usual, it was a very windy day for an exhibition jump. We were both amazed at the indicated distance of the exit point from the target.

Duffy had no costume, so he just wore a red jumpsuit to approximate the Santa Claus look from a distance. The target was on top of a department store roof so that after he landed Duffy could easily be replaced by a professional Santa in a rented costume, out of view of the large audience of kids. This "real" Santa would then climb down off the roof on a firetruck ladder in order to hand out gifts among the kids.

As we turned on jump run, Duffy turned to me and said, "I hate windy days!"

"Better you than me, pal," I replied.

"Well, I just have to remember," he said as he got ready to jump, "not to say 'fuck' in front of the (and he spelled it out) K-I-D-S !"

I was still laughing when he jumped.

John and I watched his landing while we circled in the plane. Duffy almost didn't make it to his rooftop target. He had to run downwind all the way and hook a turn at the last second, landing on the very edge of the roof.

"Well, at least he hit the roof," John said.

"I don't know, John," I replied. "It looked as if he hit awfully hard."

We landed at the small Gainesville airport to await Duffy's return. Duffy didn't arrive for the longest time, and John and I were starting to get worried. Finally a car pulled up and Duffy slowly emerged. He hobbled toward us with a very pronounced limp. He had either broken an ankle or sprained it badly.

"Well, you're up next!" he said to me.

Up until now, I had been mildly amused by the danger of jumping into the middle of a downtown area in high winds. Now suddenly I realized that I'd have to make the next jump into Ocala and somehow it didn't seem so amusing.

On our flight to Ocala, to John's dismay, Duffy pulled a bottle of scotch whisky out of a brown paper bag and started taking swigs straight out of the bottle. This was one reason Duffy had taken so long to return to the airport. He had talked his driver into a detour to a liquor store for medicinal purposes. By the time we landed in Ocala, Duffy was feeling no pain, which was exactly the effect he wanted.

I stretched out Duffy's parachute on the ground near the plane and re-packed it, which was quite a job in the high wind. Once finished, I put on the red jumpsuit and Duffy's parachute and we took off again. I had no idea where the jump site was, so Duffy had to direct us. By now, Duffy had almost finished the bottle of scotch and it was a minor miracle that we found the place at all.

Again, the target was on a rooftop and, again, the wind streamer showed a fantastically long "spot." As we turned onto jump run, I made sure that Duffy was strapped in with his seatbelt. In his drunken condition, I didn't want him jumping out behind me without a parachute. When I cautioned him about this, he said, "I'm just drunk; I'm not stupid!"

As I got out of the plane, Duffy gave me some last-minute advice: "Remember," he shouted, waving his empty bottle, "Don't land among the little kids; if you don't have any presents, they'll tear you apart!"

With that echoing in my head, I jumped, and it was quite an experience. Up until then, all of my jumps had been over open areas: drop zones, airports, or rural land. Now I was over a downtown grid of streets, homes, and businesses. The target area was out of sight, so I turned downwind and began to speed over the landscape.

I was flying to the right of a major highway, Route 41, which ran straight through downtown Ocala and on toward Gainesville to the north. It was a novel experience to see traffic below me and, with the wind, I could see that I was moving almost as fast as they were. The shopping mall was up ahead across the highway and there was a white square on one of the mall roofs, which I knew was my target.

I was getting too close for my altitude, so I turned Duffy's Para-Com-mander and held into the wind. To avoid backing into the target with no control, the trick would be to build up speed traveling downwind and turn upwind at the last moment to counteract the velocity of the wind. But I wanted to avoid cutting it as close as Duffy had. I knew I was close enough now so everybody on the ground would be looking at me, so I made a couple of quick 360-degree turns for effect before holding into the wind for the last time.

When I judged the distance to be about right by looking over my shoulder, I turned back downwind, crossed the highway, and made my final approach toward the target. I waited until the last second and made a hook turn as I crossed over the edge of the roof. I had judged it perfectly. I made a birdlike swoop and landed standing up about two feet from the white sheet which had been tacked down on the asphalt rooftop as my target.

The wind immediately grabbed my chute before it could collapse; if I hadn't been ready for it, it would have pulled me off my feet and dragged me off the roof. As I landed, I made a pivoting turn on the balls of my feet and took four or five running steps to collapse my chute. That took me near the back edge of the roof. Just out of curiosity, I took a few extra steps and looked over the edge.

Holy smoke! The roof unexpectedly dropped off three stories to concrete loading ramps at the back of the store. The building must have been built on a steep hill because the store was only one story high in front. To hell with Duffy's warning about landing in front of the store among the kids! If I had been pulled off the back edge of the roof by the wind, I could have been killed.

Shaking my head, I walked back to the target with my chute bundled up in my arms, to be greeted by the manager of the store who had stationed himself on the roof to watch the jump. He was surprised that I wasn't Duffy, but he was overjoyed with the performance. I was overjoyed with still being alive but, pretending that it was no big deal, I apologized for not landing directly on top of the target.

"Oh, that's all right," the manager said in jest. "I'm going to pay you guys anyway!"

At least, I *think* he said it in jest.

Years later, I, too, was able to sell exhibitions in two different cities on the same day. I had started an exhibition team which I called "Skyquest Parateam." By that time, John Clement had moved to Costa Rica in Central America and we weren't jumping in Englewood anymore. Rather than depend on a jump plane out of Tampa or Zephyrhills to fly for my demos, I had found another local pilot, also named John, who owned his own plane. John Tunstall was a neat guy. He was a former race car driver and now he owned his own pipe-laying company in Sarasota. John was an adventurous type of guy, and flying a bunch of crazy skydivers appealed to him.

It was the 4th of July, and the first of my two demos was scheduled in the early afternoon in downtown Tampa. After that jump, we would have just enough time to get a ride back to the Peter O'Knight Airport on Davis Island about five miles away, repack our chutes, and fly back to Sarasota for our exhibition jump right before the fireworks celebration at dusk. For these events, I had two other jumpers besides myself for the first jump and four others for the second.

The first jump in Tampa was going to be tricky. It was into a little bar right on Dale Mabry, a major thoroughfare running north and south through downtown Tampa. Our landing site was a little parking lot in back of the bar. There was nowhere else to land. The rest of the area consisted of traffic, buildings, power lines, parked cars, homes, concrete posts, and fences. You either hit the target area or you died.

I had driven up to Tampa alone to look over the site, so the other two guys on this jump, Chris Brown and Jim Beck, were lucky; they had no preconceived notion of how bad the target area really was. I remember, just before we jumped, how easy it was describing the "spot" to them because of the downtown grid. Usually with lots of pointing, there was an in-plane discussion that began, "The spot's just past that lake over there."

"Where, that small one over there?"

"No, the large one — there!"

In this case it was a concise, "The spot is three blocks to the north and four blocks to the west."

We were all jumping "squares," ram-air parachutes, and because of their forward speed, I knew that we'd have to really sink them out in order to get into that tiny parking lot surrounded by power lines. I was last out of the plane, so I had the advantage of being able to watch how the others landed and make any adjustments to my approach. I was jumping a little square called a "Unit" which was difficult to slow down when landing. It was also very easy to stall out when it was flying slowly, a situation which could be very dangerous near the ground.

I saw the other two guys below me land in the parking lot which left only myself, the team captain, to make it a perfect exhibition. In my eagerness to land on target, I misjudged my final approach and turned too early. I immediately realized that I was too close but I had to live with it — or try to. I was too low to go around to set up a new approach. I was totally committed with no place to go. I was flying toward a power pole directly ahead of me, so I kept pulling my steering lines further and further down, trying to slow my forward speed. I must have still been ten to fifteen feet in the air when I finally reached the parachute's stall point and just dropped out of the sky onto the rough asphalt. I hit so hard that I skinned both knees and both elbows. With a huge crowd of people watching, it was all I could do to pick myself up, smile, wave, and walk into the bar without limping. I had to wash the blood out of my jumpsuit in the men's room to get ready for the next jump.

We landed at Jones Aviation at the Sarasota Airport to pick up my other team members, Kenny Rolfe and Ben Hall. Our next jump was onto the tip of a small peninsula called Island Park that curved out into the middle of Sarasota Bay. Before our Tampa jump, we had all considered the Island Park jump to be dangerously "tight." But the green grass of Island Park was a dream compared to that small asphalt parking lot in Tampa. It was amusing that the most dangerous of the two jumps was for a relatively small crowd of maybe fifty people, while the Sarasota jump was before tens of thousands of cheering spectators and hundreds of boats sounding their air horns.

My red smoke and American flag set the mood for the patriotic event. Our jump was right at dusk, and a fantastic fireworks display traced our flight path back up into the night sky, topping off a very memorable day.

Another memorable day was when I was hired one time to make a Santa Claus jump into a football game on the island of Grand Cayman. My good friend Bruce Harting had introduced me to this beautiful island previously — but more about that later. At this time, Bruce had long since moved back to Florida, but his friend Reed Dennis had called me from Cayman to make all the arrangements. When Rose and I arrived on the island, our bag with all of our scuba gear was missing, but, to our relief, all of my skydiving gear arrived safely. The following day was the big annual football game and, as usual, it was very windy. It was December, but the temperature was in the 90s, normal for an island in the Caribbean. I had rented a professional Santa outfit in Sarasota, and the pilot's wife loaned me a pillow for my belly to fill it out. The pilot had never flown a skydiver before and he was a bit nervous. On jump run, when I turned to him to shake his hand good-bye, both his hands were locked on the control wheel and his attention was straight ahead, so I just patted his shoulder instead and jumped out of the plane, probably much to his relief. Because of the wind, my exit point was way out over the ocean; I felt very incongruous floating high over the blue-green Caribbean Ocean on a hot day dressed in a fur-lined Santa costume. I also felt very uncomfortable being that far out over the water encumbered in the heavy material of the Santa suit, even though I was flying a ram-air parachute. I had a feeling that if I accidentally landed in the water, I'd end up on the bottom before I could get out of all the clothing.

As I flew my parachute toward the land, the Santa beard kept blowing up into my face and obstructing my vision. This was not good, since I knew I'd have a hard enough time as it was, trying to land in the target area. The football field was a perfect rectangle cut out of a dense jungle of extremely tall Australian Pines. The wind was very turbulent and, as I made my final turn over the western edge of the trees, I flew into a strong downdraft. My parachute took a nose dive and, suddenly, I found myself horizontal, flying directly toward the ground. In alarm, I pulled on full brakes and my parachute leveled out just as I hit ground. My feet slipped out from under me on the slippery grass and I slid to a stop on my butt at the exact center of the field. Santa had made a spectacular landing and the crowd went wild.

Rose, my wife, was the announcer for all of my exhibition jumps and she was very good at it. But this time, she really outdid herself. By the time I touched down, she had most of the Caymanian kids, who had never seen a skydiver in the first place, actually believing that I was the real Santa Claus in person. When she met me mid-field, she slipped me a bag of candy which I handed out to the excited, cheering kids as if I had brought it along on the jump. Finally, with the candy all gone and the huge crowd of kids disbursed, I walked off the field to change clothes. As I walked down the sidelines toward the field house, one kid trailed along behind me, telling people, "He's not really Santa Claus." When I entered the empty field house to revert to my normal identity, I realized that the kid had followed me into the locker room.

"You're not really Santa," he said to me matter-of-factly as if I didn't know.

I took his shoulders, gently turned him around, guided him out the door, and locked it behind him. It wouldn't do to have him actually see Santa changing clothes.

"He's not really Santa," I heard him say outside the door to no one in particular.

I had jumped for a demo over water long before that, but not in costume. Duffy and I once parachuted into a beach wedding for a friend of his. It was held on Coquina Beach on the island of Anna Maria east of Bradenton.

Duffy was always experimenting with smoke bombs and other pyrotechnics for exhibition jumps. On this day, he had a couple of new hand-held flare guns to try out. They were the size and shape of an ink pen. The tiny tube was loaded with a flare cartridge and you pulled a lever back to cock it. Holding and aiming it with one hand, you simply pushed the trigger mechanism with your thumb to fire it. Duffy gave me one and we made plans to fire them in freefall.

"All right," I said. "I'll be on your right, so you fire yours to the left."

"No problem." Duffy replied.

"I mean it," I emphasized. I knew how cavalier Duffy was around explosives. "I don't want to be eating a flare in freefall!"

The wind was from the southwest, off the water, so our "spot" was way out over the entrance to the pass between the islands which in Florida are called "keys." As we jumped, it was a beautiful sight. To our left, the long straight beach of Longboat Key stretched out in front of us for miles. Behind us was Anna Maria Key, and, to our right, as far as the eye could see, was the blue sparkling expanse of the Gulf of Mexico.

My appreciation of the beauty spread before me in freefall was abruptly cut short by the curved track of a flare passing just below my face.

Damn it! Duffy was at it again! *Okay,* I thought, *if he wants to play, let's see how he likes this.*

I turned and fired my flare gun toward Duffy. We were still laughing at our aerial duel as we opened our parachutes at 2,000 feet. Even though we were way out over the water, Duffy's "spot" was good and we landed right on target among the wedding party on the beach. They were delighted when one of us delivered a bottle of champagne to the groom and the other a bouquet of flowers to the bride.

About five years later, Duffy's friend, the groom, unexpectedly committed suicide, and Duffy got the sad task of dispersing his friend's cremated ashes from a plane over the Gulf of Mexico where we had jumped. For some reason Duffy couldn't make the flight when scheduled and I was out of town, so he asked another Mission Valley Skydiver, Dan Liddy, to drop the ashes for him.

Later, Duffy said, "Boy, I hope that's the last time I have to arrange anything like that!"

"Why?" I asked, expecting to hear some poignant statement about the sudden loss of a friend. I should have known better.

"Because Liddy took the lid off the box too early and half the son of a bitch blew back into the airplane! It took me an hour to clean the ashes out of the plane after it was back on the ground!"

Nothing was sacred to Duffy.

Chapter Ten

JIM

Jim Shockley was a small, neat, well-educated young man. He was always immaculately dressed in what would now be called "preppy" clothing. He was quick to smile, but he was always a bundle of nervous energy, and all his movements were quick and sudden. When he walked, he looked as if he were bouncing along on his toes. Jim was studying to be a doctor of some sort and was quick to inform anyone of that fact. Duffy hated this attitude and disliked the lofty airs that Jim constantly exhibited. Jim never simply talked; he expounded and enlightened his subjects with lofty concepts and multisyllabic words. This never appeared to bother anyone else. We just took it all with a grain of salt. But for some reason it just seemed to get under Duffy's skin. Also, Jim never looked like a skydiver, at least on the ground. In our minds, we tended to equate ourselves with combat-hardened paratroopers. Jim never came close to our self-image; he was too well dressed, too well spoken and, well, he just didn't look rough and tough enough. What was worse, he didn't act like a skydiver. He never got drunk, and the closest Jim ever got to swearing was an emphatic "darn" or "gosh."

But despite all this, Jim was a damn good skydiver, and he and I became close friends. One of the best freefall photos I ever took was of Jim in his bright red jumpsuit, bubble goggles and silver helmet sharply focused against a deep blue sky. It was one of those perfectly composed pictures that I could never seem to improve on.

Jim was a good jumper and a very likable guy, but Duffy just couldn't let it go at that. Duffy never let an opportunity pass to taunt Jim, and the two of them were verbally at each other's throats all the time. Duffy took great delight in baiting Jim with some common piece of knowledge that any *medical student* ought to know, and Jim rose to take the challenge every time. Jim should have known better. Duffy may not have had as formal an education as Jim, but he was the cleverest guy I knew. It was like a gym-trained boxer trying to take on a street fighter.

One time, in Barney's Bar, Duffy came up with a classic. It was a typical after-jump evening with ten or fifteen of us jumpers causing havoc in the crowded bar. "Hey, med student," Duffy's voice could be heard above the din. "You're good at pronouncing things, aren't you?"

All the jumpers perked up and quieted down, sensing another battle of wits.

"Yes, I believe I am able to articulate and enunciate the English language with more acuity than most rational beings," Jim waxed elegant with a grandiose wave of his arms.

"Well, enunciate this: *Fuck you!* Har, har," Duffy laughed.

There was a ripple of laughter around the table but everyone had clearly expected something more clever. Jim just rolled his eyes as if saying, "What else would you expect from a peasant!" But I could see from the sparkle in Duffy's eye that he was far from through.

"No, seriously, Jim," now he had the attention of the entire table, "Do you pronounce the capital of Kentucky, '*LOUIE* - ville' or '*LOUIS* - ville'?"

Jim, lulled by the supposedly trivial question about pronunciation answered without thinking, "Why, '*LOUIE* -ville', of course, my good man."

"No, I'm sorry, Jim," Duffy sprung his trap with delight. "The capital of Kentucky is pronounced," he paused for effect and said the name slowly with exaggerated pronunciation of each syllable ... "FRANK-FORT"!

Jim was a good skydiver, but at times he drove us to distraction with his fastidious habits. Everything about his jump gear had to be perfect and he was the antithesis of the rest of us, whose motto was "Pack it and cut off any excess hanging out of the pack!" If we thought we might have packed in a malfunction, it never occurred to us to re-pack. We just jumped it to find out. Not Jim — he would never have made an error in packing in the first place. Duffy always claimed that Jim ironed his canopy at home before he packed it.

For this reason it was unusual for me to pick Jim for one of my crazy experimental jumps. We all had talked about the possibility of saving an unconscious jumper in freefall. I had no doubt that one jumper could deploy another man's parachute by flying in to him in freefall and pulling his ripcord; no problem. I just wanted to take this idea a little further. I thought that if the subject were conscious, as he got opening shock, he could open the other guy's pack automatically simply by holding onto the other man's ripcord as he fell away. Later, this concept was exactly how one type of student cutaway system was designed.

My first choice was Billy Revis, but he wasn't at the drop zone that day. As hard as I tried I couldn't talk anyone else on the DZ into attempting it with me.

Finally I swayed Jim by, "Don't be a wimp! Trust me, I know what I'm doing."

After talking it over carefully on the ground and reassuring Jim that nothing could go wrong, we got in the plane. John, our pilot, knew something was up because of Jim's nervousness, but as usual he never questioned me. He figured I was going to screw up just as well without any advice from him. Besides, he could see that we weren't carrying any strange extraneous objects, as we were wont to do.

We went out at 7,500 feet. The first part of the jump went just as I had planned. We flew together in freefall, grabbed hands and changed grips to each other's harness straps high on the chest. Then, once stabilized, we carefully reached across with our right hands and got each other's ripcords out of their respective pockets. As planned, I nodded at Jim and pulled his ripcord. Then expecting his pack to open, I let go of him with my left hand as he let go of me. I saw his backpack open and his pilot chute spring out. But for some reason the pilot chute didn't catch air and pull out Jim's chute as it was supposed to do. It just fell back onto his back and flopped around.

While I was watching this, with both of us still freefalling at 120 miles per hour, I suddenly realized that I was backsliding. I had now moved far enough from Jim that my ripcord, which he was still holding, had reached the end of its slack. Without warning, my backpack opened and started its deployment just as Jim's pilot chute finally caught air. Our chutes opened together with the two of us only a few feet apart. My parachute deployed up inside of Jim's, and went out through one of his steering slots. We found ourselves entangled and all hell was breaking loose! Even with our parachutes deployed, our falling speed hadn't been slowed by much. I remember vivid flashes of action as if in a stop-action dream, almost as if things were happening so fast that my brain couldn't record every frame.

Jim and I were see-sawing past each other ... his white nylon lines were whipping past me so fast they had an audible hum ... I was reaching out with my bare hands warding them away from me, not really aware that the lines were burning through my flesh like band saws ... Jim flashed past me not two feet away and at such a speed that I knew that we both would have been badly injured had we collided ... I threw off more lines. I looked up and saw that my canopy was out through a slot and I realized that if I could make my way up through there, we would be free of each other. I really wasn't sure if that goal was only a wish or a real possibility, but I was going to give it a try. I figured we must have a little altitude left. I was still desperately trying to avoid getting entangled in those lines whizzing past me at the expense of my lacerated hands. Jim flew past again almost horizontal to me and I yelled, "Hang on, Jim, I think I can get free!" I never knew if he heard me because an instant after that he cut away.

He may have saved both our lives. He did what he thought best and it worked. That's what it's all about. At any rate, once he was clear, my canopy opened with no trouble. I surveyed the situation. My canopy looked undamaged but I had three or four lines burned away. My hands were badly cut, but since they were also burned by the friction of the nylon, they weren't bleeding too badly. My chute seemed to be holding me up okay even with the missing lines, so I decided to land under it. Good! After all that, I certainly didn't feel up to cutting away and having to cope with opening my reserve, not at this low altitude. With that settled, apprehensively, I looked to see what happened to Jim. Had he been able to open his reserve — or had he fallen to his death?

I was overjoyed to see him directly under me floating down under his small white reserve. I yelled, "Hey, Jim! Are you all right?"

His reply floated clearly up to me in a voice higher pitched than normal and quavering in emotion: "Keep away from me!! This is the only chute I've got left!"

Chapter Eleven
JUMPING BLIND

I felt foolish sitting on the ground with my back to the pine tree, a strip of cloth tied around my head covering my eyes. It was a hot Florida afternoon and sweat was trickling down my neck and forehead. The blindfold was my idea. I wanted to acclimate myself to being sightless before I made my "blind" jump.

This was another one of my brilliant ideas. About a month earlier, we had been sitting around talking about — what else — skydiving. Somehow we began speculating about the possibility of surviving a long freefall without vision. The other guys were dubious but I said I was so certain it could be done that I'd bet my life on it. I must have thought I was indestructible because I immediately began making plans to make a blindfolded skydive.

For weeks I practiced counting silently against a stopwatch. I got so good at estimating thirty seconds, give or take half a second, that I was winning free drinks on bar bets after having been acclaimed by my friends as some sort of idiot savant of time. At least they had the "idiot" part right. Now, at the drop zone, the moment of truth had arrived.

Before putting on the blindfold, I had a serious talk with everyone on the drop zone. This was more life-threatening than usual, so I wanted everybody's help and cooperation. Everyone was to understand that this was no joke; it was very serious stuff indeed. Once the blindfold was in place, there was no turning back. I was to be left alone for half an hour and no one was to interrupt my concentration. Only Duffy and Bob Malott were to help me suit up, escort me to the plane, and go along to both jumpmaster me and to monitor my jump in freefall. Both they and I understood that if anything went wrong, there would not be much that either Duffy or Bob could do to help me. They would be observers only and it was every man for himself when it came to opening altitude. This experiment was my idea and if I were killed, this was my testimonial that they were to be held blameless.

Knowing both Duffy and Bob, I took them aside for a private talk. "I know how your minds work," I said. "It would be really easy to put a blindfolded man in the plane and after taxiing down the runway, run the engine up to make him think the plane was taking off. Then a couple of guys on each wing tip could rock the plane every so often as if the plane were in flight. But," and I looked each of them directly in the eye one at a time, "If I get out on the step and jump, only to find that we're still on the ground, I'll never forgive you." I was never this deadly serious, so they knew I meant what I said.

With all this expressed and understood, I put on the blindfold and settled down to thirty long minutes of self-contemplation and concentration on the task at hand.

When I got into the plane with the blindfold in place, John never said a word, but I swear I could feel him look at me and shake his head. It was a comfort to me to have a competent and faithful pilot like John at the controls. I knew he, at least, would have no part in a practical joke at my expense. I told Duffy that I was determined to go for a full thirty seconds in freefall so he had better be sure that we were at 7,500 feet on jump run or I was dead. Duffy assured me that I was not to worry one bit about altitude; he would take care of that and also give me a good spot so I'd land on target. It was then a long, long plane ride to altitude.

I was surprised that there was no small talk as usual between Bob and Duffy. They were respecting my wishes for total concentration. Finally, I heard Duffy giving John jump run corrections. I heard the engine slow as John eased back the throttle. This was it!

After a moment, Duffy put a friendly hand on my shoulder and asked in my ear, "Are you ready?"

"All set," I nodded.

"Good luck!" he said. "Have a good jump."

I was calm and collected on the outside, but inside things were humming.

"Get out on the step!" Duffy commanded over the motor and wind noise.

I couldn't afford any doubts that we were indeed at 7,500 feet, so I put it out of my mind. I reached out and, with one hand on the doorjamb, grasped the strut with my right hand. Awkwardly, I pulled myself out into the slipstream and stood crouched on the step, both hands holding the strut like a runner at his mark. I waited for what seemed an eternity but was, in actuality, only a few seconds as Duffy double-checked the spot.

"GO!" he yelled and slapped my backpack.

To his surprise, instead of doing a flat and stable student exit, I rolled off backwards and made one, two, three backloops before stabilizing out into a normal face-to-earth position.

It was weird. On the one hand, I was trying to keep a slow steady count running in my head; not too fast; not too slow.

... four thousand, five thousand, six thousand ...

On the other hand, I was trying to fine-tune my senses and consciously experience this once-in-a-lifetime event. I was never going to do it again, however it turned out, so I wanted to get the most out of it that I could.

... eight thousand, nine thousand, ten thousand ...

Actually, it was very peaceful not having any visual input or stimulation.

... twelve thousand, thirteen thousand, fourteen thoi

I was a lot more conscious of the sound of the win 120 mph. On most jumps I never paid any attention to the all.

... sixteen thousand, seventeen thousand, eighteen thousand ...

I wondered where Duffy and Bob were. I hoped they stayed clear of me when it came time to open.

... twenty thousand, twenty-one thousand, twenty-two thousand ...

I was having absolutely no trouble at all staying stable. We had discussed this as a potential problem.

... twenty-four thousand, twenty-five thousand, twenty-six thousand ...

Well, if Duffy had shorted me on altitude or if I was counting too slowly, I'd never know it; I'd just abruptly slam into the ground and that would be that.

... twenty-eight thousand, twenty-nine thousand, THIRTY thousand ... what the hell, thirty-ONE thousand...

And I reached, automatically found my ripcord handle and pulled.

Since we didn't have any ground-to-air radios, we decided right off that I wouldn't attempt to land blindfolded.

I got opening shock, removed the blindfold and got another shock. My altitude was fine, I was right at 2,000 feet, but when I checked my canopy, I saw that the dirty bastards had switched my parachute. While I was blindfolded on the ground, Duffy and Bob must have opened my pack, removed my Para-Commander sport parachute and substituted an old surplus "double-L" cheapo.

Ah, well, I thought, *boys will be boys.* Now that I was still alive, I was feeling very charitable. In all fairness, I had really never mentioned anything about switching canopies.

Now, I thought, *If I can just manage to land this old junker without breaking any part of my body.*

Chapter Twelve

BILLY

Y ou never knew about jump students. Some turned out to be good and others, for no apparent reason, didn't turn out at all. When I first met Billy Revis, he was such a quiet, unassuming kid, I thought he would never make a good skydiver. I was training students almost every week and I thought I could spot the talented ones. I was never more wrong.

Nowadays it takes a boatload of money to learn how to skydive. Training has become much more standardized and commercial. Back in the '60s, the instruction was more personalized and one-on-one. We trained people for free just to get them into our skydiving club. The student had only to pay for their jump as well as their jumpmaster's ($4.00 each) and rent the student gear from Duffy.

Since there was almost no reward for the jumpmaster except for a free low-altitude jump or two, I began to pick and choose who I would train, sloughing off the ones I didn't think promising to other jumpmasters.

One day my friend Jim Shockley said that he had two new students and asked if I would train one of them. He explained that they were two teenagers with their parent's permission to begin jump training. I wasn't too keen on the idea and I agreed only if I got to pick the one I'd train after I met them. You guessed it. I picked the dud. Jim took Billy, who became a skydiving legend in his own time.

In attitude, Billy reminded me of myself when I was a little younger. In other words, he was a wild and crazy guy. As I did, he had this premonition of an early death. His came true, however; mine didn't. Billy was a natural. He was small in stature and shy, but for some reason he had all the right moves and all the natural instincts to make a great jumper. He became the best skydiver I ever knew, without exception. The funny thing was, he was a very quiet, very private individual. He rarely spoke and when he did, it was usually so low and unassuming that you had to strain to hear him. He was short but well proportioned; good-looking with jet-black hair and a laid-back, devil-may-care attitude. He normally had a slight smile on his lips as if he knew a secret no one else did. He always did exactly what he wanted, but never made a big deal out of it.

When Billy did something dangerous, which was practically every jump, Duffy or I would offer fatherly advice in an attempt to temper his wild nature. I didn't have much to stand on since I was one of the worst safety offenders in the club, but I did my best.

Billy would politely listen, agreeing good-naturedly with us, then, on his next jump, do whatever he damn well pleased. We tried threats; we tried persuasion; we tried reward; but nothing worked. You can't influence a guy who just doesn't give a damn. The one constant in life seemed to be that Billy was his own man.

There was not much Duffy or I could say because most of Billy's stunts we had tried ourselves in some fashion in the past — or wanted to. And the threat of grounding him didn't work either. Hell, we had a hard enough time getting him to stick around our DZ as it was. Billy was always on the move and he was constantly going to other DZs all over the state.

For such a small, quiet guy, Billy was also quite a lover. Even as a teenager he always had a girlfriend, and not just on the basis of a schoolboy date, either. Many times he'd leave the DZ early and go park out in the woods to make love to his girl. For a while, we'd buzz his car with the jump plane and make crude jokes when he was around, but we never got a rise out of him. He'd just give us his sad little smile and not say much. We finally gave up on that topic out of sheer boredom.

Billy worked with his father in the family roofing business and apparently made pretty good money. He was the only jumper I knew who owned three or four complete rigs all packed and ready to jump every weekend. He could easily make six to ten jumps a day if he wanted because he could be on almost every load.

The general rule at most DZs was that a jumper had to be packed in order to manifest. That meant that most jumpers with only one rig could never get on two loads in a row. The most jumps I ever made in one day with my one rig was eight, and that almost killed me.

Occasionally, I used to make an intentional cutaway jump using an old reserve. I would attach it to my harness above my reserve on "D" links installed specially for that purpose. Billy, however, found several canopies somewhere that were solid colors — red, green and blue. On one jump he had so many canopies packed up that he ran out of containers, so he packed the last one in a grocery bag. On jump run, he turned to me and said, "Hold this for me, will you?" He handed me a large paper bag holding one of his canopies and jumped out of the plane, deploying the first canopy to open out of the bag I was left holding. He then cut that one away and deployed four more in a row, cutting them away each in turn after they deployed. It was a big surprise to all the people on the ground since, typically, he had told no one in advance. For all I knew, that was a record for the most number of cutaways performed during one jump. But Billy wouldn't have cared even if it had.

A couple of years after my entanglement with Jim Shockley, I decided to attempt the same stunt again and asked Billy if he'd do it with me. Without hesitation he said, "Sure, if you'll work with me first on a stunt I have in mind."

He wanted to put a student's static line on his main pack and jump with it in freefall. In effect, it meant that his main parachute wouldn't open unless the static line was attached to a fixed object. Here's where I came in. He wanted me to hook up with him in freefall so he could snap his static line onto one of the special "D" rings on my harness I used for my cutaway rig. When I pulled my ripcord and deployed my parachute, I would become his "fixed object," thereby opening his static-lined pack.

We decided to make our "stunt jumps" back-to-back on the same day with Billy's first. On jump run, as Billy left the plane, I paused in the door, startled by the sight of a twin-engine airplane right below us. It was off to one side, so I bailed out anyway. By this time, Billy was quite a way below me and I had to dive to make up the distance I had lost. As I was getting close, my left arm went out of joint from an old injury, as it would do from time to time. It wasn't the pain as much as the lost of arm strength which made me pull out of my dive prematurely. Still in freefall, I could see Billy just below me with the end of the static line in one hand waiting for me to get down to him. We were running out of altitude, and he was going to have to pull his reserve if I didn't reach him in time. I pulled my arms and legs in as tight as I could to my body in an effort to protect my bad shoulder, but still keep gaining on Billy. Although I was falling at over 130 mph, all Billy could see was my slow ten-mph approach relative to his 120-mph freefall velocity toward the earth. Slowly I dropped to his level for a tardy but smooth hookup. I could see the relief in Billy's eyes as he snapped the static line onto my harness and signaled he was ready. I immediately pulled my ripcord and the two of us opened —bang, bang — one right after the other. His pilot chute popped up out of his backpack so close I could have grabbed it. Except for my trick shoulder, it was a perfect jump. Now it was my turn.

Another friend of ours, Brant Snyder, went along for some relative work in freefall before Billy and I did our second stunt. We flew together in freefall to make a three man "star" before Brant broke off high at 4,000 feet to leave Billy and I to ourselves as planned. Foremost on my mind was the wild entanglement with Jim Shockley caused by my first attempt at this stunt. Billy and I carefully got hold of each other's ripcords and with a nod, I pulled his. As his parachute deployed, he held onto my ripcord which opened my pack as I fell below him. This time it had worked perfectly with no problems. After two years, I finally felt vindicated. Of the same adventurous spirit, Billy and I made many weird jumps of this nature, each trying to outdo each other with new and novel ideas.

Billy must have owned one of every type of parachute available. He even had one of those triangular jobs called a "Thunder-Bow," which had a bad reputation for malfunctions. (My friend Jack Spahr died using one of these in 1979.) Billy even talked me into jumping his "T-Bow" once. Once is all it took! It opened hard and landed hard. And since it didn't have any improved handling characteristics, I had no use for it.

When the amazing new ram-air parachutes came on the scene, Billy was one of the first to get one. But Billy didn't just use one to get to the ground — he

61

immediately came up with innovative ideas long before their time. The new "square" parachute would literally fly rings around the old-style "round" ones. Even the PC (Para-Commander) had only a twelve-mph drive compared to the square's phenomenal 30-mph.

Billy delighted in flying his square directly at some student who was having a hard enough time simply coping with getting to the ground alive. At the last moment, just when the student knew a mid-air collision was imminent, Billy would pull on the brakes to create lift and fly up and over the top of the student's canopy, sometimes walking over it as he went. This was enough to scare even me with all my accidental collisions and entanglements. But in this respect Billy was almost visionary. Canopy relative work, known as CRW, has become a sport unto itself today. Right from the start Billy had innately recognized the potential of utilizing the square's mobility in new ways.

Billy had an almost magical union with his parachute equipment. To the rest of us, a parachute was just a necessary evil, a way to get to the ground alive after doing RW (Relative Work) in freefall. But Billy used his parachute with grace and style. I've never seen anyone before or since who was so comfortable and at ease with his gear.

Several hundred feet up in the air before landing, Billy would slide his butt back in the "saddle" in order to safely undo his leg straps. He'd unhook his reserve and swing it out of his way on one connector and then undo his chest strap. Now, with nothing holding him in his harness, he'd fly into the packing area with his legs crossed at the ankles, as if relaxing at home in a reclining chair, step out of his harness as his feet touched ground and casually walk away. His parachute, as if surprised at the sudden loss of weight, would surge for a moment, still flying, and then collapse backwards onto the ground. This was really a spectacular landing and it startled both spectators and jumpers alike. I saw a few other people do it later, but never with that completely casual manner of Billy's. Theirs was a "Hey, everybody look at me!" compared to Billy's, "Ho, hum — another day at jumping."

Billy was always so laid back that often, before anyone even realized what was happening, he would pull off some amazing stunt that nobody had ever conceived possible. One time we all drove over to DeLand to enter an accuracy meet. "Accuracy" was a competition based on parachutists landing on a small canvas target one foot in diameter in the middle of a pea-gravel pit. It was pretty intense since, as opposed to a normal upwind landing to minimize impact, accuracy landings were made flying downwind for improved canopy control. However, landing downwind was extremely dangerous since the jumper hit the target area fast and hard, with his legs outstretched reaching for the target. That was the reason for a pea-gravel pit; the sliding stones cushioned the impact. Even so, in those days, there was always at least one broken leg during a meet, not counting the lesser back injuries, dislocations, or bad sprains.

So there we were, all standing around watching one of Billy's approaches when, without warning, only a couple hundred feet up, Billy hand-deployed his reserve. This was highly unusual at that low altitude, especially since his main looked good and was flying all right. We all commented on the fact that he was taking a big chance of entangling both chutes, but once he got his reserve opened, he cut away his main, one riser at a time, transferring smoothly onto his steerable reserve. Then, to our surprise, he continued on into the judging area for a "dead center" target-landing in the peas. Billy's answer as to why he did it was simply, "Just for the hell of it."

In our minds, the "reserve" was used only to save your life, and it never occurred to us to use one as a normal canopy and land on the target. It gave us that uneasy feeling of "crying wolf." It also went against all our training to test out a procedure like that during a meet — and that close to the ground to boot. Besides, everyone else was having to concentrate intently on what they were doing from the time they left the plane until they hit ground, just to get close to the target. And here was this upstart young kid, screwing around in the air and still getting great accuracy scores! In his personal quest to "push the envelope," Billy was redefining the sport in his own quiet, unassuming way.

Everyone had their own favorite "Billy" story. I remember a couple of DC-3 loads at Zephyrhills, when he really surprised a few hard-core jumpers. Once during jump run, while everybody else was nervously checking gear and getting their head together for the jump, Billy was checking out the small emergency exit over the wing. Often we'd pop this hatch open in flight to take photos of team exits, but it was so small, no one had ever thought of climbing out of it. It would be impossible anyway, with all your jump gear on.

As the other guys lined up in the door, Billy casually slipped his harness half off and, squeezing out through the small opening, stood out on the wing holding on with one hand while readjusting his gear. The team made their exit and as they left the door everybody was startled by the sight of a jumper standing on the wing where no one ought to be. Billy patiently waited for his normal place in line to exit, then ran off the trailing edge of the wing to join the formation.

Later, several other guys made a big deal of going out the emergency hatch, but once Billy proved to himself it could be done, he lost interest in it. There was really no point to it after that. Grandstanding was just not his style.

About that time, everyone was into eight- or ten-man RW competition teams, and to many it became very serious stuff. They organized permanent teams that showed up early at the drop zone to practice. They'd jump both Saturday and Sunday, and each member had to commit to a certain minimum number of team jumps per weekend. As for myself, it seemed like they were making what was supposed to be fun into hard work. I stayed as far away from it as I could, continuing to jump at Englewood and only going to Zephyrhills for the big meets. But Billy liked the action, the big planes, and the big freefall formations. He began to hang out at Zephyrhills almost every weekend and was such a good relative worker that he was always sought after as a team member.

At the time, a guy named Jim Hooper, known to all as "Hoop," was the manager of the Zephyrhills DZ. Hoop was a relatively small individual, but so aggressive and sure of himself, he was occasionally accused of having a Napoleonic complex. He did run the DZ with an iron hand, but he was an excellent skydiver and organized one of the better teams. His team won many meets, but Hoop was such a disciplinarian, he was not as popular on the drop zone as he was respected.

Hoop recruited Billy as a team member, but, as hard as he tried, he could never get Billy to take it seriously. Billy was never on time for ground practice and he skipped days whenever he felt like it. But what infuriated Hoop the most was that Billy totally ignored all of the pseudo-military discipline that Hoop considered essential to creating a top-notch team. As a result, when Billy showed up late one day as the team was getting ready to load the plane, Hoop grounded him. Billy didn't say a word but simply stowed away secretly in the tail-hatch of the DC-3.

On jump run, when the team made their exit, Billy popped out of the hatch and followed them out the door. In freefall, Hoop was very surprised to see Billy smoothly fly in to his normal slot and hook up into the formation. Hoop was even more surprised when Billy casually reached over and pulled Hoop's reserve ripcord handle. Hoop was immediately jerked out of the formation by the opening reserve chute and, as the whole formation continued its fall away from him, Hoop saw Billy expertly close the gap as if Hoop had never been there at all.

Hoop was left hanging at 10,000 feet under a nonsteerable reserve floating off on the wind. Hoop landed miles away, and it took him over two hours to get back to the drop zone. He was furious and kicked Billy permanently off the team, but Billy couldn't have cared less. He was tired of team competition and was ready to move on to something else. Besides, with his own unique style and without saying one word, Billy had already gotten even by temporarily making Hoop the laughingstock of his own drop zone.

Tragically, about a year later, Billy died in the crash of an airplane he had recently bought and learned to fly. He was only twenty-four years old.

Chapter Thirteen

THE STUDENT WHO ALMOST DIED

When I started jumping in 1964, skydiving was a rough, tough sport. If you didn't come home bleeding, you hadn't jumped that day. The gear was old; it was what the military had phased out or thrown out. It was heavy, difficult to pack, and prone to malfunction. A parachutist could be injured during a jump in many ways. The most common were by a freefall collision in midair, the opening shock of the parachute, or the landing impact with the ground — or all three.

The relative speed between two freefalling skydivers could be as high as eighty miles per hour. The only real protection from serious injury was a motorcycle helmet. A good friend of mine, Bill Dondanville, one of the original Mission Valley Skydivers, was involved in a midair collision in freefall with another jumper. He managed to pull his ripcord before he passed out. His parachute opened and he floated unconscious toward the earth. As he neared the ground, he regained consciousness long enough to turn his parachute upwind before passing out again. He recovered from his injuries to jump again, but that was the beginning of the end of his jumping career. I was sorry to see Bill leave the sport. He was a great guy and one of my favorite jumpers.

Other friends of mine weren't so lucky. In 1968 Paul Duncan was knocked out in freefall and never regained consciousness before he impacted the ground. He was 33 years old. In 1976 Tony Patterson was also knocked unconscious in freefall and never had a chance to open either parachute. In 1977 John Conway was killed when he cut away a malfunction, and was unable to open his reserve. Both were in their thirties. In 1979 Jack Spahr's reserve entangled with his malfunctioned main parachute. He was 37 years old when he fell to his death. They were all good friends and good skydivers and were sorely missed. Skydiving was not only rough and tough, it was relentless. But we could grieve for only so long. We all knew the risks and had accepted the dangers. We had to live with them as well as die by them. The best memorial was to put on our gear and go jumping again. Skydiving was not for the faint of heart.

In those days, even if everything went perfectly, a skydiver could be injured just by the opening of his parachute. It is really difficult to believe how hard the opening shock could be back in the early days when we were jumping with surplus military gear. When the ripcord is pulled, a freefalling skydiver goes from a velocity of about 120 mph to virtually zero in a matter of seconds. The person's weight, plus that of the gear, times the velocity, resulted in a tremendous momentum that created enormous stress loads. The problem with early parachutes was not so much getting them to open as it was getting them to open slowly enough for human tolerances. I had permanent bloodstains in all my underwear from the harness's leg straps cutting into the sides of my crotch during opening. During freefall, I always had in the back of my mind that, at some point, I was going to have to pull the ripcord and take that tremendous impact of opening shock. It was not something to look forward to, especially if you were jumping with a camera bolted to your helmet. Nowadays, the modern ram-air parachutes open much, much easier.

And then, no matter what, a skydiver always had to return to the ground. Landings back then were mind-bogglingly fast and hard. Just before impact, the ground came up at you at an alarming rate. I always found myself emitting an audible "Ahaaaaaaaa..." in anticipation of the impact that I knew was coming.

We always compared parachute landings to the impact of jumping off the roof of a house. In fact, I got hurt more often at parties demonstrating the proper landing technique than in a parachute at the drop zone. Luckily, being half drunk kept the injuries to a minimum when I came hurtling off a roof for the enjoyment of the party guests.

Jumping off a roof was an extreme case of demonstrating what was known as a PLF, short for Parachute Landing Fall. Normally, we trained students by having them jump from a three- to four-foot-high platform into a sawdust pit. Instead of taking the whole jolt of the landing in his legs and back, the student was taught to think of his whole body as a one-piece unit. As he hit and rolled over his shoulder, only five points of the body were to make contact with the earth; the toes, calf, thigh, butt and shoulder. In this manner the impact of the downward momentum could be spread over the entire body and the direction of the force could be changed from vertical to horizontal. Using this technique, the human body could withstand a tremendous downward impact without injury.

We made students practice PLFs until they were sick of them. But until the jumpmaster was assured that a student could do a perfect PLF while falling in any direction, he was not allowed to make his first jump. It had to be second nature; a completely automatic reflex. I can attest to its worth. A good PLF saved my life many, many times.

Skydiving equipment is, in theory, very simple. But in actuality, it is a very complex arrangement of material and hardware which has been engineered and developed over years of experimentation at the cost of many dollars and many lives. It is vital that each element of this apparatus function properly and in the right order. In the early days, if the opening sequence did not occur exactly as prescribed, malfunctions were bound to happen with potentially disastrous consequences. Even when the parachute was properly maintained and carefully packed, malfunctions happened at an alarming rate for no apparent reason.

On his first five jumps, a student was hooked to the plane with what was called a "static line," which opened the pack automatically as the student fell away. Assuming that the jumpmaster "spotted" his student's exit point at the proper distance from the target and on the correct wind line, and that the parachute opened correctly, there were still many potential dangers to be faced by the student parachutist. The student still had to steer his parachute into the designated target area. These were skills which were difficult to teach and had to be acquired by trial and error. In the meantime, the list of landing dangers was long: power lines, tree landings, water landings — all had their particular hazards and their corresponding recovery techniques. And all of them had to be taught to and mastered by a student before his first jump even if he contemplated making only one jump.

The trick was to try to teach students to think during an emergency, but we had to assume the worst and instill the right reactions if they didn't. All it took was one jump to kill a person; it was difficult at times for instructors to keep this in mind when training a "one-jump wonder."

Even if the student reached the target area safely, the danger was not yet over. If it were windy or a sudden gust grabbed the chute, there was the possibility of injury by dragging. Students had to be taught how to recover to a standing position while being dragged along the ground so the chute could be collapsed. This technique was best taught on windy days when no one could jump and we had nothing better to do. Besides, it was great entertainment to send some hapless student dragging off on a wild ride across the field.

Of course, we had to watch new jumpers closely even after they were off "student status." I saw one new jumper heading for the plane to make a jump when I stopped him for a routine pre-jump equipment check. Everything looked OK and I was about to let him proceed, but something bothered me. I took hold of his harness and, to his surprise, gave it a good yank. It practically came off in my hands. It seems that he took his new harness home the week before and neatly trimmed off all the excess lengths of straps which are normally just stowed with rubber bands. He didn't realize that without the ends which were double folded and sewed, the straps would easily slide through the buckles holding everything together. He is no longer involved in skydiving but, to this day, whenever I bump into him, he reminds me of that day I saved his life.

As for the mental attitude of new students, they had to be advised strongly that although it was a sport, skydiving was something to be taken seriously. It was as dangerous as it was unforgiving. Nothing changed a person's outlook on this subject as fast as seeing someone falling to his death.

One day a group of art students from a local college showed up at the drop zone. Neal Smith, known to all as Smitty, was the ringleader. He knew Duffy and had made all the arrangements for one of their friends to make one jump. Apparently Duffy had trained him during the previous week and they were all at the DZ to watch the guy jump. I finally overheard the whole story. Several of them had made a cash bet that their friend wouldn't have the guts to jump when he went up in the plane.

Hearing this made me mad. A bet was no reason to induce a person to skydive! They were calling this guy a coward and putting his life in jeopardy to make him prove otherwise. The whole thing stunk. I took it on myself to teach them all a lesson. I went over and added my name to the manifest along with the student and jumpmaster. Then, when no one was looking, I got my old cutaway rig out of my car and slipped it into the back of John's plane. The student got his last-minute instructions and we all got in the plane; me in the far back seat behind the pilot, the jumpmaster next to me, and the static-line student in front of him on the floor. All the art students gathered around to see him off, shouting last-minute jokes. I just smiled. We taxied off to the far end of the runway and John turned around for takeoff. I asked John to stop a minute. In this position, we were out of sight of everybody in the packing area, so I was able to quickly switch places with the jumpmaster with no one the wiser. As far as they knew, the student was to be the first one out of the plane and I didn't want to change this illusion. I got my spare rig out of the back of the plane and hooked it on as we took off. This was an old beat-up reserve that I used off and on to practice cutaways when I wanted to scare myself. Today it had a different purpose. Today it was going to double for a poor first-jump student apparently falling to his death. I told John of the change in plans, that I was going out on the first pass instead of the student. Although this was highly unusual, John just smiled and took it all in stride. He knew what I was up to.

We went on jump run and I said to hell with the correct spot, squeezed past the student who didn't have a clue as to what was going on, and rolled out the door directly above the packing area. We were only at 3,000 feet, normal altitude for a static-line student, and, although this was my usual opening altitude after a practice cutaway, I was determined to take this jump very low for maximum effect. I opened the chute right away to make it look like a normal static-line jump. I knew the people on the ground were laughing right then and saying, "Well, I'll be darned, he *did* jump after all!"

About that time, I released one riser, the chute suddenly collapsed, and I began a rapid descent, trailing the flapping chute over my head in what skydivers called a "streamer." I checked my altimeter. I was passing through 2,000 feet, the legal minimum opening altitude for experienced jumpers. It was still too early to let them off the hook. I held on and kept plummeting earthward. At 1,500 feet I released the other riser and went back into freefall face to earth. I was having a good time. I counted five seconds and pulled. My gold PC blossomed out overhead and I began a leisurely descent to the drop zone. I looked down at the packing area to see if I had made any effect.

Holy smoke! There were people running in every direction! I could see a police car screech to a halt on the dirt road with his flasher going. He jumped out and stood outside his patrol car, looking up while talking on his radio.

What's going on down there? I thought. It looked like an anthill that had been stirred up.

I landed right where we had boarded the plane. The whole drop zone now had realized what had happened and everyone was furious at me: the art students because I had scared the hell out of them and the jumpers because I hadn't told them what I was going to do. Only Billy commented quietly, "Nice jump!" as he sauntered past.

About that time, the real student made a very anticlimactic jump from the plane and landed with no problem.

Later, Duffy showed me the heavy sweatshirt he had been wearing. Apparently, standing behind him, Smitty had taken a death-grip on it when I had collapsed my cutaway. Then when I had dropped away from the streamering chute, Smitty, still looking up, had raced off — I guess to catch the falling student. Unwittingly, he had neglected to release his grip on Duffy's shirt and left a huge ragged hole torn out of the back of it.

Funny ... under normal circumstances, a circus strongman couldn't have torn that material.

Chapter Fourteen
THE FIRST NIGHT JUMP

It was right out of a James Dean movie. There was supposed to be a full moon for our first night jump, but a high solid overcast had turned the night into an ink pot. We drove our cars out onto the unlighted air strip and, lining them up at spaced intervals, we tried to light the limits of the grass runway with our headlights. There was a note of urgency to our actions because John was due to land his Cessna at any moment. It was unusually cold for Florida and our breath, frosting with every exhalation, punctuated the night with ghostly exclamation points. Duffy sent a wood-gathering party into the nearby trees and soon we had a roaring bonfire burning which reached high over our heads, lending a surrealistic quality to the already charged atmosphere. John ought to be able to see a beacon like that, we thought.

Buchan Airfield in Englewood was known as a dangerous place to land even in the daytime. Several planes had crashed in the recent past. The first one was on September 12, 1965. I remember it as if it were yesterday. Phil Todd was flying the jump plane that day. He was a veteran of World War II with over 2,500 hours of flying experience. He was 52 years old, married, and a father of two children. DeWitt Coburn, a friend of mine, one of three jumpers, was the last to leave the plane.

I can't remember what I was doing at the time. I was probably packing my parachute or just standing around the drop zone talking to someone. All I remember was hearing the plane engine revving up, getting louder and louder. I looked up in amazement and saw the jump plane flying straight for the ground. This was very unusual because a jump pilot had to be very careful of the plane's engine temperature as he came back to earth. Too rapid a descent could cool the engine too fast and crack the block. I kept expecting to see the plane pull out of the dive and level out for a landing, but that didn't happen. Instead, the plane went into a slow roll, still vertical to the ground, and the engine noise was getting even louder as it neared the ground. Everyone on the drop zone had frozen in place: some packing their chutes; some suiting up for the next load; some just talking or lounging around. They all were looking up at the plane in astonishment. The noise of the engine was winding up to an impossibly high pitch. When the plane impacted the ground, time stopped. We couldn't believe our eyes because the sound of the engine still continued. Since the point of impact was at least 300 yards away, it took a couple of seconds for the sound of silence to roll across the packing area. The silence was like a thunderclap. Everyone remained frozen in place. It was as if we were waiting for the restoration of reality when everything would return to normal. But it didn't.

I jumped into my 'Vette and raced down the dirt road toward the woods near the junction of the two runways. I skidded to a stop, jumped out of the convertible without opening the door, and raced into the woods. I was the first one on the scene and I didn't know what to expect. In my heart, I knew there were no survivors. I wouldn't have known what to do if there were. I pushed through a dense thicket of palmetto and pine and stumbled to a stop in a small clearing. I was standing before a huge lump of twisted metal. It was unrecognizable as an airplane. I knew it was the plane only because of one wheel sticking straight up in the air. There was no smoke; there was no fire; there was no movement; all was quiet. It was as if this particular piece of metal had always been there, sitting quietly in the woods. There didn't seem to be anyone in what was left of the cockpit. I circled the wreckage slowly, not knowing what I was looking for and yet frightened of what I might find. I stopped. There was a baseball cap hanging on a bush as if it had been purposely placed there. I stood looking at it, my mind numbed. It was only then that I realized I was standing before what must have been the body of the pilot lying on the ground. I backed away. I don't remember much after that, only that I was sick at heart for many, many days.

It was thought that Phil had experienced a heart attack and was dead before the plane reached the ground. It was good to know that the accident wasn't caused by pilot error, but it didn't seem to ease the sense of loss.

A year later, on October 16, 1966, tragedy struck again. Ron Zimmerman, age 31, a pilot from Venice, was flying Duffy's Cessna 180. He had a passenger, Warren McLennon, age 45, who had gone up to watch the jumpers. After the jumpers left the plane, Ron descended to land. As he made his final approach, the late afternoon light must have fooled him into thinking a clearing in the trees was the landing strip. He tried to power out at the last minute, but the landing gear clipped a tree and the plane cartwheeled into the ground, killing them both.

All of this was on the minds of the veteran jumpers as we heard the sound of a lone airplane approach from the south. As the sound got closer, we heard the slight frequency change signaling the plane's reduction of power to set up for a landing approach. Our eyes strained in the darkness but we could see nothing. Then we saw John's landing light, but, by the line of his approach, we could tell he had misjudged the position of the runway; he was right on top of us and powering out in an attempt to miss the electric power lines at the end of the runway.

I jumped into my Corvette and, fishtailing down the dirt road, skidded to a stop where the airport met the highway. I flashed on my high beams across the end of the runway to show John where the power lines were. Someone else drove down to mark the opposite end of the runway. There was nothing else left to do but wait and sweat it out. I knew if anyone could land here at night, John could. If not, he was smart enough to abort and fly up to the airport at Venice where they had lights marking the paved runways.

I heard the engine roar again as John, on his second pass, gave his engine the gas and the plane flashed over my head in the dark, the wing lights streaking the blackness. Holy smoke! It looked like his wheels had cleared the power lines by inches.

Give it up, John, I said to myself. *It's not worth it. We can make the short drive up to Venice.*

But, no — here he came again for the third pass, the engine loud in the black cold air. I heard John totally cut the engine and commit to a landing by simply dumping the plane on the ground.

John didn't even have to taxi. The plane just rolled to a stop in its customary parking space near the big pine tree. Whew! If the jumping was as exciting as the landing, it was going to be quite a night! The first thing John said after acknowledging our excited greetings was that the second load of jumpers would have to drive up to Venice because there was no way he was going to land in the dark again. We all agreed. Nobody blamed him a bit.

The first load — Billy Revis, Stan Stanton, and I — suited up. I was scared to death. Somehow, jumping at night just didn't seem natural. None of us were really properly prepared with lights for relative work in freefall so we weren't going to do anything fancy. We were able, however, to rig small lights on our altimeters so, at least, we could read our altitude in freefall. We were just going to get out of the plane at 7,500 feet and space ourselves out for thirty seconds of freefall alone.

I took a flashlight out of my car as well as a signal flare. I just stuffed them unceremoniously into the front of my jumpsuit. The hand-held flare was an MK-13 marine signal flare which we had obtained through devious means from the military. Either end could be activated with a ring pull; orange smoke came out of one end for daytime and the opposite end burned brightly for night use.

We were ready to go. I attributed the slight shaking in my body to the cold temperature. Going up in an open plane at night was a brand-new experience. It might have been interesting if it weren't so damned dark outside. The ride to altitude was over ever so soon, and, before we realized, it was time to jump.

I was to be last out of the plane. After the other guys jumped one at a time, I counted slowly to five before I gave John a "good-bye" pat on the shoulder and followed Billy out the door. The blackness swallowed us up, like stepping into a well. As usual, once I was free of the plane and on my own, my nervousness disappeared. There was nothing to do and nothing to see, so I just watched my altimeter. At 2,500 feet, I pulled my ripcord and got a very gentle opening. Too gentle; something didn't feel quite right. It was hard to tell in the dark without any references, but it felt like I was turning. I unzipped the top of my jumpsuit and got out my flashlight. Tentatively, I shined it up into my canopy, a brand new Para-Commander which I had bought only a few weeks previously.

Oh my God! In the glow of my flashlight, I could see that half the parachute was wadded up in a ball, entangled with some lines. Even as I quickly evaluated the problem, the turn accelerated into a full-fledged spin. More and more I was being thrown outward at an angle by the centrifugal force. I saw that there would be no way to clear it. Oh, hell! My first night jump and I was going to have to cut away and open my reserve. How was this possible?

I knew very well how it was possible: sloppy packing. Earlier that day, I had been two hundred miles away on the other side of the state jumping in Indiantown at South Florida Parachute Center. This was a drop zone run by Paul Poppenhager, who was one of skydiving's most famous personalities and known far and wide simply as "Pop." I had been on a film job in West Palm Beach, so after spending the night at my sister's, who lived there, I was on my way home. As usual, if I passed through Indiantown, I stopped off at Pop's to jump with my friends, the Delray Aerial Circus. It had been late afternoon when I was finished jumping and I realized that I would have to really move to make it to Englewood in time for our night jumps. It was the first time we had ever attempted skydiving at night and I wanted to be on the first load. I did the fastest parachute packing job in history before hopping into my Corvette and roaring off in a cloud of dust. That was when I must have packed in the malfunction.

My 'Vette was the second fastest car in Sarasota at that time. I had taken my car up to speeds of over 130 mph several times with acceleration to spare, so I knew I could make it to Englewood in record time if I didn't run into any police. There were no interstate highways at that time so I thundered across the back roads and through the small rural towns of interior Florida at breakneck speed. Driving like this was probably more dangerous than skydiving, at least if you took the time to pack your parachute correctly.

It was already dark by the time I went flying through the tiny community of El Jobean just west of Port Charlotte. I was still at least ten miles from Englewood and I thought I would be very late. But when I skidded onto the dirt road at Buchan Airfield, everyone else had just arrived. I must have set a speed record for crossing the state of Florida.

Now, here I was, at God-knows-what altitude, in a violent spin, plummeting downward into the blackness of the night. My first thought was that I couldn't cut away with a flashlight in one hand. This was long before the modern single-point release invented by Bill Booth which could be activated with only one hand. At that time, we had only the standard World War II "Capewell" releases attaching each riser to the harness which, incidentally, are still being used by the military to this day. These were heavy-duty metal connectors which were activated in two stages. First, reaching both hands up to your shoulders, the Capewell covers had to be pulled down, which revealed the squeeze pulls. Then, with thumb and forefinger, you had to squeeze the buttons at the top of each device while pulling down at the same time. If this was done correctly to both sides at the same time, your main parachute would detach from the harness at the shoulders and you would fall away, free to open your reserve chute without fear of entanglement. If you did not activate both Capewells at exactly the same time, there was a good chance that the added stress to the one remaining would lock it up, and you'd have to struggle with both hands in an attempt to free it. Naturally, during an emergency, this was undesirable.

Long before, I had filed off the tits on my squeeze pulls so I didn't have to squeeze them at all. They just smoothly pulled down with the slightest pressure. Technically, this was illegal, but it was my life at stake and I figured in sport jumping, this was one edge that might save my hide.

I calmly stowed my flashlight back into my jumpsuit. I knew I was going to need the use of both hands and I didn't want to lose a perfectly good flashlight. Hoping that I still had enough altitude to cut away, I reached up and, in two quick movements of my hands, activated my Capewells. Instantly, I fell away from the malfunctioned parachute, and the centrifugal force threw me at an angle outward into the night. Immediately I reached in toward my stomach and pulled my reserve's ripcord. Even in the dark, I had performed a textbook cutaway, putting my legs out in front so I would fall away on my back. In that attitude, my front-mounted reserve chute would be properly oriented to deploy upward, away from my body without the risk of entanglement

Since I had pulled so quickly before building up any freefall speed, my reserve deployment was slow and smooth. I couldn't see it in the dark, but I could feel the "blip," "blip," "blip" of the lines pulling out of the rubberband stows on the inside of the reserve container. The small parachute opened gently, swinging me upright, and I found myself once more suspended in the blackness of mid-air.

Hesitantly, I got out my flashlight again. I almost didn't want to shine my light into the little canopy which was somewhere in the blackness over my head. I was torn between the desire to confirm that it had opened properly and the fear of seeing another malfunction. There would be nothing I could do if this chute were tangled also; it was definitely my last chance.

I got out my light anyway and flashed it into the canopy overhead. Aha! I knew it all the time. It looked fine. It looked better than fine — it looked great! Relief flooded over me. I was going to live after all. But, wait — where in hell was I? I looked around. It was like looking around a pitch-dark room. I could see nothing. Did I have my eyes closed, or what? There should be a huge bonfire on the airport somewhere under me. I couldn't see any bonfire, I couldn't see an airport, I couldn't see anything.

Oh my God! I thought. I must be so far from the airfield that I was miles out in the woods — or worse, miles out in the Gulf of Mexico. Oh, great! If I didn't drown, I'd freeze to death on a night like this. No, the best thing was to think positive and consider how much trouble I was in over *land*. My imagination went into overdrive, coming up with countless possibilities: ponds, trees, power lines, buildings — the list of obstacles representing injury and death was endless. It was funny, my mind came up with everything but safe, flat, open ground.

Then I had a brilliant idea. I had a night flare right there in my jumpsuit. I could ignite that and it would light up everything. I quickly got it out and, awkwardly, because I was still holding the flashlight, pulled the ring tab. All of a sudden, I was holding the end of a spouting volcano. It lit up everything all right — to about twenty feet. I was in the middle of a brilliant ball of light beyond which was pitch blackness. The flare was dripping a white-hot molten material. I immediately held it at arm's length, as far away from me as I could get it. My God, if any of that stuff blew back toward me it could easily burn right through my nylon lines. On the other hand, I didn't dare drop the flare for fear of starting a forest fire should there be trees below.

To my relief, it finally burned out, but in the dying light I saw the tops of pine trees rushing up from below.

"Oh, oh!" I dropped the burned-out flare and immediately went into a tree-landing position; feet together to avoid straddling a tree limb, arms up gripping the inside of the risers, and face turned into the shoulder. I gritted my teeth and got ready for a bad landing. To my surprise, I came down between all the pine trees and almost did a stand-up landing in the soft brush. Piece of cake!

It was hard to believe that only two or three minutes had gone by since I had left John in the plane. Reality was starting to sink in that, while I had made it to the ground alive without a scratch, I had lost my new five-hundred-dollar Para-Commander.

In the past, we had lost parachutes in the woods during the daytime and, despite seeing where they had gone down, were never able to find them. Losing one at night was hopeless. With a sinking heart I gathered up my gear. Hell, I had not only lost my main, I had managed to lose myself in the process. I had no idea where I was or in what direction to start hiking.

I flashed my light around through the surrounding trees in an futile effort to identify where I was. I don't know what I hoped to accomplish; one pine tree looked like all the rest. But, lo and behold, there was my beautiful gold Para-Commander hanging from a tree branch not twenty yards away. One end was only three or four feet off the ground, so I just walked over and pulled it down with no trouble. Then, just when I was about to bemoan to myself how lost I was, I heard close by, "Mike, hey, Mike!" It was Bob Malott. He walked in through the trees to help me with my gear. Boy, did he look good to me! I was amazed to find that I was across the highway only a few hundred feet off the east end of the runway. The flare had helped after all. Bob was able to find me very easily by watching the track of the glow.

When we walked back to the field, the bonfire was still huge. I never figured out why I couldn't see it from the air. My skydiving was over for the night; not only did I need to get my reserve re-packed, I had had enough excitement for one evening. So I popped a beer and warmed up by the fire.

The next load scheduled was Duffy, Bayliss Faiella, and Dan Liddy. They had already left for the Venice Airport to meet John. Twenty minutes later, I was still unwinding from my brush with death when we heard the plane high overhead. We could hear John cut the power and knew that the guys were getting out of the plane. For thirty seconds there was nothing. Then the night was punctuated by the "whump," "whump" of two canopies opening at 2,500 feet. Where was the third one? We waited, straining our ears, but could hear only the crackle of the fire. Then we heard the unmistakable sound of a body in freefall. It was like a toy on a string being whirled round and round; a distinctive kind of buzzing. Once you hear it, you never forget it. It was the skydiver's jumpsuit being flapped at an abnormally high frequency by the tremendous rate of fall through the air. The buzzing got louder and louder. Whoever it was, he was falling toward us, directly overhead and, by the sound, was extremely low. We all listened in terror, knowing that the next sound we would probably hear would be the awful, flat thud of a body impacting the earth at 120 miles per hour.

"Crack!" It was the loudest canopy opening I had ever heard from the ground. A few seconds later, Bayliss came flying in out of the darkness as silent as a bat and landed near us by the fire. He made a spectacular stand-up landing with a loud thump of his jump boots on the hard earth. My God, he must have opened less than two hundred feet up. I went over to see why he had opened so low. Once I was close, I could smell the alcohol on his breath.

Jesus! Drinking before a jump was not only stupid, it endangered everyone else in the plane and on the ground. We had a strict code of no drinking before or during jumping activity, which no one had ever before challenged. I found out later that Duffy hadn't smelled it because he had a slight cold. Bayliss had slipped by our rules this time, but he was put on strict notice that if he ever drank before jumping again, he'd have to find a new drop zone. As far as we were concerned, he could go somewhere else to kill himself.

The third load went off without a hitch, and we all retired to our current bar to expound on the events of the evening. I knew one thing: Night jumps would never again terrorize me. It was like combat. Once you lived through the worst, what more can happen to you?

Those events, like the bonfire, burned themselves into my memory and to this day, over thirty years later, I remember them as if it were yesterday.

Chapter Fifteen

PAUL

In a lineup, Paul Pollaro would have been picked as the one most likely not to be a skydiver. He was a small, skinny guy who was a hairdresser by trade. He weighed maybe 120 pounds soaking wet. He was a sharp dresser, which, combined with his pencil-thin mustache and his slicked-back hair, made him look like a Hollywood gigolo. He was married to Roberta, a beautiful girl with long black hair styled like the singer/actress Cher. Paul was very overprotective and jealous of Roberta with no apparent cause. She seemed to be content with their marriage and a good mother to their two young daughters.

Paul was the comic of our group. When he got excited, which was often, he'd dance around, gesturing with his arms while talking a mile a minute. He was rarely serious, and because he clowned around so much it was hard to tell when he was earnest or just acting as if he were. He knew he made people laugh, so he made the most of it.

Because he weighed so much less than the average guy, Paul had a hell of a time doing relative work in freefall. He was of such a light weight his natural falling speed in freefall must have been less than 110 mph. The rest of us fell at rates of 120 mph or higher. Everyone else fell so much faster than Paul, he was always left behind, floating above. When a whole plane-load of us jumped and flew together to create a freefall formation, Paul would still be hovering a few yards above us when it was time for the group to separate and open their parachutes. He tried wearing weights, but with his slight build that made for dangerous landings, so he gave up on that idea. While the rest of us would be maneuvering together in a stable face-to-earth position (like lying face down on a bed with arms and legs outstretched), Paul would be in almost a vertical head-down body position which he had a hard time controlling. Sometimes he'd be fine but then, on the next jump, his approach would be just as radical as ever. As hard as he tried, he just never could become consistent in freefall. This meant he didn't get a lot of the positive feedback from a good skydive that the rest of us thrived on.

That's one reason I respected him so much. Despite all the failures and the kidding, Paul hung in there and stuck with it when lesser men would have quit. Also, while most of us got accustomed to the danger, I think Paul was apprehensive on every jump. Despite all this, he continued jumping. He probably had more guts than any two of us put together. This was something that most of the other jumpers never considered.

Paul was a scrappy kind of guy and could party with the best of us. During one drunken party, he got mad at Duffy; the two of them, both hardly able to stand, went outside to settle it like men. Now, Duffy outweighed Paul three or four to one, so when Paul started slugging Duffy in a furious volley of punches, it didn't faze Duffy at all. But, even drunk, Duffy knew if he ever hit Paul he'd kill him, so, tired of taking punches, he put a hand on Paul's head and held him at arm's length. Paul kept swinging away like a windmill, not landing a blow. It was right out of an Abbott and Costello movie and we all stood around, drinks in hand, laughing until we cried. Paul ran down at last and the two of them went back inside to continue drinking, arm-in-arm, the best of friends.

Paul was a bundle of nerves on a normal jump, but when we all decided to go on a night jump during a meet at Zephyrhills, Paul was like a toy with its spring wound too tight. Hell, we were all scared to death, but I guess we worked harder at not showing it.

We were in a DC-3 which, with its interior stripped out, held about fifty jumpers. We had formed our own little group of twelve skydivers, one of three groups crowded into the plane. The pilot was going to make three separate jump runs and we were to be on the last pass, the last ones to jump out of the plane. That would give us more room to line up in the door, but it would also give more time for our nervousness to increase.

Normally, during the climb to altitude, everyone clowns around and yells jokes to each other over the roar of the engines. On this load, however, everyone was so busy checking their lights and double-checking equipment that it was dead quiet. We all had strobe lights mounted on our helmets as well as little altimeter pen lights on goosenecks rigged on our reserves, enabling us to read our altitude in freefall. A few of us had chemical sticks, plastic tubes of cold green light which had to be activated at the last minute by bending them in half to break the glass vials inside. We sure were all better prepared than when I went on my first night skydive with only a hand-held flashlight. The Zephyrhills airport was also many times larger than the one in Englewood, which gave us plenty of safe landing room, even if we ended up off-target in the dark.

Finally the other teams jumped and the big plane was making its third lumbering turn onto jump run. It was our turn to get ready, and we wished each other good luck as if we might never see each other again. Everyone was hyped up as we lined up in the door; Paul looked as if he were going ballistic. I was last in line and it was going to be a relief to get out of the plane and into freefall.

As I dove out the oval doorway right behind the man in front of me, I was shocked by how dark it was. There was a full moon and I expected to be able to see something, *anything*, but it was pitch black. Apparently, a high cloud cover had obliterated any moonlight. The prop-wash on a DC-3 is horrendous and it tends to flip jumpers over as they exit. Also the one-hundred-plus mile-per-hour velocity on jump run tends to string out a group of exiting skydivers into a long vertical line.

Even on a daytime jump, the last men out of the plane can usually never see the "base" men. These are the first few guys out of the plane who form the "base" of the formation. They have had ten to fifteen seconds of freefall by the time the last guys exit the plane and by then, they are several hundred feet below and behind the airplane. So it's a game of "follow the leader" for the last out of the plane as the freefallers track downward at a high rate of speed. If everyone follows the person in front of him, eventually, thousands of feet below, all the jumpers get together into one formation.

This routine is especially true at night. But on this particular night jump when I got out of the prop-wash and gained stability, I couldn't see anyone in front of me. I couldn't even see the ground — just blackness. I went into a steep dive hoping to see someone or something, but it was like swimming in a bowl of ink.

At last I saw a circle of lights forming below me. My God, they were way below me! I put my arms all the way back and went screaming down through the blackness trying to catch up before we ran out of altitude. I must have been hitting speeds of 180 to 200 miles per hour but I was damned if I was going to be left out of a night formation! All of a sudden, without warning, I saw the shapes of bodies loom up blacker than the darkness of the ground. It seems that I had been looking at their helmet lights thinking they were far away, when, in fact, I was right on top of them. In panic, I flared out my arms and legs in a desperate, last-second attempt to slow down before I crashed into them. There was no time to do anything else before my outstretched hands hit and grasped the arms of two jumpers. I had put the brakes on just in time and had fallen perfectly into a slot between two skydivers. With the same momentum, I pulled their grasp apart and merged into the formation in one smooth motion. I was the eleventh man to enter the circle of jumpers.

To my left, in the dark, I could make out the silhouette of one lone man still trying to reach the formation, but he was floating high. It had to be Paul.

The altitude was gone. It was time to break off, do a 180, track off, and open. We each had to get clear of each other in order to open our chutes without collisions or entanglements. What was difficult in the day was nerve-racking at night.

My chute opened okay, and, as I floated quietly down through the darkness, I could see other ghostly parachute shapes at various altitudes around me. At last I could make out the lights on the target, and all I had to do now was try to land without crashing into someone else.

It really was an outstanding jump, but I felt very sorry for poor Paul who couldn't really enjoy the celebration afterward; he was the only one of our group who hadn't made it into the formation.

As for myself, I basked in the compliments: "That was the hottest approach I ever saw, and at night, too!"

For some reason, I never got around to confessing to any of my friends that the best dive of my life had been a complete stroke of luck.

Chapter Sixteen

DON

Don Bell was one of the most likable guys I've known. He had a way of looking at life in a very humorous way. He was one of those people you could always count on to make you smile, and he was a comfortable person to be around.

Compared to the rest of us, whom our pilot called "the wild bunch," Don was such a normal-looking, pleasant, easygoing guy, that any person who didn't know him would never guess that Don was one of those crazy skydivers. I always asked Don along on a jump when I needed a competent jumper I could count on.

Don was a liquor salesman and must have made very good money, because he never seemed to have financial problems like so many of us. The interior of his house was fascinating because it was always festooned with the latest motorized or lighted point-of-purchase displays that were normally seen only in lounges or liquor stores. As would be expected, Don always had a well-stocked liquor cabinet; for that reason, his house was our favorite party place.

One year, Don hosted a Halloween party which he required us to attend in costume. At first we thought it was a little silly, but it was so much fun that it became an annual event which we always looked forward to with great anticipation and planning. We all tried to outdo each other with our costumes — the more outrageous, the better. The ultimate test was to show up at the party and not say a word, to see how long it took anyone to recognize you. Once, Duffy persuaded a friend of his, whom no one else knew, to attend the party. All night we kept asking each other, "Who's the weird-looking guy over in the corner?" Duffy got a big laugh out of that and we never did find out exactly who it was.

The next year Duffy came as "The Hunchback." He made a gigantic "hump" that he strapped to his back, and he used professional stage makeup to create a horrible face. He covered over one eye with some kind of plastic skin and then, over it, re-created the eye socket with a false eye hanging down on his cheek. It was very realistic. Somehow we found out about it beforehand, so when he appeared at the party all hunched over and dragging one leg, we all said nonchalantly, one by one, "Oh, hi, Duffy. Couldn't find a costume for the party, huh?"

For some reason, Don always put up a Confederate flag at the drop zone. Since he was as far from being racist or red-neck as one could get, I guess it was because his family originally came from one of the "Old South" states. I used to look at the "Stars and Bars" flapping in the breeze to judge the wind direction as I came in to make a parachute landing. That is, until the guys on the ground got wise and tied a string to it to see if they could induce me to crash-land downwind by manually changing the direction of the flag. That was their idea of a big joke. I never got hurt, but I'm sure they would have thought it even funnier if I had broken a leg.

About that time, the movie "Gypsy Moth" began playing at the movie theaters. It was a classic movie about barnstorming skydivers, starring Burt Lancaster. We had always been very cavalier about taking foreign objects into the air with us, but this movie seemed to liberate our latent ideas. Emulating the movie, we began taking various objects such as flags and ropes into freefall with regularity. Don used to attach his Confederate flag to the middle of a rope about twenty feet long. He and his friend Rusty Fornes would jump out of the plane first and stretch the rope out between them. With them hanging on to each end, the drag of the flag in freefall would cause the rope to bow up in the middle. I would then fly down and try to grab the rope in the middle near the flag. Once, when I was making my approach to the rope, they shifted over for no apparent reason, which put the flag right in my face. At 120 mph the flag nearly flapped me to death. Then when I finally got one hand on the rope, they became unstable and whipped around, changing places almost in unison. This little maneuver nicely put the rope in a half hitch around my wrist. It didn't worry me until I realized that I couldn't let go of the rope and, if I pulled my ripcord, it would probably take my arm off. Don was supposed to hold on to the rope at the end of the jump and I was afraid, since he didn't realize I was tangled, he might pull at any time and take my arm with him. I quickly tucked up and fell into the rope, thereby creating enough slack to untangle myself with no harm done.

If there were only two of us on a rope jump, we used to have fun pulling each other around the sky. We'd get the rope stretched tight and then one of us would give the rope a big tug. This would fling the other guy across the radius of an imaginary circle until he hit the end of the slack. It would then be his turn to give the rope a pull. I figured out that if I balled up, I could drop below the other guy and literally hang on the rope below him. I did this one time near the end of our freefall. Don looked at his altimeter, saw it was time to break off and simply let go of the rope. There I was, hanging on the end of this rope in freefall at 120 mph, and when Don let go, I got the distinct "elevator-going-down" sensation of falling, something rarely experienced in skydiving. With a shock, the thought flashed through my mind, *Oh, my God, he dropped* me! Then my mind caught up with reality. What did it matter if he let go of the rope — I was falling to begin with! A little embarrassed by my initial reaction, I regained stability, gathered in the rope, and opened my parachute with no problem.

It was always a long drive from Englewood back to the nearest bar in Sarasota, so after jumping, we got in the habit of stopping in the nearer town of

Venice. There was a bowling alley there called Myakka Lanes. The owner was a big sports fan and in his lounge he had the walls covered with sports photos. I made a few enlargements of some of my skydiving pictures and he proudly hung them in the lounge. Then I began to think up new photo ideas especially for Myakka Lanes. We borrowed a bowling pin and made several photo jumps with it. Those pictures were interesting, but when the manager mentioned that he had an old bowling ball we could borrow, we really got excited.

We had never heard of anyone jumping with a bowling ball before. Of course, we hadn't heard of anyone jumping with a bowling pin either, but getting out of a plane with a heavy bowling ball seemed to fire the imagination. A person couldn't help but have "Tom and Jerry" cartoonlike images of the big black ball dragging a skydiver earthward, like a boater jumping overboard holding an anchor. As it turned out, however, our preconceptions were all wrong.

When we took possession of the bowling ball, we found, to our surprise, that a hole was drilled completely through it. It must have been used previously for some display purpose, exactly what, we never found out, because a wooden broomstick had been forced through the hole, thereby creating handles on either side. This was perfect for our purposes, since a naked bowling ball would have been very difficult to handle in the air.

Before asking anyone else to jump with such a potentially hazardous item for photography, I planned to test it myself. Actually, I just wanted to be the first, but Billy Revis talked me into letting him hold   the ball while I took photos. It was a little tricky getting it out of the plane, but once in freefall, Billy had no problems. He was even able to hold on to it during the increased gravity loads caused by opening shock. To our amazement, instead of pulling a man head low, the bowling ball floated. In other words, it fell slower than a skydiver, so it held Billy a little head high. I got some unusual photos, but I still wasn't satisfied.

For some reason, I fixated on taking a freefall photo of Duffy in midair bowling the ball toward bowling pins held by Don, Rusty, and Billy. It never occurred to me that the idea was totally impractical and that it would be a difficult picture to compose even on the ground. Instead, it became a challenge. To my credit, I realized immediately that the bowling ball itself wouldn't work. But our old experiments of taking fruit into freefall came to mind.

We had discovered that an average grapefruit fell at about the same velocity as a skydiver in freefall. In other words, an object's rate of fall was not as much a question of weight as it was the ratio of its mass to the cross-section of its area. When gently pushed toward another freefalling skydiver, a grapefruit would float magically across the space between the two jumpers while both skydivers and grapefruit were falling earthward at 120 mph. With this in mind, it seemed perfectly logical to me that a black grapefruit could stand in for the less practical bowling ball. It could then be pushed toward the bowling pins in freefall and still remain in my camera's field of view while I took the picture.

After work one day, it was a simple matter to spray-paint a grapefruit with a flat black paint. Once it dried, I rushed over to Duffy's house to show off my handiwork. He was very impressed with my "stand-in" bowling ball and we had a drink or two as we sat around talking about it. Several other friends stopped by, and, as usual, an impromptu party began. When another jumper walked in, we had almost forgotten about the black grapefruit sitting on the coffee table like some ultramodern centerpiece.

Without so much as a greeting, the new arrival immediately asked, "What's that?," pointing at the grapefruit.

"It's a grapefruit, obviously!" Duffy replied sarcastically, as if the guy should have known.

"How'd it get black?" the guy asked bluntly, not to be put off.

Duffy was the master of spontaneous jokes but he looked at me to see what I'd say.

For an instant, I was caught off guard, but I wasn't about to repeat the whole complicated story once again. Without thinking, I began to make up a story as incredulous as I could on the spur of the moment.

"Well," I began, "first you go to the grocery store and pick out a perfect grapefruit. You have to be careful, though, that it's not too ripe."

"Uh, huh," the guy nodded.

"Then you have to have a bowl deep enough to hold the grapefruit because you have to totally submerse it."

"Submerse it!" the guy exclaimed. "Why do you want to do that?"

"Do you want to know how I got it black or not!" I chided him.

"Okay, okay," he said, reluctantly agreeing to shut up and listen.

"Let's see — where was I?"

"You were about to submerse it!" the guy said, not being able to restrain himself.

"Oh, yes. You take a fifth of gin and pour it over the grapefruit. Normally, if you've picked one that's not too big, a fifth just covers it. But it depends on the bowl, too," I corrected myself, "so use more gin if you need to."

The other guys had drifted into the kitchen to refresh their drinks but now, overhearing, they drifted back into the living room; this was getting interesting. They couldn't believe that this guy was listing raptly like a gourmet watching a cooking show.

"So then what?" he was asking.

"So then you put the bowl into a dark closet and wait for about a month."

"A whole month?" the guy exclaimed.

"Yeah, it takes about a month for the grapefruit to soak up most of the gin."

"Oh, of course," the guy agreed, as if he had known all along but had just momentarily forgotten. "Then it's black?"

"Oh, no! You have to take another fifth of gin and fill the bowl again and put it back in the closet."

"For another month, right?"

"Right. You've done this yourself, haven't you?" I asked him.

"No, no," but he looked pleased that he had guessed correctly. "So after the second month what happens?" He was beginning to get restless.

"Well ..." I was running out of imagination. I thought he would have caught on by now that I was putting him on. Besides, the other guys were about to lose control and break out laughing. "Well, you take the grapefruit out of the bowl and eat it. Then while you try to sober up, you take another grapefruit and spray-paint it black." I ended the story in a rush. Then, amid all the laughter, I had to explain the real story to our bewildered friend.

The following weekend Duffy had a falling out with the manager of the bowling alley and moved our after-jumping activities to another bar. After all my preparation, I never did get a chance to try out my bowling ball stunt. It was just as well; it was a dumb idea anyway.

Along with his Confederate flag, Don Bell also used to bring an old bugle to the DZ — God knows why. Off and on, he'd attempt to play "Charge" or "Taps" when someone was landing or taking off. I finally talked him into attempting a "bugle-pass" — passing the bugle from one to another in freefall. I had a secret agenda. When I got the bugle, I was going to be the first one ever to play a bugle in freefall.

After jumping from the plane, Don and I passed the bugle with no trouble, but when I tried to play it, nothing came out. Admittedly, I could barely play the thing on the ground, but I had expected something to come out of it, even if it was only an unmusical squawk. I couldn't even get a note out of it after I had opened my parachute. Oh, well, at least I was the first to *attempt* to play a bugle in the air, and don't anybody forget it!

I was successful, however, in making the highest punt in the history of football. Don could be counted on to always have something to fool around with at the drop zone between jumps. So one day I borrowed his football and, stuffing it into the front of my jumpsuit, took it along on a skydive. When I got into the plane, John, our pilot, looking at the bulge in my jumpsuit, made some comment about how he didn't realize that I was "in a family way."

After I had opened my chute, I waited until I had drifted over the airfield so I didn't lose the football in the woods as I gave it a kick. Hanging under a parachute and encumbered with harness straps, it turned out to be the feeblest of kicks. But as far as I was concerned, I went into the history books as one of the greatest place kickers of all time. From that point on, in any bar, I could truthfully brag that I had kicked a football 500 feet high!

Don eventually moved out west and got out of skydiving. I hear from him occasionally, however. Every six months or so, he drinks a little too much, gets maudlin thinking of the good old days, and calls me. There's one thing I don't understand, though. Why does he always call at 3 a.m.?

Chapter Seventeen
THE WATERMELON

As he got into the plane, John paused, looked at me and shook his head. "Tell me I didn't just see a watermelon in the back of my plane," he said.

"I can explain ... " I started to say.

"Nope — I don't want to know about it." John waved me off and got ready to fly. I was in the far back seat with Don Bell sitting next to me. The watermelon sat on the floor between my feet like a giant green egg. Even to me it seemed totally out of place in a jump plane.

I don't know how I talked Don into holding the watermelon for me in freefall. I guess he took pity on me because no one else had the nerve to help me. Where was Billy with his bowling ball experience when I needed him? At any rate, here we sat in the plane, climbing to altitude to attempt the world's first watermelon pass.

This idea, like most of my hair-brained stunts, started out innocently enough. Over a long period of time, we had taken a tremendous number of objects out of the plane and into freefall for a record number of "firsts." We were big on "firsts." It never dawned on us that we were first many times only because no one else was stupid enough to attempt something that dumb. We had jumped with ropes, flags, bugles, bowling pins, bowling balls, footballs, champagne bottles, and a lot of other objects that were not tied down or that someone was not watching.

It all started out in California when two jumpers made the first contact in freefall. Prior to that no freefalling skydivers had ever touched each other in the air. Steve Snyder (later to become a big name in the manufacture of skydiving equipment) and Charlie Hillard (who later, as a pilot, became a national aerobatic champion) passed a baton to each other in freefall, forever changing the course of skydiving. So passing a baton like aerial relay runners became the "thing to do" in the skydiving world of the '60s.

When I first started jumping, one day Bob Malott and I decided to pass a baton. When we got airborne, however, we realized we had left the baton on the ground. Up to now it had never occurred to us that we could pass anything else but a baton to each other in the air. As we climbed to altitude, I made a search of the back of the plane and came up with a half-used pencil. I broke off the point for safety, and, voila˜, we had a teeny-tiny baton. Bob looked skeptical that we could pass anything that small but, once in freefall, we made the delicate hand-to-hand switch with no problem. It was a real mind opener. From that point on, we passed everything we could get our hands on. The only taboos were kids and pets.

Of course, the reason for the taboo was that we weren't always able to hold onto all of these objects which we took into freefall. And once something got away from us it was almost impossible to catch. Even a round shape would not fall straight as might be expected but would accelerate toward earth in an unpredictable spiral. All of this activity with inanimate objects which might end up freefalling to the ground was only possible because there were no homes around our Englewood drop zone at the time; only many square miles of palmetto scrub and pine trees. By the time of the watermelon pass, however, a few scattered homes had sprung up, as well as a trailer park on the north edge of the field. But that was okay. Despite the wind direction, I knew I could shift our exit spot so we would be over empty land during our jump.

Don wasn't nervous because he knew he had the easy job. All he had to do was hold the melon and fall. I was the one who had to fly down to him, get a grip on it, make the transfer and then hold on to it as I opened my chute.

I wasn't worried either because I thought for a man of my skills it would be a piece of cake. Besides, it really didn't matter if we succeeded or not. What was the worst that could happen? If we dropped the melon we might wipe out a palmetto bush or something — no big deal!

When we went on jump run, Don moved to the floor next to John so I could move over and "spot." Because of a bad crosswind, I had to give John several direction corrections to put us past the trailer park. I gave the "cut" and Don climbed out the door. Standing on the step, Don had to let go of the strut with his left hand so I could hand him the melon. Now, this was a large water-melon that anyone would have had a hard time holding even on the ground, so it was quite a trick to pass it out the door of a plane in flight. I held it until Don put his free hand under it, then he switched his other hand from the strut to the top of the melon as he fell away holding it in front of him. I immediately dove out of the door after him.

Once I got stable, I could see our true vertical position in relation to the ground.

Oh my God! Somehow we had drifted over the trailer park! I couldn't believe this was happening! I realized in a flash that now I *had* to get that melon and I *had* to hold on to it or we were in big trouble. I dove down to Don and flew in to hook up in one quick, smooth move, wasting no time. I don't think Don realized that we were over the trailer park because he had a big smile on his face. He was having a good time.

I grappled with the melon, got both arms around it, and, with a nod, signaled Don that I had it. He let go, turned around, and flew off. In my peripheral vision, I saw a flash of upward movement as Don pulled his chute.

My attention was totally on the watermelon now. It was only then that I realized the melon was on top of my ripcord. I couldn't pull. It didn't matter anyway. It took both hands to clutch the damn thing to my chest. If I let go of it with one hand in order to pull, I would lose the melon. In this position, I was tilted head-to-earth and had really picked up speed. I must have been falling at over 180 mph. My mind was working frantically. How was I going to pull? I was damned if I was going to give up and let go of the melon!

I worked one hand around and, hooking my ripcord out of its pocket with one thumb, I tried to pull it. Nothing! From that arm position I had no leverage and no strength. The ground was starting to rush up at me. I had to do something even if it was wrong. I hooked both thumbs in the ripcord and extended both arms as far out as I could while still cradling the melon between my elbows. I felt my pack open and I knew opening shock would follow momentarily. I tried to re-grab the melon but it squeezed out and over my arms as the opening sequence of my parachute began to slow me down. I felt like the "little engine that could": "I think I can, I think I can."

My hands were reaching and fumbling like a pass receiver trying to make the winning catch during the last play of the big game. It seemed to never end. I had my hands on the watermelon but I just couldn't seem to get a grip. The deploying chute was slowing me down but the melon was still falling at the same speed as before.

Wham! Opening shock hit me and the melon whizzed downward out of my hands and was lost to my sight like the coyote in a "Roadrunner" cartoon. I watched for the impact in vain, but even from an altitude of 1,000 feet, the sound of the explosion reached me. I could see that I was still over an edge of the trailer park but it was impossible to tell exactly where the melon had impacted.

Even though I had opened low, I was able to land right on target at the DZ. I was in a panic. I knew how serious this could be if it got out of hand. Even if there was no damage, John could lose his pilot's license, the DZ could be closed, and I could end up in jail. I said something unintelligible to Duffy about the trailer park, hopped in my 'Vette, and raced down the highway to the trailer park. Don followed in his own car after he landed.

I went straight to the manager and explained everything. I told him that I was at fault and was totally responsible. If there were any repercussions, they should fall entirely on me. I put myself totally at his mercy. By that time Don had arrived and the three of us went to the west edge of the park to survey the damage.

One resident had been walking his dog nearby and had witnessed the explosion. He was puzzled by what might have caused it. He assumed something had fallen out of the plane which he saw flying overhead at the time. We looked at the area he indicated. There was an oval impression in the ground about a foot long. I was amazed to see a fairly large piece of melon rind still lying in the impact crater which was about 2 inches deep in the hard ground. I heard later that they found pieces of the watermelon rind all over the park. The manager let me off the hook with a stern lecture and made me promise never again to bomb his park. Even so, it was truly one of the worst days of my life.

It took me years before I would talk about it, but the rest of the guys took great glee in relating the episode to other jumpers who hadn't been there. There were endless debates in numerous bars about what might have happened. Most of the scenarios were, of course, in bad taste. For example: "What would the park resident have thought if his dog had suddenly turned magically into a pile of watermelon seeds?"

I never had the heart to take part in these questionable discussions, but some of them were pretty funny, even to me.

For a long time after that, anyone who landed out in the woods, upon returning to the packing area, would inevitably relate incredulous tales of huge watermelon patches growing in the wild. They never reported these wondrous things directly to me but somehow they always made sure that I was within hearing distance.

Chapter Eighteen
GOING LOW

I called John Saturday night and asked if he could arrive at the drop zone the following morning earlier than nor mal. "Sure," he said. "What's up?"

"Oh, I just want to do a little filming before everyone else arrives."

John suspected that I was up to something strange, as usual, but he was agreeable to being in Englewood an hour early.

A curious new phenomenon was being experienced in skydiving at that time. Maybe it wasn't all that "new," but it was happening often enough to warrant its own name. It was called "ground rush." Strangely, when a person jumps out of a plane and goes into freefall, there is no sensation of vertigo such as you would get by standing on the top of a building, for example, and looking over the edge. Even as one falls toward earth at 120 mph, there is little or no feeling of height or apparent ground movement. It has to do with the human eye and the physics of sight. Only when the eye's peripheral vision is entirely filled with motion does the brain sense abnormal speed and set off mental alarm bells.

It's like driving into a tunnel. The car is still traveling at the same speed as before but now, enclosed by the tunnel walls, the car seems to be going a lot faster.

In skydiving this effect becomes apparent only at altitudes well below our normal and "legal" opening altitude of 2,000 feet. Only somewhere around 1,200 feet does the horizon fill the vision and the relative motion between the ground and the jumper start to become exponential. To a jumper still in freefall, the ground will appear to "rush" up at him; thus the name "ground rush." It is a startling and frightening effect adding to the woes of a skydiver experiencing a malfunction or an accidental low pull. In many cases it may have been the final disorientation culminating in a fatality.

In skydiving circles, it became "cool" to casually mention "ground rush" in a harrowing jump story. It signaled, for people in the know, that the storyteller was describing, true or not, an abnormally low-altitude jump without him bragging openly about it.

Being a dedicated movie maker and having "gone low" myself on many occasions, I wondered if "ground rush" could be captured on movie film. I figured that I'd have to use a fairly wide-angle lens in order to approximate the human eye. That meant that the cameraman, myself in this case, would have to go very low to fill the lens with the "rushing" motion of the earth.

I had seen many student jumpers mimic the dangerous habits of experienced skydivers without the student having the skills or knowledge to get out of a tight jam. That's why I wanted lots of privacy when I did my ground rush filming. I didn't want some student thinking that it was a neat thing to do. I also didn't want to seem to be "grandstanding" in front of the other, more experienced, jumpers. It was better this way, to do it on my own.

John was right on time and I was waiting on the empty airfield, all suited up and ready to go. I explained what I was doing and John was his usual stoic, unflappable self. I offered to pay triple price to compensate for the two empty places in the plane, but John wouldn't have it. He said that this jump was on him.

I checked my movie camera as we climbed to 3,000 feet. It was mounted on the top of my helmet with the off/on switch routed down my sleeve to my hand. I had zeroed my wrist-mounted altimeter to the field "ground zero" and I double-checked it against the plane's instruments. They matched exactly, which was comforting. The plane banked around to come on jump run and John expertly put me right on the spot without my having to give flight corrections.

John cut the power and we shook hands solemnly. I swung my legs out the door and put my feet on the step. Without going through the normal procedure of getting out on the step and holding the strut for a stable exit, I switched on the movie camera and rolled out of the plane. I made a single front loop and stabilized out. I could hear the grinding sound of the movie camera even over the wind blast of freefall. I bent my arms inward further than normal so I could read the altimeter on my wrist without having to turn my head, which would have moved the camera.

I was going to fall flat and stable with the camera aimed at the ground, but my eyes focused on my altitude until the needle read 500 feet. I was counting on having packed my parachute perfectly since, at that altitude, I'd have no time to handle any type of malfunction before impact. My chute had to come out of the pack cleanly and swiftly for me to survive. It was very difficult for me to keep my concentration on the dial of my altimeter and not look around for visual cues as to my altitude. Falling at a rate of 120 mph, which would translate to 176 feet per second at terminal velocity, I figured I'd have a fraction over 2 1/2 seconds for my parachute to open. I was gambling that my altimeter was going to be reliable and accurate.

The ground came up like a freight train. I clenched my teeth and watched intently as the altimeter needle swung ever so slowly toward the 500 mark. It would have been so easy to pull the ripcord early. Who would know? I'd know! I kept falling. I reached in, pulled the ripcord handle out of its pocket and held it, still falling, ready to pull like a cocked spring.

The instant the needle touched the little black line indicating 500 feet I pulled the ripcord with all my might and looked over my shoulder for the pilot chute.

On many jumps we had experienced what we called "pilot chute hesitation" which was caused by the small pilot chute becoming trapped in the vacuum that forms over a falling body. The pilot chute would come out of the pack and flop around over the skydiver's back for a few seconds until it happened to catch air, inflate and deploy, finally performing its function of pulling out the parachute. I had found that just by looking for the pilot chute, I automatically dropped a shoulder which caused a momentary disruption of the vacuum and the pilot chute would never hesitate.

This was one jump that I couldn't afford a few seconds slack. There was no pilot chute hesitation this time and immediately I got a hard opening shock which, for once, I didn't mind. I was so low I couldn't believe it. I had only enough time to check the canopy, get hold of the steering toggles, and turn upwind before landing right in the packing area.

I stretched out my parachute on the ground and was half packed when a strange car came speeding up the airport road in a cloud of dust. It screeched to a halt opposite me and the man leaned out of the window to ask, "Did you just jump out of a plane?" John was just landing behind me.

"Yeah," I said. "Why?"

"Well," he said, pointing, "I live right over there. I was out in my yard watching you jump when you fell behind the tree line. I thought you hit the ground without opening your parachute. It scared the hell out of me!"

"No, I'm fine," I assured him. "I was just filming a low-altitude opening." By that time John had parked the plane and had joined us.

"It was all planned," I continued. "I knew exactly what I was doing." John didn't say anything but just winced.

The neighbor seemed mollified and drove off. I opened the back of my movie camera and checked the 50-foot film cartridge. "Christ!" It had jammed. What a disappointment!

About that time, everyone else began to arrive for a day of jumping. Like conspirators, John and I smiled at each other. Only he and I knew what had transpired that morning.

Movies or not, I never had the nerve to try filming it again. It would have seemed to be tempting the fates. I never went that low again ... at least, not on purpose.

Mike Swain about to make jump #247 on May 12, 1968 at Buchan Airfield, Englewood, Florida.

Bruce Harting exits Dave Allyn's antique Lockeed Electra at an altitude of 10,500 feet on March 12, 1972. This was the second skydive ever made over the Caribbean island of Grand Cayman. (see Ch. 22 - Bruce and Ch. 21 - Dave)

photo by Mike Swain on his 732nd jump

Mike filming in freefall from 10,500 feet while falling at speeds of over 120 mph during jump #338 on January 12, 1969. The 16mm movie camera is mounted on  the helmet, the white power cable routed to the two home-made battery packs on each hip, and the on/off switch is in his left hand. (See Ch. 20 - Photography)

photo by Harry Sowry using author's hand held still camera

Bob Malott and Duffy Nathan making a 60 second freefall from 12,500 feet over Zephyrills, Florida on August 11, 1968. (see Ch. 3 - Duffy and Ch. 4 - Bob)

photo by Mike Swain on his 279th jump

Although Mike had only 47 jumps on August 21, 1966, he thinks this is one of the best freefall portraits he ever took.

His logbook said, "After taking a great photo of Jim Shockley and opening my parachute, I landed south of the drop zone in the palmetto bushes." (See Ch. #10 - Jim)

photo by Mike Swain over Englewood, Florida from 7,500 feet

Mike opening his parachute at the end of a 45 second freefall from 10,500 feet over Englewood, Florida on May 25, 1969. The champagne bottle in his left hand is to celebrate jump #400 while his right hand is outstretched pulling the rip-cord. This was a complicated skydive involving a three-way bottle and camera pass with fellow jumpers, Billy Revis and Duffy Nathan.

photo by Billy Revis using author's hand held still camera

Billy Revis opens his parachute at 2,500 feet over Englewood, Florida after a 30 second freefall from 7,500 feet on June 22, 1969. (see Ch. 12 - Billy)

photo by Mike Swain on his 416th jump

Competition "accuracy" landings were fast, hard, and dangerous. Usually during these meets there were many injuries involving bad sprains, dislocated joints, or broken bones. This photo taken on December 29th, 1968 was at Paul "Pop" Poppenhager's annual New Year's meet at his famous drop zone in Indiantown, Florida. (see Ch. 8 - Landings)

jumper - unknown, judge - Lester Ruper, photo by Mike Swain

Chapter Nineteen
BIG PAUL

Paul Healy was a big man. When he was on a diet, which was rare, he weighed an even 300 pounds. He was almost six feet tall and about half that lying down. With his weight and girth, he was one of the most unlikely candidates for skydiving you could think of. At the drop zone, if you were standing nearby when he landed under a parachute, you could literally feel the ground shake. But as imposing as he was physically, Paul was the nicest guy you'd ever want to meet and one of my favorite people.

At one skydiving meet in DeLand, a bunch of skydivers met in town for breakfast before going to the drop zone. It was a lively mixture of guys from our group in Sarasota who jumped in Englewood; the Tampa Skydivers, including Paul Healy, who jumped in Zephyrhills; a few of the local DeLand jumpers; and others from various DZs throughout Florida. These were all young, active, and healthy men who ate huge breakfasts with gusto. That is, until Paul arrived. At first the waitress thought it was a joke when Paul ordered two dozen scrambled eggs, a loaf of toast, a skillet of hash-brown potatoes, and a pound of bacon. It was no joke, even though this was not what Paul always ate for breakfast. Actually, he was trying to cut down.

The other guys took no notice, taking Paul's voracious appetite for granted. But when the food arrived and Paul began consuming it, the picture changed. I began noticing a few guys hurriedly leaving for the drop zone without finishing their meal. As Paul kept eating without pause, others turned sickly, made excuses, and left. I was used to it, so the spectacle didn't affect me at all, and I stayed to keep Paul company. But I got a chuckle out of all these macho guys who couldn't take the sight of someone eating a little breakfast.

Despite his obvious weight problem, Paul asked for no sympathy or special treatment and we gave none. However, he rarely did any relative work in freefall because he fell twice as fast as anybody else. In fact, he told me sadly one day that he had never hooked up with anyone in the air. He had gone up several times with some very good jumpers, but nobody could catch him. I thought I was the best skydiver in the world, modesty notwithstanding, so without hesitation I said, "No problem, let's go do a 'two-man.'"

On the climb to altitude, I told him that if he just got as flat and stable as he could and held a heading, I guaranteed I would hook up on him. I was so confident because I had lots of experience going last on large loads, taking movies as I dove to the formation at speeds of over 200 mph. For a long time, I never wore goggles on those jumps. I just let my eyes water and let the wind clear my vision by blowing the tears away in freefall. I did that until one day, during a "hot" dive, I went so fast that my right eyelid suddenly blew up like a balloon from the pressure. The trauma may have ruined that particular jump for me, but luckily it gave me no permanent eye damage. It did, however, give me a lot more respect for the dynamics of high-speed diving. From that point on, I always wore goggles and continued to dive faster and faster. This was why I was sure I could catch Paul if he remained stable and patient.

When we left the plane, Paul dropped away from me so fast I couldn't believe it. I went into a max-dive with my arms at my sides, my legs together, and toes pointed. I was flying straight down, my body vertical with my head thrown back in order to keep visually zeroed in on Paul. I could see I was catching him and, when I was about to crash into him, timing it perfectly, I flared and swooped in for a precision hand-to-hand hook-up.

Most jumpers fall with their hands cupped, but Paul, in an effort to grab all the air he could to slow his fall, had his fingers spread wide apart as if clawing the sky. When our hands met, our fingers meshed together like matching gears. To my surprise, instead of me grasping him and being able to let go at will, our fingers interlocked as if engaged in some kind of strongman contest.

I had done exactly what I had claimed I could: I had hooked up with the uncatchable Paul, but I was totally unprepared for what happened next. Now that I had pulled out of my dive, my speed decreased to about half that of Paul's. I began flapping over him like a flag in a strong wind. Paul, who was having the time of his life, wasn't about to let go. He had a death grip on my hands. Meanwhile, my fingers were being bent backwards to the point of breaking. I was in tremendous pain and was screaming "Let go! Let go!" But naturally, in freefall, Paul couldn't hear me. With a big grin on his face, he was oblivious to it all and the two of us, one laughing and one crying, continued to hurtle toward the earth.

To my great relief, our altitude ran out and Paul, reluctantly disengaging his fingers from mine, turned around, moved away, and pulled. Hoping I still had the use of my hands, I managed to get enough of a grip on my ripcord to pull it.

Well, I thought, *the worst is over.* Little did I know.

Back on the ground, Paul in his exaltation of making his first hook up, tackled me in a great bearhug and, as we fell to the ground, rolled over me with all three hundred pounds.

As in the cartoons, it took me a while to get back to normal again.

Chapter Twenty
PHOTOGRAPHY

I started taking pictures on my third static-line jump. I had a rinky-dink snapshot camera and I asked my jumpmaster if it would be all right for me to take it along on my next jump. He said he didn't see why not. From that point on, I was fascinated by capturing my skydiving experiences on film for others to see. No one else in normal life seemed to be interested in skydiving, or at least, when I described it, knew enough about it to exhibit any interest. But when they saw a picture — wow! It really got their attention. Later, after I joined my father in his motion picture business, it was an easy transition for me to start taking movies in freefall.

At that time, there were only a handful of skydivers doing freefall photography, and only a few of those were professionals. We were all solving the various technical problems in the isolation of our individual drop zones with little interaction except at the big meets. But common problems called for common solutions, and soon we found that we were all coming up with many of the same answers.

Freefall posed some very severe limitations, so some of the choices were obvious. For example, all skydivers used their arms and legs in freefall for movement and control in the air. The rest of the body was taken up with a harness and parachutes. So, by process of elimination, that left only the head as the logical place to mount a camera. Besides, the helmet provided a convenient hard platform on which to bolt cameras as well as eyesights. The head also could then act as a tripod for tilting and panning to compose a shot. Where the cameraman looked was what the camera saw. This, in itself, posed several safety problems. While a cameraman was filming, he couldn't look where he was going or at his altimeter to keep track of altitude to avoid going low. He had to keep the eyesight fixed on the subject at all times and use his body to fly, moving closer or further away, higher or lower, in order to make all the subtle aspect changes as the scene changed and the composition varied. It became quite an art. In my case, I was shooting movies before I had mastered all the skills of skydiving. Duffy used to joke about all my weird body contortions in freefall while filming other skydivers. "But," he would say in admiration, "the camera was always level and rock steady."

Everyone loved to be in front of the camera and tended to get so involved with the "acting" that they forgot to watch the altitude. But the cameraman needed extra altitude in order to set up, head-high, to avoid whiplash when he opened.

No matter how often I explained that to other skydivers before the jump, inevitably we ended up below a safe opening altitude and I was the one to suffer for it. As a result, I developed a little clock in my head. I would know automatically when it came time to open. I didn't have to look at the ground or my altimeter, or depend on other jumpers to wave off; I just backed away, set up, and pulled.

The other major problem with having a camera on your helmet was the weight. A normal opening shock could cause severe neck injury if precautions weren't taken. A hard opening could cause death. I know of at least two freefall photographers who died in the air of a broken neck. There were probably more. The opening force of a parachute swings the body from the horizontal falling position to a vertical upright position in a few seconds. Since the parachute is connected to your harness at the shoulders, the tendency is for your body to swing one way and your head another during the opening sequence. A cameraman's neck becomes the fulcrum point because of the heavy weight attached to his helmet.

I experimented with various ways to lessen the opening shock on my neck. One thing that helped was body position. Opening with the body in the normal flat position, parallel to earth, was not good. It accentuated the whiplash effect. I found that taking the time to set up in a head-high position before pulling my ripcord helped to align my neck and spine to the vertical forces of the opening shock. Holding the helmet with both hands had absolutely no effect. You had no leverage with your arms since they were undergoing the same forces. If that sounds funny, try holding a weight at arm's length inside an elevator and see what happens when it starts or stops. There is no way you'll be able to keep your arm parallel to the floor, no matter how strong you are.

But I discovered the simple law of lever action was the real solution. By grabbing my risers as high as I could immediately after pulling my ripcord, I could change the fulcrum point of the opening stresses, from below my head at the neck where my risers attached to the harness, to above my head where my hands held the risers. Actually, it didn't even take much strength. The trick was just to change that fulcrum point. Whether I was wearing a camera or not, I got into the habit of reaching as far back over my shoulders as I could after I pulled the ripcord on each jump, in order to grab my risers.

I remember very distinctly one time that I did this out of habit and kept right on falling. For a moment, I didn't understand what was going on. When I pull the ripcord and grab my risers, the parachute is supposed to open. I went through it again in my mind: Pulled the ripcord ... check! Grabbed the risers ... check! Parachute opened ... no check. Hmmm, this definitely was where the problem lay; the parachute hadn't opened yet. I double-checked my theory by looking at the ground. Yep, it was still coming straight up at me. Hmmm, I'd have to do something about this situation. I looked over my shoulder to see what in the world could possibly be causing my pack not to open. I got the shock of my life. I was looking directly at my pilot chute only a few inches away. This was probably the only time I had ever seen my own pilot chute in freefall. I was holding it in my hand. Apparently, my pilot chute had come out of the pack, gotten trapped in the vacuum over my back and flopped up over my shoulder just as I grabbed my riser. Without realizing it, I had grabbed it, also. No wonder my chute hadn't opened. I don't know how long I fell, looking at my pilot chute like an idiot, but when the realization finally reached my brain, I opened my hand and let it go like it was a hot potato. I could then complete my inventory: parachute opened ... check! No problem. After that, I didn't grab for the risers quite so fast.

Even using all the safeguards, many times I experienced muscle pulls and neck injuries due to heavy camera equipment. Some of them were bad enough to cause me to lay off jumping for several months until my neck healed. When I wore two movie cameras, I got into the habit of wearing a double set of neck braces. I looked foolish and it was uncomfortable to wear, but they enabled me to avoid further neck injuries.

Movie cameras for skydiving had to be small, lightweight, and rugged. Spring-wound cameras had too short a film run to be practical, so battery power was a must. Since normal movie cameras were much too heavy to mount on a helmet, there was only one choice: gun cameras from World War II fighter planes. These were developed at the start of the war to verify fighter "kills," presumably because fighter pilots were sometimes known to exaggerate. These small 16mm movie cameras were mounted in the plane's wings and activated by the pilot's machine gun trigger. They were engineered and manufactured under government contracts through two companies, Bell & Howell and Fairchild. These miniature cameras shot all the air-to-air dogfight footage that we've all seen in the movies and on television depicting air battles. I often wondered if my cameras had shot any of that footage.

There is a limited amount of this historic film in the archives and if you are attentive, you can spot identical shots used repeatedly. "Baa Baa Black Sheep," the TV series based on the life of World War II fighter pilot Pappy Boyington, must have used every available foot of archival gun camera film. Even though they used the same scenes over and over again, it was a good show and I enjoyed it. I get a little put out, however, when movie directors think that their audience is stupid enough to accept dogfight footage for something else, such as a bomber's point of view. In my opinion, it shows the director's lack of acuity rather than the audience's.

The most common gun camera was designated "N-6." These held slide-in film magazines holding only 50 feet of film. They were designed so that even the most unskilled aircraft ground crew could remove an exposed film cartridge and slide in a fresh one with no trouble. All they had to do was remember to close and lock the door on the back of the camera. This was the type of gun camera I used because I could find them so easily and buy them so cheaply. All the parts were interchangeable so I could salvage a bad or damaged camera using spare parts. The other camera, the "N-9," had a 100-foot film magazine, but was a little larger and heavier. I could never find any of those at a price I could afford, but I knew of other cameramen who were using them. At that time, Kodak still loaded and sold movie film in the standard 50-foot magazines. The buyer was supposed to return the exposed film to the lab in the metal magazine, but I kept all of mine and built custom equipment for reloading them with bulk film at less than half the cost.

There were no manuals for these cameras since I found them in the dusty back rooms of Army surplus or used camera stores. So I would tear them apart to study the gear ratios in order to compute the shutter speeds. Most of them had three set speeds available on a click-stop dial. They were calibrated in frames per second (fps) and the only speeds were 16, 32 and 64. Since the "normal" shutter speed of any modern movie camera is 24 fps, the gun cameras recorded scenes either in slow motion (64 fps), slightly slow motion (32 fps) or at a speeded-up rate (16 fps), somewhat like the old silent movies. I liked to shoot skydiving in slow motion, so not having available a normal speed of 24 fps didn't bother me a bit. One Hollywood camera company I knew of bought up a lot of these cameras, refurbished them, replaced the gears for 24 fps and sold them for thousands of dollars each.

I was also able to use my gun cameras in my film business to get those occasional odd-angle shots when I needed to mount a camera in an unusual or risky place. For example, driving a car over the lens was impossible for the normal movie camera, which had too high a profile. When I made a movie for my friend Dave Allyn about his antique biplane, the N-3-N, I used two of these gun cameras for wing and tail viewpoints. I would duck down in the front cockpit to be out of the picture and switch on the cameras as Dave did loop and roll aerobatics. We got excellent results with this idea. On the movie screen, it was startling to see Dave in the cockpit of the biplane remain static in the middle of the shot as the earth circled behind him.

I remember one flight from Sarasota to Englewood when we were on our way to do aerobatics with mounted gun cameras. I looked out and saw that the 85 filter on the lens of the wing camera had worked loose and was about to fall off. I motioned to Dave that I could walk out on the wing to retrieve it, but he shook his head "no." I thought he was worried that I didn't have on a parachute. I found out later he was just scared that I'd put a foot through the wing fabric. The filter finally fell off over Venice. I always thought that one day, I'd bump into a person who would mention the strange day that a piece of colored glass fell out of the sky. But it hasn't happened yet.

The trick to getting good footage with these cameras was not the camera speeds or the gear ratio; it was the lenses. Originally, these war surplus cameras had fixed lenses bolted on the front. Not only were they "long" lenses designed for shooting objects fairly far away, which was no good for skydiving, but most had deteriorated badly. They had a fixed focus and, instead of f-stops, had only "D, H, and L" designations. I couldn't figure that out for the longest time but, after seeing that the "D" setting had the largest aperture and "L" the smallest, I came to the conclusion that the wartime ground crew could set the lens before a flight according to the type of day it happened to be: Dark, Hazy or Light. All this didn't matter anyway because I never used these lenses. At one point, some camera company had manufactured a new front plate for these cameras with a standard "C" mount. This was very important because it meant that any professional "C-mount" lens could be screwed onto the camera. Depending on the job, any lens, from wide angle to telephoto, could be easily and quickly interchanged on the camera. Good photography depended on good lenses of the proper focal length. For skydiving, I used mostly wide-angle lenses from 15mm to a 5.7mm "fisheye"; my preference was 10mm. So the trick was, on my tight budget, to buy or trade for a gun camera with a "C-mount" modification. Several times I found the front plates alone for very little cost.

Another piece of information I learned from my friend Bill Cole in Canada. Very few people knew that while most United States war planes were based on a 24- to 28-volt battery, the Canadian war birds had a 12- to 18-volt power supply. The camera manufacturers had supplied gun cameras to the Canadian military with 12-volt camera motors. I went around Canada and bought up all the Canadian gun cameras I could find, whether they worked or not. Soon I had switched the motors in all my gun cameras. None of the other freefall cameramen could understand how I could use such a small, lightweight battery pack. Until I explained, it never dawned on them that I needed only half the power they did.

I used to delight in trying to dream up new camera angles. One day I decided to film my own backpack opening so, rather than go to the trouble of rebuilding my helmet mount, I simply turned my helmet around backwards. I got Billy to fly in and hook up on my legs to give the scene some action. I told him to wiggle my feet with his hands when he was ready and I'd pull the ripcord. That turned out to be a smart move on my part because, once out of the plane, my helmet, being on backwards, rode down and covered my eyes; I couldn't see a thing during the whole jump. I just waited for Billy's signal to pull my ripcord. I got the sequence on film, but I was kidded a lot about how silly I looked.

Then I got obsessed about trying to go a step further: to film the opening sequence from inside the parachute. This posed some very interesting problems. First, it meant that I had to attach the camera to the inside of my parachute and actually pack it into my parachute container. The average parachute was a very tight fit as it was. With the extra bulk of a movie camera, I needed a couple of extra guys to help me close my pack. Every jump I made with this arrangement was a "hard pull"; I needed the full strength of both hands to pull the ripcord. I also had to string a power cable from the camera in the parachute down the lines to my battery pack inside my jumpsuit, so I could turn on the camera at the proper moment. I'd jump out of the plane, get stable in freefall, turn on the camera switch and struggle to pull the ripcord. It took me a few jumps to work out the bugs. It seemed that the camera would tangle up in my parachute lines, causing a spinning malfunction. Every jump I'd have to cut away my main and open my reserve. I didn't mind cutting away as much as disconnecting the power line which turned off the camera. I hated to miss the shot of myself falling from the jettisoned canopy. Despite all these problems, I refused to give up. I was determined to get this shot. Others might have called it foolhardy, but I was damned if I was going to let a mechanical problem get the best of me. It had become a point of pride.

We were jumping at Zephyrhills at this time and I experienced several weeks of multiple malfunctions back to back, as I made subtle adjustments as to how I rigged the camera. My malfunctions happened with such regularity it got to be a tradition at the drop zone for everyone to stop everything and come out from under the packing shed to watch my jump.

There was always something for me to learn. Usually it was how dumb I was. On one of the first of these jumps, I used ordinary clothesline rope to tie the camera into my parachute. For some reason, it didn't dawn on me that the tremendous forces that developed as the parachute opened would break the clothesline as if it were thread. During the opening on this jump, I happened to be at a slight angle off of vertical. An instant after I took opening shock, I heard a "buzz" flash past me like an angry hornet. I looked up to see no malfunction, mainly because my camera was gone. That "buzz" had been the camera going past me, still falling at 120 mph. If I had opened straight up and down as usual, the camera would have gone right through my helmet and embedded itself in my brain. It probably would have served me right! After that, I always used nylon cord or webbing for parachuting rigging.

I found the camera, by the way, on the ground just off the runway. To prove how rugged these cameras were, I took off the bent-up housing and put the guts of the camera into a spare body. It has worked fine ever since. I finally got the shot I wanted but, after all the trouble and the danger, the results were anticlimactic. The film was black until the parachute opened and then the first few seconds after that were blurred due to the vibrations of opening shock. Once everything settled down, the movies were fine, but I might just as well not have gone to the trouble to pack the camera in the chute after all but, rather, hoisted it into the canopy after it had opened. But then I would have missed all that excitement!

Chapter Twenty-one
DAVE

Dave Allyn was rich. At least that's how he appeared to us at first. He had a wealthy and famous father and we assumed he was born rich. Actually, that was an injustice. Dave was a self-made man who despised rich kids who played with their parents' money. He left home at the age of 18 and worked as a roughneck in the oil fields for $300 a month. He then went to sea as an able-bodied seaman, rising to the rank of 3rd mate before going to flight school. Before he started Dolphin Aviation, a fixed-base operation at the Sarasota Airport, he had become extremely successful in another local aviation business which rebuilt World War II vintage P-51s.

At any rate, it didn't matter to us skydivers that he had money or not. We liked Dave right off because he was a true aviator. He loved everything about aviation and so did we. I guess what Dave especially liked about us was that, like him, we didn't care about superficial things. The only things we cared about were guts and glory.

Dave was a big bear of a guy. Kind of gruff to strangers, but a wonderful guy to those who knew him. Dave was in the process of acquiring a whole fleet of antique aircraft to start his own museum of aviation history, and he delighted in flying each of his acquisitions when time permitted. He later moved the whole museum out to Santa Fe, New Mexico.

Since Dave was doing so much flying, he became interested in learning how to skydive for his own safety. He became acquainted with the Mission Valley Skydivers through Rick Fulwider, one of his employees. Rick was a nice, easygoing young guy who had joined us earlier and had quickly become a good skydiver. Although he was more serious and not as wild as the rest of us, he was well liked by us all.

One day Dave and Rick flew into the drop zone at Englewood in Dave's Stinson Trimotor. This was a beautiful aircraft, and it happened to be the only one left in the world still flying. There were quite a few of the Ford Trimotors still around, but the Stinson was even more old-fashioned looking and a lot smaller. The interior looked like a trolly car with benchlike seats and weird structural pipes spaced throughout the cabin from floor to ceiling angled out into the aisleway. Even with the two big noisy engines, it was underpowered and very slow to climb.

It was somewhat of an ugly duckling but we all thought it was neat and immediately fell in love with it as a jump plane.

We were in luck. Dave was going to let Rick jump from it to test one of his pilot's emergency chutes before having it repacked. Dave saw all of us drooling over the Trimoter and very generously invited all of us who wanted to go along for a free jump. We, of course, literally jumped at the chance. It was a unique experience and we all had a great time. All, that is, except Rick. He went into freefall for about 15 seconds to reach terminal velocity with Dave's emergency pack and pulled the ripcord. It opened so fast it damn near took him apart.

This particular rig was undoubtedly to be used only for an emergency. You used it only if you had no other choice for getting to the ground alive. It sure wasn't for sport jumping. At least that was Rick's opinion, and he paid the price to find out. He was sore for several weeks. I was the unofficial club "test jumper," but in this case I was glad I wasn't offered the job. From that point on, any time Dave felt like flying the Trimoter, he'd give us a call and whoever wasn't busy would go along for the ride and get in a unscheduled jump.

Then came the day that another one of Dave's emergency packs came due for a repack and Dave again wanted to make sure that it indeed did work before he actually needed to use it for real. Rick said there was no way he was going to jump it! I also declined. I was crazy, not stupid. So Rick called to say that they had decided to strap it to a big metal barrel and static-line it out of the plane over Englewood. I immediately stopped what I was doing at work, swung home to pick up my jump gear, and met them at the airport. This was something I wanted to see. Gail Davis, one of the few female jumpers in our group, was hanging around the airport at the time and went along for a jump.

It was only a short flight to Englewood and Rick, Gail, and I bailed out to watch the big event from the ground. Dave flew the Trimoter around for another pass to give two of his employees time to get the barrel ready to toss out the door.

Our jump went fine. It was nice to be playing hooky from work on such a nice Florida afternoon. We all landed halfway down the north-south runway and, slipping out of our harnesses, left our rigs on the ground for later once the barrel was down. There the three of us stood, in the middle of an empty airfield on a lazy afternoon, looking up at the circling plane like a bunch of refugees waiting for an airdrop of supplies.

We wondered what was taking so long. Maybe the guys in the plane were having trouble getting the barrel rigged up in the doorway. The doorway of the Trimoter was not the roomiest in the world. Finally the plane circled again and we could tell it was lining up for another jump run. About that time a car pulled off the highway and started down the airport road.

"Who the hell is that?" I wondered.

Well, I had no time for that now; the barrel was about to be dropped. The plane passed overhead and still no barrel appeared. The car kept going and instead of stopping where the road ended, it drove out onto the runway. What the hell was going on? And where was the damn barrel? My head swiveled up and down, from the car to the plane and back again. The car stopped in the middle of the two crossing runways and just sat there. I never did find out what the car was doing there.

The plane was now directly over the car and, naturally, this was the exact point that the barrel was ejected out of the plane. And, naturally, this was the time that the parachute chose not to open. We couldn't believe it. It didn't take a genius to draw an imaginary line from the falling barrel, trailing the streamering chute, straight down to the car directly below it.

We must have been at least 100 yards away from the car but once we recovered from the shock of these unlikely events, we started running down the runway like idiots screaming, "Move the car! Move the car!" We could see that it was going to be no contest. We'd never reach the car in time.

The barrel was hurling downward relentlessly and we were no track stars. As I got closer, I could tell that the car was a Cadillac.

Oh, great! I thought. *It couldn't be an old junker, it had to be an expensive Cadillac!*

About 100 feet over the car the parachute opened unexpectedly. We could see that it wouldn't have hit the car after all but now, under parachute, given the current wind direction, it might drift into the car and still do major damage.

Our headlong run had slowed when the chute had opened but we now sped up again, spurred on by this new danger. We had no breath left for shouting. We were still quite a distance away when the barrel slammed into the ground just a few yards from the car. We finally arrived at the car, huffing and puffing, dreading the outraged lecture that was sure to come from the car owner.

We stood there trying to catch our breath and gather our thoughts as to how best to explain.

The car door slowly opened. An elderly lady gradually emerged from the Cadillac. We stood there glancing down at our boots like thieves caught in the act.

With a concerned look, the lady asked, "Is the man in the barrel all right?"

Chapter Twenty-two

BRUCE

B ruce Harting, along with Duffy, was one of the original founders of the Mission Valley Skydivers. He was a handsome, rugged former Marine and, although not much older than me, he always impressed me with his military bearing and serious attitude. An expert in karate and weapons, he had the reputation of having a bad temper and I was a little in awe of him at first. Later we became good friends.

I had experimented with using a variety of cameras in freefall and soon I became known as our club photographer. One day Bruce came to me and said, "Mike, in all my jumps, I don't have any pictures of myself in freefall. Do you think you could get some of me?"

I was flattered that he had asked and we agreed to make a photo jump the next Sunday. I felt that he was phasing out of skydiving and it was now or never for getting pictures of him in the air. Since Bruce wasn't jumping much at that point, he didn't have all the gear except his old main, but there was never any problem in borrowing equipment at the DZ. That's why I thought nothing of it when, that Sunday, Bruce borrowed a jumpsuit, reserve, and helmet to make our jump. He and I went to 7,500 feet and, although he was a little rusty, we had no problem flying together in freefall as I took a whole roll of what I thought were good photos. I got them to a lab as soon as possible and in a few days I had the prints. I was right. I had taken some great pictures. Bruce would be very pleased. Even if he quit jumping, he now had some nice photographs that he could enlarge for display. There was only one problem. I had not noticed it until it leaped out of the photos at me ... the helmet that Bruce had borrowed spelled out in big letters across the front: "**CHUCK**"

Bruce was an engineer and draftsman dealing with water treatment plants and occasionally he moved from one job to another on various development projects. When he called to say that he and his wife had moved to Grand Cayman, my initial response was, "What are you doing out in Arizona?"

"No, no," he said, "that's Grand *Canyon*! This is Grand *Cayman*, an island in the Caribbean just south of Cuba."

Bruce was calling to see if we wanted to make the first skydive in the history of the island. Damn straight we wanted to! I still had no idea of where it was, but a skydiving "first" was a "first"!

Soon all the arrangements were made. Dave Allyn had volunteered to fly us in his antique Lockheed-12 at no cost. Thank God for that, as most of us were broke as usual.

The island of Grand Cayman was a British protectorate and for some reason parachutes were equated with military maneuvers. There were some kind of antiquated laws left over from World War II that forbade any parachuting activity without prior approval from England. Bruce waded through a couple months of red tape but finally the date was set.

There were seven of us: Dave Allyn, our pilot; Dale Zigler, his employee who was flying co-pilot; Rick Fulwider, a jumper friend of ours as well as an employee of Dave's; Duffy Nathan, infamous skydiver; Joy, Duffy's wife; Jo Anderson, my girlfriend, and me.

Dave's plane, although classified as an antique, was, in its day, designed far ahead of its time. With its advanced air frame and its silver metal skin, it looked like a modern aircraft, and Dave kept it in tip-top shape. With two engines, it was a safe and reliable airplane to fly over water, even though it was the same make and model aircraft flown by Amelia Earhart when she was lost over the Pacific.

Since the most direct route from Florida to Grand Cayman lay directly over Cuba, Dave had filed a flight plan and had gotten permission to fly through the designated international airspace that ran in a narrow corridor through the middle of the island. It was called the Giron Corridor because it ran in a north-south direction from the town of Varadero on Cuba's north coast to Playa Giron on the south coast near Bahua de Cochinos, the infamous Bay of Pigs. Nothing could stop us now -- we were on the way.

The instant we took off from Sarasota, Duffy pulled out a large thermos of mixed drinks and the party started, excluding the pilot and co-pilot, of course. We were in good shape when we made our first stop in Key West to refuel, but Duffy's thermos had given out long since. While Dave and Rick took care of the plane, we made a beeline for the airport bar.

In a short while, Dave and Rick came in with down-at-the-mouth expressions. Dave had checked his flight plan with the FAA and, to his surprise, found that the permission to fly over Cuba had been cancelled without warning or explanation. He figured the rest of us might as well have one more drink and then he'd fly us home.

But we weren't about to give up yet. We spread out air charts over the cocktail table and charted alternate routes to Cayman around Cuba, both through Jamaica and through Cozumel in Yucatan, Mexico. After much discussion, Dave vetoed both plans because they more than tripled our flight-time over water. Our hopes sank; the only thing to do seemed to be to turn around and go home.

Then Duffy, in an alcoholic haze, came up with his brilliant plan. "Let's call Cuba," he said, "and talk to that son-of-bitch Castro!"

We all laughed until Duffy went to the bar phone and got the international operator on the line. Dave was petrified, but I took him aside and rationalized that even if Duffy could get through, he probably wouldn't be able to reach anyone of any importance.

"Besides," I said, "Who would be better suited to talk to them than Duffy?"

Dave seemed to agree and we rejoined the group at the bar. By then, Duffy was trying to talk to a non-English-speaking operator and, at the same time, order another drink. I still wasn't exactly sure if he was serious about calling Cuba. Finally, after going through several operators, to our amazement, Duffy seemed to be talking to somebody in the Cuban "Air Ministry." We could only hear Duffy's side of the conversation. It was funny as hell! Duffy would be talking with extreme politeness into the phone one minute, "Yes sir, that is affirmative ..." and the next, covering the mouthpiece with his other hand, saying, "That fucking Communist son-of-a-bitch" aside to us. We were struggling to keep the laughing to a minimum so the guy on the other end wouldn't hear us, but we weren't doing such a good job. Dave, worried to death about losing his pilot's license over an international incident, was about to have apoplexy as he tried to shush Duffy's verbal abuse on one hand and our laughing on the other. But Dave wasn't able to keep a straight face either. This was Duffy at his best: able to switch from drunken prankster to shrewd diplomat and back again in a heartbeat. Even so, I was sure that he was going to get mixed up and say the "fuck" word into the phone while telling us politely, "That is affirmative." And that made it even more funny. Even the bartender overhearing all this was cracking up.

At last Duffy hung up. Our laughing subsided as we realized we may have screwed up big time. There was a long sober silence. Then Duffy said, "Well, everything is all set."

We all cheered and ordered another round.

Dave refused to believe it until he checked with FAA and, sure enough, our clearance was official. We were on the way.

The flight over Cuba was uneventful except for the MIG fighters which were scrambled to escort us over the interior of the island. We all had to struggle with Duffy to keep him from photographing them. We could just imagine ourselves spending a year or two in a Cuban prison because of Duffy's drunken hijinks.

The only other little accident occurred when one of the girls used the "relief" tube, a little funnel and rubber hose device, whose other end had inadvertently been disconnected from the drainpipe. Oh, well, every flight can't be perfect.

Bruce met us at the airport, and going through customs was a breeze. The only hitch was a flurry of native laughter when the customs agents discovered Duffy's address to be on "Grand Cayman Street" in Sarasota.

Cayman at this time was a charming undiscovered paradise, still unspoiled by rampant tourism. Our first stop was a local bar/restaurant for a tropical island lunch that Bruce had arranged as a gesture of welcome.

Previously, over the phone, Bruce had promised that all our expenses of food and lodging would be paid for by sponsors which he would arrange before our arrival. With that in mind, we all went into a food frenzy, ordering shrimp cocktails, lobster and escargot without regard to cost.

Bruce's wife, Anne, with a worried look, took me aside and quietly explained that the sponsorship idea had not worked out after all. Bruce was quietly going to keep his promise by paying for everything himself without telling us. I made the rounds to all the guys at our table and quietly relayed this information. Touched by his gesture, we immediately agreed among ourselves to go dutch on everything. Dave said that he'd back any of us who were short on cash until we got home. Our food order immediately reverted to normal, less exotic fare. But once the islanders found out who we were, many of our drinks were paid for and we were invited to many private parties.

Late that afternoon we packed our chutes along the side of Bruce's little house. For us it was very exotic to string out our chutes among banana trees and flowering tropical plants, a real change from our normal flat, empty, Florida DZs. We wanted to be completely packed and ready since the next day was our designated jump day. Because of all the long-distance red tape, we realized it was our only window of opportunity to make any skydives while we were here. We even cut the partying short and got a good night's sleep for once so we'd be fresh to make the first jump on the island of Grand Cayman.

The next morning dawned to a clear, typical island day. The only problem was that a "typical" island day was like a hurricane to us. We were known for jumping in bad winds, but this was ridiculous. We were fearless, but even we had never jumped in winds like this. Nevertheless, this was the only day we could jump, so our favorite expression applied: "It's a dirty, dangerous job, but somebody has to do it."

First we loaded all our gear and rode in the back of Bruce's truck out to the drop zone. The target area turned out to be a disaster in the making. It was the land site that Bruce's employer was clearing for development. I have to admit that it was a nice flat open site with no hazards like trees or powerlines. The only hazard was the DZ itself! It consisted of hard limestone bedrock recently cleared of mangroves. Scattered randomly across this forbidding surface were grapefruit-sized pieces of coral rock which the bulldozer had "smoothed" off of outcroppings throughout the site. I couldn't think of a worse place to make a parachute landing even on a good day. Bruce had thoughtfully marked out a huge circle on the ground as our proposed target.

Hell, in this wind, I thought, *we'll be lucky just to hit the island!*

Duffy pulled the pin on a smoke grenade and tossed it out onto the target area to see what the wind was doing. The gale was so strong, the purple smoke streamered out across the hard ground and never got more than a foot high before it dissipated. Standing there with our clothing flapping in the high wind, we all turned pale and made gulping noises. We assured Bruce that it was indeed a perfect DZ and made for the airport. It was time to "do or die" and it was beginning to look like the latter.

The only ones not worried were Duffy and Dave, who were going to land in the water. Duffy was sporting a broken foot from his last jump back in Florida. He was planning a nice soft water landing out in the bay, but he was beginning to realize that, in this wind, even a water landing could be dangerous. Dave was a bit heavier than the rest of us and had very few jumps. It was obvious that he would never survive a landing on that target site in this wind, thus the reason for his water jump.

An island-based jump plane had never materialized so we had to jump from Dave's Lockheed with its tiny oval door and high flight speed. Since Dave, our pilot, was planning to jump, Dale, our co-pilot, had to fly, and he had never flown jumpers before. Dave gave him last-minute instructions. It was sizing up to be one of our typical "balls-to-the-wall" jumps. It was March 12, 1972.

During our flight to altitude, everyone was hyped and we were making our usual silent promises that if we were just allowed to make it to the ground alive this time, we'd never jump again. Jump run emotion was a mixture of "I don't want to do it" and "Let's get it over with."

At 13,000 feet the island looked extremely small, surrounded by a very big ocean. We could barely see our target circle on the ground, but the target area itself was obvious. It was the big bare white scar devoid of any natural greenery on a narrow piece of land between the bay and the Caribbean. Several skinny fingers of land stood out against the blue of the bay where the developer was creating more "waterfront" than was naturally available for their more expensive homes.

With his goggles on, Duffy knelt at the door and stuck his head out in the wind stream to line up the plane for the jump run. The wind stream swept his hair straight back and rippled his cheeks like it did in freefall. Occasionally he would duck his head inside and call "five right" or "five left" degrees of flight correction which we would relay up front to Dale in the cockpit. Duffy assured us that he'd give us a good long upwind "spot" to compensate for the high winds.

Since Bruce was our host, he was given the honor of being the first out the door. Don't think that it didn't cross our minds that once Bruce left the plane we could have kept on flying back to Florida. But then there was the question of our baggage and the girls we had left on the ground.

"What the hell," we said. "It's a dirty, dangerous job, etcetera."

We all jumped, one behind the other, through the small door, and started a long 65-second freefall toward our doom. I was shooting both 16mm helmet-mounted movies and 35mm hand-held stills. I was worrying about landing in the water and ruining my movie camera but then I thought, *Hey, no problem, I'd probably drown anyway!*

Despite all this, it was a beautiful freefall through the crystal clear Caribbean air. Once I had opened, I looked around and counted canopies. Rick's blue canopy was off to the right at my same level only 50 yards away. But I could see only two others at a higher altitude. Where was the fifth one? Then I saw way below a red-and-white reserve. Someone must have had a malfunction.

Later we were to learn that Dave couldn't find his ripcord which had accidentally gotten out of its pocket. He had gone very low fumbling for it and finally pulled his reserve. As the reserve opened it had snagged the errant main ripcord and momentarily hung up until it tore loose. It had left a large gash in the small canopy all the way to the skirt. Luckily, the lower lateral band around the bottom edge of the canopy had held, or Dave would have been history. Also, with that hole spilling air, it was lucky that Dave was landing in soft water rather than hard land. But Dave's trials weren't over yet. After he landed in the North Sound, quite a distance from shore, his reserve re-inflated in the wind and began towing him underwater. He thought he was going to drown until, in desperation, he pulled on a riser with all his might and miraculously re-surfaced. He was rescued by two guys fishing in a small boat.

Duffy, making his water jump as planned, landed in Governor's Harbor and was picked up by a Caymanian in Bruce's boat, stationed there for just that purpose.

Rick hit hard in the target area and was dragged for quite a distance. In the process, he cut open his arm on a coral rock from his wrist to his elbow. He was immediately hauled off to a local hospital.

Bruce hit and dragged but he was only slightly bruised and cut up by the rocks.

I hit ground like a ton of bricks but dragged only a short distance before I made a textbook recovery, rolling to my feet unhurt to collapse my chute. I was disappointed to discover my movie camera had jammed, but I had taken some good stills with my trusty Nikonos.

Once Duffy and Dave were returned to the target area, we blew up Dave's reserve in the wind to see the damage. We were all amazed by the size of the hole in it. Dave was lucky to be alive.

With a huge crowd of Caymanians looking on, Bruce and I repacked our chutes. It was quite a trick, considering the wind conditions. Finally with our gear all packed, Bruce and I looked at each other, shrugged, and got back in the truck. With Rick in the hospital, Duffy's gear all wet, and Dave's reserve ruined, we were the only two left able to make our second jump of the day.

It was a long quiet ride back to the airport. The wind was picking up. Since we had lots of room in the plane, Reed Dennis, Bruce's former Marine buddy, decided to go along. He published a local newspaper, *The Cayman Compass*, and he wanted to take pictures of our exit for the next issue. With only two of us to jump, we only went up to 10,000 feet for a 50-second freefall.

I had decided to leave my movie camera on the ground this time and concentrate on 35mm slides of Bruce. I went out the door first, turned over to fall away on my back, and took a classic photo of Bruce exiting the Lockheed in a spread-eagle pose. Later, I sent a couple of enlargements of this shot to Bruce. One he hung on his wall. The other he said he sent to the Queen of England as a way of saying "thanks" for the special authorization to jump. He and I like to think that it's hanging on some wall in Buckingham Palace to this day.

Years later Bruce showed me a photo taken at the same instant as mine. It was photographed by Reed shooting out the door of the plane. It was an exact reverse angle of Bruce, with me below him. Bruce had hung it next to mine. It was funny to see, side by side, the same instant of time frozen in two such different views. If you looked closely at my enlargement, you could make out Reed's head sticking out of the door of the plane. Reed's photo ran on the front page of his newspaper and mine won a minor award in a local photo contest back home.

Anyway, on this second jump, Bruce landed near the target and dragged about 50 yards across the limestone and coral. Thinking ahead, on this jump he had worn the top half of a scuba suit which protected him from too many more scrapes and abrasions. His backpack, however, was ruined where he had sledded across the rocks on top of it.

My landing was almost as spectacular. Once I got close to the ground and knew that I would land somewhere in the general target area, I turned into the wind in order to slow my horizontal speed over the ground as much as possible. I was really scared to deviate even a fraction of a degree off the wind line. If I did, I knew I'd pick up speed and land even harder than I expected. This meant that I was backing into the landing area and I kept turning my head around as best I could, trying to see what I was about to hit. Not that it seemed to matter much; I knew I was going to die wherever I landed.

The ground was coming up like crazy and I got prepared to do the best PLF I knew how. The first parts of my body to touch ground were my heels. The very next thing to hit was the top of my helmet as I flipped over backwards without stopping. From that point on it got worse. But what the hell, my opinion of a "good" landing was one after which you were able to crawl to the nearest bar and order a drink. So I guess this one qualified. I had survived with only one bruise ... my whole body.

Later, Rick arrived at the bar all bandaged up but cheerful that he had come through alive. We immediately prescribed alcohol for his pain but cautioned him not to operate any heavy machinery for several hours. Needless to say, it was party time, and we settled down for a night of revelry accompanied by the island music of "The Barefoot Man" and his calypso band at the Galleon Beach Hotel. The mission had been a total success.

A couple of years later, I was back in Grand Cayman on a job to tape-record Barefoot's first record album. Early one afternoon, Bruce, Reed, and I were sitting at a bar, reminiscing over old times. We were indulging in an old Marine pastime of chugging "depth-charges." A depth-charge, also called a "boilermaker," is a draft beer with a shot of rum dropped into it, shot glass and all. You drink it in one long swallow. We had already had two or three of these when in walked a local lightweight for whom Bruce and Reed had no use. They knew from past experience that it was pointless to try to avoid him. When he asked, they glumly agreed that he could join us at the bar. He wanted to have the same thing we were drinking so we ordered another round. We downed ours and turned to watch him. He upended his glass in a game attempt to emulate us by drinking the contents of the glass all at once. As he leaned way back on his bar stool to finish the last swallow, he continued on backwards unconscious. As one, he and the bar stool slowly fell over to crash on the floor of the bar. It was pretty funny because not one of us lifted a finger to help or showed any surprise at the outcome. Unconcerned, we simply turned back to our conversation while the startled bartender rushed around the bar to carry him off.

"Say," I said to Bruce, "do you remember our second jump that day? I was so damn scared that I would never have gone up again if you hadn't have been so dead set on it!"

Bruce turned to me in amazement. "*I* was so set on it?" he repeated incredulously, "I thought *you* wanted to jump again!"

Chapter Twenty-three

THE ALTITUDE RECORD

A s I swung my legs out of the open door of the air-plane, the distinctive triangular runways of the Zephyr- hills airport were 28,000 feet below. More than five miles under us, the enormous airport looked unbelievably small as Duffy and I sat side by side in the doorway and made the final preparations for our record-setting jump. We were in the domain of the huge commercial jets but, unlike them, we had no pressurized cabins with comfortable temperatures and normal oxygen levels.

We were attempting to reach 34,000 feet, but the turbo-charged Cessna 210 from Zephyr Aviation just wouldn't climb any more. We had been at 28,000 feet for the past 15 minutes, so, resigned to this compromise which was still establishing a new altitude record (the previous record was 22,500 feet), we had commenced our jump run.

I knew that our pilot, Paul Rice, was talking to a Miami air traffic controller. For some reason I never could quite fathom, we were on Miami's air traffic radar and needed their final clearance to jump, even though we were 30 miles north of Tampa and 240 miles northwest of Miami.

The view was unbelievable! The door of the Cessna 210 had been removed on the ground in preparation for this jump so we had an unbroken, 180-degree view of the horizon. No amount of peering through a tiny plexiglass window of an airliner could prepare us for the stark beauty of this unique vista. We could actually see the curvature of the earth and the indigo color of the sky above where it was beginning to merge into the blackness of space. What a feeling of exhilaration and wonder! We were flying due east into the prevailing 12-knot wind which gave us a fantastic view of the whole Tampa Bay area and beyond, including a vast section of the Gulf of Mexico.

Inside my head I could hear the raspy sound of my every breath, magnified by my oxygen mask. I was so cold I could barely think. I couldn't feel my hands any more and, a little ashamed of myself for being such a wimp, I began worrying about frostbite. I put it out of my mind, since there was nothing I could do about it. My whole body ached from the intense cold and, due to the altitude, I was having pain from nitrogen bubbles in my right elbow, commonly called the "bends" in the scuba-diving world. We should have "pre-breathed" oxygen a lot longer on the ground before the jump, to purge the nitrogen from our systems, but we simply couldn't afford it. I thought making a high-altitude jump would just be uncomfortable. I had no idea that it could be so downright painful.

With the door off, it was thirty degrees below zero within the cabin of the plane. I couldn't imagine what it would be like once we got into freefall. Common sense told me it would be even colder falling through the freezing air, even though the concept of "wind chill factor" was still an idea of the future.

Duffy sat in the door beside me, trying to "spot." His goggles kept frosting over on the inside — a phenomenon we had never considered as a potential problem or that was ever mentioned by anyone. After trying to clean them several times with his gloved hands, he gave up. We had to exit soon. Due to the cold, we had already, clumsily and laboriously, switched to our small bail-out bottles which held a supply of only four to five minutes of oxygen. I was not at all sure that mine was functioning properly. I could feel no extra gas pressure in my mask as I could with a scuba mouthpiece. If it was not working properly, I knew at this altitude I had only a minute or two of consciousness left. There was no way I could re-hook to the larger oxygen bottles in the plane. My hands had lost all function, at least for the delicate operation of connecting valve fittings. We had to jump *now* or abort the whole thing, and if we aborted, we had to immediately fly down to a lower altitude where there was a thicker, more oxygen-enriched atmosphere. Even in freefall, it would take over a minute to get down to a less hostile atmosphere which was breathable.

It was hard to believe that when we had started, only a little over an hour ago, we had been sweltering in the 95-degree Florida heat. For November, it was unusually hot even for Florida. With our heavy jumpsuits, oxygen masks, goggles, smoke grenades, cameras and parachutes, we looked like some kind of giant insects boarding the plane. On the ground we had sweated profusely, which froze in the higher altitudes and made us even colder and more uncomfortable. It seemed like a lifetime ago that a fairly sizable crowd of jumpers and spectators, gathering near the plane, had seen us off with cheers and wishes of "good luck." I remember waving to my mother standing in the crowd. She had come over from St. Petersburg with her brother, Bobby. I really hadn't expected her to make the trip, but it was just like her to unquestioningly support me in whatever I did.

My father and stepmother were there, too. As usual, my father thought I was risking my life just to irritate him and he was torn between pride and resentment. His advice before I suited up was, "Don't be a hero, son," meaning, "Don't take any chances." He didn't realize that a "hero" was exactly what I wanted to be and that taking chances was the name of the game.

Adding to the excitement was a camera crew from a Tampa TV station. I had persuaded them to cover our story with the angle of two guys attempting to establish a new altitude record for sport parachuting.

Duffy and Bob Malott had attempted to make a jump from 24,000 feet in Englewood three years previously. Flying in a Cessna 180 piloted by Bill Sack, they had been foiled by bad weather and a plane that couldn't get above 19,000 feet. Now Bob had quit jumping and had moved to St. Petersburg. I felt honored that Duffy, still determined to make a record attempt, had chosen me from all the other Mission Valley Skydivers. Duffy knew I was a damn good jumper and I had almost as much experience now as he did, with 308 jumps compared to his 456. But I had a sneaking suspicion that he had picked me primarily because of my movie-making abilities as well as my connections in the TV industry. I didn't care. I was thrilled to be involved, for whatever reasons. We had worked and trained hard for this opportunity and, as usual, we were doing it entirely with our own money. It had taken many months to make all the necessary arrangements, and one of the key ingredients was obtaining comprehensive high-altitude training.

We were very fortunate in having a major Air Force base located nearby in Tampa. Only an hour's drive from Sarasota, MacDill was the home of SAC, the famed Strategic Air Command, and it had one of the few high-altitude physiological training courses in the country which was open to qualified civilians. Months before he had asked me to join him on this jump, Duffy had arranged for a group of us to take the day-long course. I didn't know at the time why he had taken special interest that I go along. I found the training to be very worthwhile and extremely interesting, even if a person had no particular plans to put it to immediate use.

The course taught about all the symptoms and dangers of hypoxia (oxygen starvation) and the effects of rapid decompression. The training consisted of several classes in the morning on various related topics such as the atmosphere, respiration, circulation, hypoxia, hyperventilation and decompression sickness. In the afternoon after lunch, the training continued with classes on acceleration, G-forces, decompression, spatial disorientation, and oxygen equipment. We learned that between 15,000 and 18,000 feet an individual without oxygen experiences a sense of well-being, overconfidence, a narrowing field of attention, a blurring of vision, and poor memory. Above 18,000 feet without oxygen, these symptoms increase and are coupled with a loss of judgment, a loss of memory, no sense of time, repeated purposeless movements, and fits of emotional outbursts. Loss of consciousness usually occurs within minutes.

Finally, at the end of the day, the knowledge we gained was put to practical use in the decompression chamber. It's one thing to acquire good "book knowledge," but it's an entirely different matter to experience, firsthand, the bizarre effects of a unique and dangerous environment.

The decompression chamber was a huge metal tube somewhat like a giant scuba tank. It was large enough for the average man to walk into without bending over, and it had seats and equipment for about 12 people. The entrance was a hatch which could be closed, airtight, with a huge oval door on hinges. When the massive door was slowly swung closed and secured with heavy latches, it was like being sealed in a tomb. It certainly was no place for a claustrophobic person.

The air had that unmistakable odor associated with an all-metal enclosure — something of a cross between a heavy mustiness and the sharp tang of a metal oxide. Running along both sides of the chamber's metal walls were a series of small portholes fitted with heavy glass for outside viewing. The chamber was housed in a large room with adjoining rooms holding the vast amount of electrical and mechanical gear needed to suck air from the chamber to simulate the lesser pressure of higher altitudes.

It was all somewhat intimidating, and, naturally, everyone taking the course was relying on the staff's expertise to guide us through the potentially dangerous exercise. Once inside the chamber, we were paired up for safety, and, after selecting a seat, we were each fitted with oxygen masks, microphones and headphones.

Hanging from the ceiling in the middle of the chamber was an ordinary household rubber glove, inflated loosely with air, tied closed at the top and placed in a very conspicuous position. This was to be our visual cue as to our altitude. As the air was pumped out and the occupants of the chamber raised, in effect, to higher and higher altitudes, the lower pressure would cause the glove to inflate larger and larger right before our eyes, the fingers hanging down like some grotesque cow's udder. However, our demonstration was unexpectedly and dramatically enhanced by Duffy's wife, Marilyn, the only woman in our group, whose inflatable bra went from an "A" cup to a "D" cup right before our startled eyes. All of a sudden the normally deserted chamber room was inundated by off-duty servicemen peering through the portholes. Marilyn finally got so uncomfortably squeezed that she had to undo the strap and remove the magic bra from under her blouse to the delight of the young men jockeying for position outside the windows.

We were paired off, as we found out, so that each one could remove their oxygen mask to experience the symptoms of hypoxia while the other observed and acted as a safety man in case their partner became incapacitated by the lack of oxygen. One experiment, which really taught us each a lesson, was doing simple arithmetic on a pad of paper while under the influence of oxygen deprivation. After removing the mask, the normally simple procedure of starting at 99 and counting backwards by three became more and more difficult the longer one was without oxygen. As we experienced it, the numbers and the mathematics seemed perfectly logical and straightforward. But once we went back on oxygen, our pads looked like the demonic scribblings of an idiot.

The truth of the matter was pounded into our brains with the subtlety of a sledgehammer. The symptoms of hypoxia could and would sneak up on a person without warning, and no amount of courage or strength or willpower could forestall it. This was one situation where you had to play by the rules of physics or court disaster.

The last part of the chamber experience was a rapid decompression. This simulated the loss of cabin pressure at a high altitude such as the fracture of a window in a commercial airliner or, in the military, an enemy's machine-gun bullet penetrating a jet fighter's canopy. It was accomplished by the technicians temporarily pressurizing the chamber, instructing us to remove our oxygen masks and then blowing the air out to a vacuum. Since the temperature remained the same but the pressure was reduced drastically, the "dew point" of the remaining air was immediately exceeded and the cabin of the chamber was instantaneously fogged as if by magic. It was a startling way to demonstrate Boyle's law. At this point we knew we had only a certain number of seconds to don our oxygen masks before becoming disoriented by the lack of oxygen. Once safely masked, we were returned to a normal ground level atmosphere, released from the chamber and graduated back to civilian life.

The high-altitude training course was a great experience and a very important factor for our quest to make an altitude record in a safe and professional manner. Also, it gave Duffy the opportunity to gain the attention of one of the training instructors with a gift of a couple bottles of fine scotch. This enabled us later to borrow a pair of bail-out oxygen bottles complete with masks and fittings without having to go to any great expense or compromise our safety.

Even with all our training and planning, we encountered many problems. Our pilot had his own oxygen supply built into the plane's cockpit, but we had to make do with several large scuba-sized bottles of oxygen for the long climb to altitude. To keep them in place on the floor of the cabin, I secured them together with ordinary duct tape. Wrong! When the cabin temperature dropped below freezing, the duct tape became unglued and the big oxygen bottles began rolling around the cabin with every tilt of the plane. It wasn't fair. Boyle's law said nothing about duct tape! Even with heavy gloves, our hands became numb and the simplest chores, like switching our oxygen hoses from one bottle to another, became an almost impossible and life-threatening task.

I took a 16mm hand-held newsreel movie camera for documentation inside the plane which worked well at lower altitudes. Higher up, it became impossible to change film rolls and I had to abandon it. My hand-held 35mm still camera, an old beat-up Nikonos normally used underwater, worked flawlessly both in and out of the plane, but my 16mm helmet-mounted movie camera totally froze up and I got no movies at all in freefall. The biggest problem technically — physically and psychologically — was the mind-numbing cold. It became increasingly more difficult to move, think, and function the higher we climbed.

Now, as we sat in the door, struggling to start our epic dive, I knew we both had in mind the tragic death of Nick Piantanida in 1966, whose extreme high-altitude fatality was attributed to a faulty valve worth maybe half a dollar at the most. We now knew how something so simple could so easily go wrong in a hostile environment, leading to disastrous results. Well, for us, it was now time to do or die ... or do and die. It was November 24, 1969, a little after noon.

Duffy finally seemed satisfied with our "spot" and signaled me with a slap on the shoulder and an urgent "Go! Go!" which was muffled through his oxygen mask. I switched on my helmet movie camera (to no avail, as I later discovered), gripped my still camera tightly in my left hand, and awkwardly rolled out the door. I made an attempt to fall on my back as preplanned to film Duffy's exit, but with the thinness of the air at this altitude, I had no control whatsoever, and flipped over and over for several hundred feet before I was able to stabilize. I was surprised by two things I hadn't expected which were caused by the rarified atmosphere. One was the harshness of light. When I looked up at Duffy as I left the plane, I was totally blinded by the overhead sun. We got so separated at the start of the jump that I never saw Duffy again until we were on the ground. The other surprise was the speed of terminal velocity in the thin air of high altitude. "Terminal velocity" is when a falling object's acceleration becomes balanced by the air pressure beneath it. The object starts to fall at earth's constant gravitational pull of 32 feet per second per second. As its speed increases the acceleration is counterbalanced by the resistance of the air and the acceleration drops to zero. At the same time, the speed increases until it reaches a constant velocity. Each falling object, be it a man or an apple, will have its own particular falling speed dictated by its mass and the cross-sectional area it presents to the air in the direction of motion. Newton's revelation, that all bodies fall at the same acceleration regardless of their weight, is true only in a vacuum. No telling what Newton might have thought had his apple tree been taller and his apple no longer accelerating when it made applesauce on his head.

Being free of the damn plane was wonderful. I had expected to fall faster at the higher altitude, but I had figured once the air pressure under me had built up at the higher speed, it would feel just the same as always. Not so. At the start of the jump, I must have been falling at well over 200 miles per hour. I was just zipping through the air and it felt somewhat like traveling over ice; as if always being on the edge of losing control.

Duffy was nowhere in sight so I had nothing to film and nowhere to go except down. I looked at my altimeter. It was practically useless. We couldn't afford high-altitude instruments, so on the way up to altitude, our regular 12,000-foot dials had wound up over two times what they were built to indicate. Now when I consulted my altimeter, it either read 10,000 feet or 22,000 feet — take your pick. I realized I would just have to judge my opening altitude by eye.

We both carried two smoke grenades on single boot brackets. We had been advised by an Air Force officer that smoke wouldn't burn above 20,000 feet due to the lack of oxygen. When I estimated I was about to pass through that altitude, I reached down and pulled a cord taped to my leg which was tied to one of the smoke grenade pins. Instead of firing off the grenade, the entire apparatus pulled off my foot and I lost the whole boot-bracket, smoke grenades and all. So goes the best laid plans.

Duffy, I found out later, was having problems of his own. His goggles remained fogged over as he jumped and in desperation, he tried to clear them by lifting them off of his eyes in freefall. This exposed his bare eyes to the supercooled air, which caused excruciating pain and blinded him for almost a minute.

Once he got down into the warmer air and regained his sight, he ripped off the useless goggles in freefall and cast them aside. His smoke didn't work either. The pin on one of his smoke grenades bent and the other grenade failed to ignite in the rarified air.

Now, I was over a minute into my jump and I was still higher than I had ever been in freefall. *Wow! This is fantastic!* I thought. Despite the cold and the pain, I was starting to have a good time.

My bail-out oxygen seemed to be working fine except that I kept having to use one hand to keep my mask centered over my mouth and nose. I still couldn't tell that any oxygen was actually flowing but at least I hadn't passed out. My velocity was starting to slow down now that I was getting down into thicker air. I dreaded the opening shock coming up in about a minute and a half. I was so cold I felt as if any trauma to my body would shatter it.

The airport was getting larger and I could see that I was too far east of it. I was over the edge of a huge cypress swamp. I started tracking toward the west, trying to get back to a good opening point. I was getting low now. I gave up on my altimeter; it was too confusing. I started to look for visual clues as to my height; things like the relative sizes of buildings, cars, or highways. The size of people were no good; if you could see people you were way too low to begin with.

I was coming up on two and a half minutes of freefall. Incredible! That was over a minute longer than I had ever fallen in my life. It was like an endless fall!

The ground configuration finally fit the pattern in my mind for 2,000 feet so I looked up to check that Duffy wasn't over me and pulled.

"Oof!" Opening shock really hurt. My chute had opened fine and, looking around, I could see that I was going to land off the field to the east of the airport. I still couldn't feel any parts of my body except the tingling pain of my skin unthawing. I knew hitting ground was going to hurt, but there was nothing I could do about it. That was one thing about parachuting: you knew for sure that you were going to hit the ground, one way or another.

I came down in a cow pasture, and I had been right about the landing. When I hit ground, I felt like the cartoon character who, when struck by a club, shattered into a thousand pieces. My altimeter still read 1,800 feet. I was glad that I judged my opening altitude by eye! I stripped off my harness and my heavy jumpsuit and let my body absorb the hot Florida sun. Even so, it took about two hours for my body to get back to a normal temperature. I still hadn't seen Duffy. I hoped he made it all right.

I field-packed my chute, put it on my back, and started hiking. I crossed four barbed-wire fences and one creek before I reached the airport where a truck from the DZ was waiting to pick me up. Duffy was in the truck and we congratulated each other warmly. He hadn't seen me the whole jump either and thought I had "gone in." When we got back to the DZ, the TV crew filmed us opening a bottle of champagne in celebration, and that night we made the evening news.

People asked, "Was it worth all the pain, the expense and the danger?"

"Damn right!" I'd answer. "I wouldn't trade the experience for anything."

"Would you do it again?"

"Yeah, I'd like to go even higher sometime, but not real soon. I'd like to thaw out first!"

It had been one of those jumps that was so painful and difficult that it was not particularly fun at the time but it was dynamite to talk about in a bar! How many other people could say that they had skydived for two and a half minutes from 28,000 feet and lived to talk about it?

In the southeast at least, there were only two ... Duffy and me.

Chapter Twenty-four

BILL

Elizabeth, my niece, said that there was a Bill Cole on the line calling from Toronto, Canada, when she brought me the phone. I was flat on my back on my brother's couch two months into a painful recovery from my Bartow skydiving accident. I had no idea who Bill Cole was or what he wanted.

After a brief introduction, Bill said, "I'm going to make a jump without a parachute and I need a good freefall cameraman I can trust to document it on movie film."

Who was this crazy man?!

"Well, Bill," I replied. "I'm afraid I can't even walk right now, much less jump. I'm trying to recover from a bad landing." That revelation didn't seem to faze him in the least.

"Don't worry — I'll plan it around your schedule. When will you be ready to jump again?"

"Soon," I said optimistically. I didn't dare tell Bill that I had no idea when I'd be able to even walk again.

"Good," he said undaunted. "I'll start working out all the details on my end. I'll keep in touch."

What a great plan: a skydiver jumping without a chute, being filmed by a guy who couldn't walk! Hell, he didn't need a chute; he needed a psychiatrist!

When I hung up, I didn't have much hope that I'd ever hear from Bill again. But at least it gave me a goal to work toward in terms of getting back on my feet.

Two or three painful months later, I took my first step without crutches. I was so proud of myself it was pitiful. I called Bill and told him to start finalizing his plans because I was going to be jumping very soon now. I figured I wouldn't have to walk that well to be able to jump. I just had to be able to get in and out of an airplane. A couple more months passed, and I was ready to try a test jump. I was still not fully mobile, but the jump went fine and I saw that if I was careful, I'd be able to skydive without hurting myself any further. I was very relieved. For me, being condemned to life "on the ground" would have been no life at all.

I immediately started to work on modifying the mount for my 16mm helmet camera. It had worked fine for the movie jumps I had made in the past, but I wanted something more reliable and foolproof for Bill's jump. Since I had been disappointed several times in the past by camera film jams, I had also decided that I would need two cameras for such a "one of a kind" jump as Bill's. Not only would two cameras insure against missing the shot, I could also use two different lenses and two camera speeds: one normal 24 frames per second and one high speed at 64 frames per second for showing slow motion. I experimented with various configurations for mounting two cameras on one helmet.

The obvious method, for balance as well as less neck stress, was to mount one on each side of the helmet. But this did not prove to be viable because the "risers," the straps which connect the parachute lines to the harness, tended to catch on the back of the cameras during the parachute opening and give the helmet a nasty flip forward.

I had lost several helmets in the past when they were ejected off my head in just this manner. Since I could envision my head being still in the helmet as it fell to earth, I modified my helmet chin strap with Velcro so it would come off easily under stress. I reasoned that I could replace the helmet and camera easier than I could replace my head, although a few of my friends would argue the point.

At any rate, I found for my purposes the best idea seemed to be one camera on the side of the helmet and one on top. There were many other technical problems to overcome as well. One was the mounting of a World War II device called a "Newton Ring" gunsight. It had to project down from the helmet over one eye in order to properly aim the cameras during a jump. A simple cross hair eyesight wouldn't work for this purpose because a slight shift of the helmet would throw off the alignment.

The most formidable problem, however, was the need for a reliable source of battery power to run the cameras. Since this was all custom-built equipment, there were no experts to turn to; I had to figure out the problems all by myself. After trying all kinds and types of batteries, I decided on using a series of individual 1.5-volt "C"-size NiCd batteries in custom-built plastic holders. These batteries were not inexpensive, but they were rechargeable and readily available. I built two battery packs for each camera, so I always had a backup. I bought several chargers, each of which could charge four batteries at once. In this manner I could charge two whole sets of batteries at one time. I also bought enough batteries so I could have two sets on charge while I was using two other sets on a jump. I built backup power cords with interchangeable disconnects so I could quickly isolate and replace faulty parts as well as run the lines easily through my jumpsuit. I had to engineer and build all my hardware, all my mounts, and all my connections. I would roam hardware stores and commercial electrical supply houses for hours on end to come up with just the right component. I'm sure many a parts manufacturer would be startled and maybe amazed to see to what use I put their products.

I was far from ready when Bill called and asked me to commit to a date only a few weeks away. As Sherlock Holmes would have said, "The game is afoot!"

I still wasn't fully healed, but at least I could move around, walk, drive a car, and, most importantly, jump out of an airplane. Bill had no sponsors, and my film studio had no excess funds with which to speculate on a noncommercial project. But in my enthusiasm, I talked my father and my brother into allowing me a couple of weeks off and a few rolls of film from our family motion-picture business. I was really putting my professional neck on the line. I was going to attempt to film a real life-and-death documentary, as it happened, with no script, no budget, no crew, no financing, and no idea if the main character would live through it. It was one of those things that you had to go with gut feeling and not think too much about.

I ran out of time before my new helmet mount was completed. I worked on it up to the last minute, then I loaded movie cameras, camera mounts, tripods, film, changing bags, tools, spare parts, and everything else I could think of into my Corvette and headed north. With the addition of my parachutes, jump gear, and clothes, my poor little car was packed to the gunnels. Even the passenger's seat was full and covered over with a tarp. The way I was squeezed into the driver's seat, with the convertible top down, I felt like a jet fighter pilot flying out on a mission.

Bill and I were going to meet at a little drop zone in Ohio to make a few practice jumps, get to know one another, and finalize our plans. In actuality, a jump like this was going to be illegal, so we had to be somewhat secretive about our plans around other people. In fact, when we finally met, I was a little taken aback when I found out that, in order to protect all the people who had agreed to help, I was going to have to make the documentary without revealing the identity of the drop zone, the pilot, the jump plane, or any other skydivers involved in the jump. The only thing I could show was Bill Cole himself. It seemed like an impossible task, but I had no other option but to try.

Bill and I hit it off right away, even though we had completely opposite personalities. He was serious and straightforward while I tended to be funny and devil-may-care. I was a confirmed bachelor; Bill was a family man. I drank like a fish while Bill would order "milk" in a bar. Profanity was a large part of my vocabulary; Bill said "darn" instead of "damn" and "heck" in place of "hell." Bill seemed to be totally devoid of fear while I simply sublimated mine. He was interested in "numerology" as opposed to my total belief in the logic of science. Our friendship must have been based on our mutual respect of each other's skydiving talents, since it certainly wasn't an agreement of philosophy or ideas. The more we talked, however, the more we discovered similarities in our skydiving exploits. We both had exhibition skydiving teams, both had made "blind" jumps, and we both had set high-altitude records. Apparently, we each had a love of doing what no one else had ever done and doing it with style.

Bill was a tall, lanky Canadian only slightly older than me. He tended to be serious but had a dry sense of humor which I seemed to bring out in him. One talent he had that I lacked was the ability to find lucrative sponsors for his exhibition skydiving team. He was the first person I had ever met who actually made his living entirely from skydiving. Bill was extremely outspoken in his views, which polarized people — they were either for him or against him; nothing in between. He would be the first to admit that he was somewhat of an opinionated male chauvinist, but that wouldn't stop him from expounding at length about the futility of allowing women in sports, especially in skydiving. After a few friendly arguments, we gave up on converting each other's opinions and took a "live and let live" attitude with each other. I always felt, however, that his attitudes made him more enemies than friends. It was too bad, since Bill had so much to offer. Despite all our differences, we became instant friends and moved ahead to make the "chuteless jump" a reality.

Bill and I met for the first time at a little drop zone that Bill knew in Parkman, Ohio. For a "flat-lands" Florida boy, I was most impressed by the landing strip there, which consisted of bright green grass running up and down over a couple of small hills. To my amusement, their jump plane disappeared over one hill before emerging and taking off over the next. The DZ was operated by Dale Gates and his wife, a very nice couple who were old friends of Bill's. They had a big house right on the airfield which was terrorized by their pet monkey.

That night they very kindly invited Bill and me to supper to talk over our project. We decided that this drop zone, although very nice, had too much student activity and was too popular with experienced jumpers to suit our clandestine needs. We certainly didn't want to jeopardize Dale's livelihood. Bill said that he had another place in mind not far away that should be perfect.

Eventually the subject came around to my helmet camera mounts; or rather, my lack of a completed mounting system. Dale very generously offered me the use of his tool room. I don't think he knew what he was getting into because I literally took it over for the next two days. Bill had all of his specialized jump gear in order and was ready to go, but knowing how important good movies were to the success of his jump, he was very patient with me. Finally, I proudly emerged from the tool room with a professional-looking two-camera helmet mount, hand sawed and constructed out of the bar-stock aluminum I had brought from Florida and painted gold to match my helmet and jumpsuit.

We said our good-byes and moved our operation to a very small out-of-the-way drop zone in Grafton, Ohio. There were no student jumpers there, at least at that time of the year, and no "civilians" around to ask us what we were doing. Bill had also recruited a few skydivers from this drop zone to help us.

The first night in Grafton we held a meeting with all the players to map out our strategy. There was Joe Swaisygood, the pilot, John Vander Schrier, the safety man, Chuck Copp, the alternate safety man, Ken Wiechec, the reserve holder,

Bill Cole, the chuteless jumper and me, the cameraman. Up to this point, I had taken everything Bill had told me on faith. Now he revealed his scheme as to how he was going to jump without a parachute and live to reach the ground. Here was his plan:

There would be four jumpers in the plane. Bill had attached a reserve parachute to a special board with handles which would be held by the first jumper to leave the plane. The second to leave would be Bill who would be wearing a harness with no parachute but with custom risers running down his arms to his hands. These risers ended in snap connectors which Bill would use to hook onto the reserve. The third would be me, the photographer, to document whatever happened. There could be only one of two outcomes: success or disaster. The last out of the plane would be a safety man who would try to reach Bill in a desperate attempt to help if anything went wrong. The safety man would have a spare set of "D" rings installed on his harness. Bill would have to hook on to those in an emergency and the two jumpers land under one parachute. But no one really knew if a normal parachute would stay together under the opening stress of a double load. When Bill left the plane, he had to fly down to catch up to the man holding his chute, hook up with him and hook onto the reserve. He could then pull the ripcord and float safely to earth. It sounded simple and foolproof. What could go wrong?

Right from the beginning I had told Bill that I would be involved only if everything was done professionally and safely. Bill had wisely scheduled a whole week for practice jumps to work out all the potential bugs. Now after I had heard the plan, at my insistence, Bill agreed to a further stipulation that he would make the actual chuteless jump only after he had made a successful connection with the reserve three times in a row during our series of practice jumps. This would insure that, as a team, we truly had solved all the problems. I'm sure as we adjourned the meeting, each of us in our own way was thinking, "What in hell are we doing?"

Since we had little money, Bill and I retired to a little mobile tent camper that Bill had towed down from his home in Toronto. We parked it on the drop zone and lived on balogna sandwiches we made from supplies from a local grocery store. The alternate safety man's parents who lived nearby took pity on us and invited us to a good home-cooked meal almost every night after jumping and breakfast in the mornings. They also made a shower available to us, which was a godsend after long days on the drop zone. It was summer and brutally hot. Being from Florida, I thought I was used to heat, but this was like being in an oven all day. Up until now, I had no idea that Ohio could be so hot. We had no shade except the tent, and its interior was almost unbearable during the day. We jumped and packed in the heat and then jumped and packed some more.

In between jumping and packing, I was repairing helmet cameras which would break or jam on almost every jump. I had brought a big box of spare parts from Florida and, in the tent, I would strip down a faulty camera to its gears and rebuild it before the next jump. All during our practice jumps, I slowly refined my two cameras into instruments I could rely on.

But this did not solve all my problems. Over and above the freefall footage, I had to be thinking about the details of good movie making and all the little intercuts that would make a smooth-flowing film out of the major scenes. On every jump I would try to open low so I could get to the ground first, rush over and get out my professional 16mm Arri-S and get ground shots of Bill landing and discussing the jump. I was mapping out the script in my head and each day I tried to knock off some staged intercuts that I knew I'd need to make a cohesive film: scenes like Bill putting on his helmet, packing his chute, or just looking at the sky. I also needed fill-ins for the plane and pilot such as close-ups of the prop starting, the pilot's hands flying the plane and the plane's instrument panel.

Combined with the heat, the packing of chutes, the repairing of cameras, filming intercuts, and the nonstop jumping, I was totally exhausted at the end of each day. But then I had to change film in the magazines, charge batteries, make repairs for the following day, and go over the scenes I still had to film. During all this, I had to cope with the intense back pain still lingering from my accident.

At first, I didn't realize what a crazy bunch of guys the Grafton jumpers were. I thought the Mission Valley Skydivers were wild, but these guys were incorrigible. No matter how low I would go to open my parachute trying to get to the ground first, they'd open lower. Finally I had to ask them to pull higher so I could get some ground shots of parachute landings other than Bill. They said no problem. It was just habit; they always opened under 1,500 feet as a rule.

I shrugged that off, but then something happened that made me a little more cautious around them. They all knew that I was still recovering from a back injury and that I was in constant pain on every jump. I thought they were all being polite by not landing on their tiny pea-gravel target area. Several times during practice jumps as I was landing, I was tempted to turn downwind and go for the "peas," back injury or not. But I was feeling so bad, I resisted my natural impulse and made gentle landings off target. On one jump, I landed beyond the peas and walked across the target on my way back to the packing area. As I walked over the pea-gravel pit, I had expected my feet to crunch and sink into the small gravel since their whole purpose was to cushion a jumper's impact of landing. To my amazement, it was like walking across uneven concrete! What in hell was going on here? I asked the local jumpers what the deal was with the pea-gravel pit. They said that they had gotten the wrong kind of gravel. Instead of pea-gravel, they had bought some kind of cheaper lime rock. The first time it rained, it had hardened into a solid mass.

"Well," I asked incredulously, "why didn't anyone tell me it was hard as rock?"

They just laughed and said that they thought I'd find out sooner or later. One of them said flippantly, "I was wondering if you'd go for the target."

Whoa! This attitude was a little too callous even for me! Apparently they didn't care for their own safety as well as anyone else's. If anyone unknowingly had made a competition landing on that target, they'd have been in the hospital for a long time. Well, at least Bill had picked the right place to do a dangerous stunt. No one was going to get excited about us taking any chances.

Actually, they were a nice bunch of guys and we all became good friends. But they really did take a joke to the point of perversity. They took delight in telling me how they, at one point, pretended that one of them had "gone in." He had opened extraordinarily low on a jump and when they drove out to see if he was all right, found him in a field waiting for a ride back. On the spur of the moment, they decided to play a little joke.

When they brought his supposedly "dead body" back to the packing area, they thought that the corpse would immediately be seen to be obviously breathing and the joke would be over. However, everyone unquestioningly accepted the verdict without examining the body, quit jumping for the day, and left the DZ en masse. The guys "in on it" were left with a live corpse and a joke without a punchline. So they decided to take the joke a little further and hold a wake.

They rented a coffin from a local undertaker and after applying a little white makeup to the face of the deceased, invited everyone for a viewing that evening. The party was going full blast with the women all crying and the men getting drunk in grief, I was told, when the corpse, who was not too happy with his impromptu inactive acting role, got bored with the whole thing, sat upright in the coffin, and demanded a drink. This had happened over a year ago and they admitted that they may have gone too far, since some of the people fooled still weren't talking to them.

I'm afraid I may have done a bad thing. When we were all at the local bar having our customary after-jumping drinks, I discovered that they didn't know how to play "Dead Ants." I couldn't believe it! How could jumpers, even in Ohio, not know how to play "Dead Ants"? Looking back on it, I feel bad. It was like giving a juvenile delinquent a loaded gun to play with.

"Dead Ants" is a drinking game which consists of appointing an "Ant Master" at the beginning of the evening. At any time after that, the "Ant Master" was authorized to call out in a loud voice, "Dead Ants!" With that cue, everyone had to hit the floor flat on their backs with their arms and legs straight up in the air. The "Ant Master" judged who was last on the floor and that person had to buy a round of drinks for everybody. The loser then became the new "Ant Master" and could call the next "Dead Ants" any time that evening.

Usually, the first time "Dead Ants" was called in a crowded public bar, there would be pandemonium. You can imagine the reaction of the people not in on the game when half the bar crashed to the floor. They didn't know whether to hit the floor, run out the door, or call the police. The "civilians" who stayed tended to be a little "goosey" and jumped nervously at every unexpected noise.

Like a returned prodigal describing the ways of the big city to his backwoods cousins, I explained the rules to my new friends. They were delighted and nothing would do but to play right then. Normally with sophisticated players, the trick was to allow a few hours to go by to let people forget to be on guard before calling "Dead Ants." But with these guys, not a minute went by before it was called. They didn't fool around. Everyone hit the deck, overturning tables, chairs, and beer glasses. It caught me so off-guard that I was almost last, especially since hitting the floor nearly killed me with my bad back.

We had barely gotten our free drinks when another "Dead Ants" was called. Thinking it would be easier on my back if I pushed over backwards in my chair, I caught the back of my head on the table behind me and almost knocked myself out. That was good because it took my attention away from the myriad of cuts I received from all the broken glass on the floor from the last round.

When we all recovered and got seated again, the guy next to me picked up his full beer glass from the table for a well-deserved drink. As he picked up his drink, the bottom of his glass remained on the table with the beer flowing out all over the table as he lifted the top half of the glass to his lips. We were all amazed. Apparently, when he fell to the floor, his knee hit the underside of the table so hard that the shock cleanly cracked his glass at its base. It had remained unmoved in its place on the table still full of beer until he had picked it up.

The next day I was so hung over and full of aches, pains, bruises, and cuts that I looked back in envy at before when I only had my back pain to contend with. I should have known better, but that night I taught them "Cardinal Puff," a drinking game that originated with World War I pilots.

"Cardinal Puff" is a ritual that requires the applicant to drink a full glass of beer while saying prescribed words and making precise hand movements in an exact order. If the slightest mistake is made at any time during the ritual, the remaining beer must be consumed at once and the individual is required to make at least one more attempt. It was less physical than "Dead Ants," but, even so, I don't think Ohio has ever been the same since.

Within the first few practice jumps, everything that could go wrong did. On the very first jump, Ken Wiechec, Bill's friend from Cleveland, inadvertently left the plane with the reserve held upside down and Bill couldn't hook up to it. We realized if that happened on the real chuteless jump, Bill was a dead man. On the next jump, Bill lost the grip on his risers which flapped dangerously over his back, a potential deadly threat to the opening of his main chute. Bill was illegally jumping with only one chute on all these jumps. He was leaving his reserve on the ground to better approximate his real falling weight when he would jump with no chute at all. So every practice jump for Bill was a dangerous proposition.

I was having camera problems on every jump, but the practices were not a total loss in terms of the film documentation since at least one camera always worked. I was also using each practice jump to figure out a good flying strategy in order to be able to keep the cameras smoothly on Bill from the time he left the plane to the time he pulled his ripcord.

At the end of five days of practice, Bill had made a few successful passes of the reserve but not two in a row. We were getting tired and discouraged and broke. That night in the tent Bill quietly told me that the next day he was going to make the actual chuteless jump. I protested that we weren't ready and reminded him of his promise. He said that he was out of money and out of time. He was also tired of risking his hide with only one chute during practice. Tomorrow was the day. He respected my reservations and he wouldn't hold it against me if I didn't go along. But, movies or not, he was adamant about making the jump with no chute. Bill had me. He knew I wouldn't let him jump without me.

The next morning we held a meeting and broke the news. Once everyone knew that Bill was determined, they all agreed and the jump was on. I asked Bill to leave us for a moment; there was something I needed to discuss with the other guys.

Once Bill left, I explained that of all four of us on the jump, Bill not only had the least number of jumps, he had the least amount of freefall time. The brutal fact was, there was at least a 50/50 chance that Bill might not get the reserve; he might die in the next hour. That's why I didn't want Bill to hear this. He didn't need any negative images or thoughts if he was going to do this jump. But the other people involved, who would be alive if things went wrong and who would have to face the authorities, had to, beforehand, face reality and discuss the "what if"s.

I asked everyone for their word of honor that if the worst happened, none of us would reveal the name of the jump plane pilot. His pilot's license and his income were at stake. The fact that Bill and the rest of us were doing this of our own willingness would make no difference to an FAA board of inquiry or the police. We all agreed that we'd take our lumps and keep our mouths closed. If the unthinkable happened, we were to try to save Bill down to an altitude of 1000 feet; after that, as hard as it would be, we'd have to abandon Bill and save ourselves. When we left the meeting to go make jumping history, the guys were all a lot more quiet and reflective than I'd ever seen them. Bill never asked me what we discussed.

The previous day, I had already filmed Bill chuting up for the actual chuteless jump. In the world of film, this was not cheating or untruthful. It was simply practical filmmaking. I was a one-man crew and I couldn't stop now to film trivial things. I had enough on my mind, as did Bill. We all quietly suited up. Bill put on a 20-pound weight belt to help make up for the loss of his parachute weight. Weight would be critical in catching Ken and making a stable reserve transfer. Bill had cut holes in the top of his jumpsuit at the shoulders so he could wear his harness under the jumpsuit. He thought it would look better for my movies if we emphasized the fact that he was wearing no parachute. I helped Bill tape his special risers to his arms so he wouldn't lose them again as he had on the one practice jump. As I was doing this, it hit me like a ton of bricks that these risers would now be Bill's only connection with life. Reality was starting to set in with a shortness of breath and a quickening of the heart.

I doubled-checked all my camera equipment for the third time. I didn't want to screw up in any way. Excuses would be meaningless, especially for me.

The plane wouldn't start. The battery was down again, so Joe had to hand-prop it, standing in front of the plane and flipping the propeller through one revolution. I always hated that. It looked so dangerous and, in fact, if done wrong, it could be fatal. The engine started and Joe walked around and got into the pilot's seat. The drop zone was empty except for us. There were no cheering crowds. No one but us and a handful of local jumpers knew what was about to happen.

We all shook hands, wished each other luck, and boarded the plane. Only Chuck, the alternate safety man, was staying on the ground. We all had that haunted look of unspoken feelings and mixed thoughts. All but Bill. He looked totally relaxed and unconcerned. How could he do that?! I had two chutes and a passive role in this jump and I was a nervous wreck. We had started a train of events in motion that no one could stop now even if he wanted.

We all sat without talking on the way to altitude, lost in our thoughts. We were each going over in our minds the freefall scenario of the impending jump. I kept nervously wiping the sweat from the palms of my hands on the legs of my jumpsuit. We had to make this work. Failure was no longer an abstract concept. Failure meant death for Bill.

All our practice jumps had been made from an altitude of 7,500 feet, giving us a working time in freefall of 30 seconds. For this jump we were climbing to 12,500 feet to give Bill a full 60 seconds. One minute could be a very long time or a very short time, depending on how you look at it and how well you used it.

We were climbing past 10,000 feet now and, sitting on the floor next to the pilot with my back to the instrument panel, I looked out the open door at the Ohio countryside, a patchwork of farmland. The air, although cooler at this altitude, was extremely hazy and I couldn't make out a distinct horizon. All of a sudden the plane was slowing and I realized that Bill was spotting. We were on jump run already. Oh, God, this was it! Bill said "cut" and Joe pulled the throttle back as far as he could without stalling. Bill looked at me, smiled, and said quietly, "Let's do it." The date was July 20, 1972.

I took a deep breath and got out of the door onto the step. I got a grip as far out as I could, swung out and hung off the strut. I was looking back at the doorway and as I hung there, the forward speed of the plane, about 90 miles per hour, pushed my legs slightly toward the tail of the plane. Bill moved up and let Ken get past him onto the step. After Ken had gotten himself situated and turned halfway back, Bill handed him out the reserve. I saw Ken double-check himself that he was indeed holding the pack right-side up. Technically Bill could still abort the jump. He could, but I knew there was no way Bill would stop now.

I started one camera. Since each camera held only a 30-second film magazine, I had to stagger the starting of each camera so I could document both the start and the end of the jump. God help me if one of my cameras failed now. Hopefully, I would have overlapping footage from both cameras only during the middle part of the jump. It was tricky because, in addition to flying in freefall trying to follow Bill's every move and concentrating on composing the constantly changing scene, I had to keep track of the elapsed time in my head and remember to turn on the second camera at the proper moment. While you're falling at 120 miles an hour, it is a lot to think about. The good thing was that, once in freefall, I wouldn't have time to worry about Bill. I would have my hands full concentrating on my job of taking good movies.

Bill knelt at the edge of the door and nodded his readiness to Ken. Ken pushed off the step, holding the reserve in front of him with both hands. He dropped away from the plane like a brick. Bill paused a moment to give a good separation between them and dove out the door without touching the step. He looked different from the practice jumps. Then I realized why: Bill was wearing no parachute this time.

Everyone had to do his job perfectly. If something went wrong, no matter how minor, this time Bill would have no second chance. The chuteless jump had begun.

Chapter Twenty-five

CHUTELESS

— Altitude: 12,500 feet —

When Bill Cole dove out the door of the plane without touching the step, it caught me a little off-guard, since he had always put one foot on the step before exiting during all the practice jumps. But, despite the little surprise, I was able to keep the camera's eyesight fixed on Bill as I let go of the strut and dropped away from the plane right behind him. No matter what happened or how my body had to twist and contort to keep up, I was determined to keep the bull's-eye locked on the man without a parachute.

Bill had just 60 seconds to catch up with Ken, hook onto the reserve, and open it at a safe altitude. At this point, I didn't even consider the disastrous consequences if he failed. I had to totally concentrate on my job: documenting the jump on 16mm movie film.

After about 12 seconds of falling and picking up speed, we both stabilized out at terminal velocity of 120 miles per hour. I was in a perfect position, slightly higher and behind Bill. All of our practice jumps were coming into play. I knew exactly how to fly to remain at the proper distance and keep Bill centered in the lens. I was also drawing on years of freefall camera work and hundreds of jumps to make this footage perfect from the start to the finish.

— Altitude: 11,000 feet —

From my end, everything seemed to be going great. From Bill's standpoint, however, I was starting to worry. He was still very high, seemingly not in any big hurry to get down to Ken, who was holding Bill's reserve chute. Ken looked awfully far below to me. Bill had better get moving. He was going to need that reserve very soon to get to the ground alive.

— Altitude: 10,000 feet —

I put those thoughts out of my mind. There was nothing I could do about it anyway. My job was to keep Bill on the movie screen for as long as I could, and that was exactly what I was going to do to the bitter end. If anything went wrong, I was going to film until I got ground-rush. Then my brain's self-preservation mode would kick in, my hand would automatically pull the ripcord, and I wouldn't have to consciously make the decision to leave Bill to his fate. Hell, I had this thing all figured out; psychological atonement even before anything bad happened.

— Altitude: 9,000 feet —

Now, at last, Bill was making his move and starting to dive. Having his jumpsuit outside of his harness looked neat but it seemed to be slowing him down and giving him a little difficulty flying. Instead of diving directly toward Ken in a straight line, Bill was sliding slightly to his right. At least it was away from me, making it easy for me to follow. I synced my fall with his, and the two of us traced a lazy spiral through the hazy air down toward Ken and the sprawling Ohio farmland further below.

— *Altitude: 8,000 feet* —

Boy, this was starting to get dicey! By this time on most of our practice jumps, Bill had already made contact with Ken and was working on the transfer of the reserve. Right now he wasn't even close to Ken. Maybe the 20 pounds of weight Bill was wearing wasn't enough to compensate for the lack of a parachute. I caught a glimpse of the safety man way above and behind Bill. What was he doing there? He was supposed to be behind me out of camera range but close enough to get to Bill in an emergency. He was way too high. He'd never get to Bill in time if he were needed. *Never mind,* I thought. *Concentrate!*

— *Altitude: 7,000 feet* —

Ken was doing a great job. He was just lying there patiently waiting for Bill and keeping the reserve facing toward us, no matter from which quadrant we approached. Bill had corrected his slide and was now moving in on a straight line. My mental alarm clock went off and I reached over with my right hand and clicked on the switch for the second camera on the back of my left hand. I had to do this with absolute clarity of thought since I didn't want to turn off the first camera accidentally thinking I was turning on the second.

— *Altitude: 6,000 feet* —

Bill was now closing in on Ken and had eased out of his dive. I could see that the risers had ripped the tape holding them to Bill's arms and were flapping from wrist to shoulder adding an additional drag and slowing Bill even more. At least Bill still retained the ends of them in each hand in readiness to snap on to the reserve. If he lost grip on even one of them it could spell disaster.

— *Altitude: 5,000 feet* —

Bill was flying as small as he could get with his arms and legs pulled in, trying to match Ken's speed in order to dock with him. He was agonizingly close but seeming to hover about 10 feet above and in front of Ken. The weight differential was becoming a major problem. I was at a 45-degree angle to Bill's left and trying to close in at the same speed while keeping them both centered in the lens. We were running out of time. There were only a couple thousand feet left to normal opening altitude.

— *Altitude: 4,000 feet* —

I knew I was getting the best footage I had ever shot. Bill dropped to Ken's level and as he slid closer, he reached out his left hand as if to grab the reserve. My mind did an instant replay of one of our practice jumps where Bill had made the exact same movement. My heart skipped a beat, because on that jump, his outstretched arm had thrown Bill into an unintentional back loop and it had taken several thousand feet to get lined up again. In skydiving, Newton's third law of motion — "For every action, there's an equal and opposite reaction" — is ever so true. Bill must have remembered the incident, too, because he instantly retracted his hand and flew in with his whole body instead.

— Altitude: 3,000 feet —

Contact! Bill had one hand on the reserve. They bobbled a little for a heart-stopping moment as he and Ken fought for control. This was like trying to pass a watermelon during a downhill ski race. In my head I was pleading, *Careful, don't blow it now, guys!* Disaster was still only one slip away. Then Bill swung in and had the reserve with both hands. Ken gave the reserve stability as Bill struggled to snap on his risers. To me it seemed to take forever. He got them attached, reached to the sides to get grips on the board's handles, and nodded to Ken. Ken let go of the reserve and as he turned to move away, he looked at the camera and smiled before he moved out of camera range.

— Minimum Safe Opening Altitude: 2,000 feet —

Without Ken's weight, Bill was suddenly much lighter than I was and floated up and almost out of my frame as I slowly sank below. I grabbed all the air I could to slow down and, with my head as far back as it would go, tilted my body head-high in an attempt to keep Bill in the camera lens. In that position I started sliding backward and lost even more altitude in relation to Bill.

— Altitude: 1,600 feet —

Just as I was about to lose sight of Bill, he pulled the ripcord and his opening was recorded on film as he was instantly jerked up and out of sight. I immediately pulled my ripcord, but my own parachute's opening seemed anticlimactic.

— Altitude: Ground zero —

We landed in a beautiful field of wheat. Far from my other movie cameras, I took off my helmet, pulled a fresh film magazine from my pocket, reloaded the helmet camera and, just holding the helmet in my hands, filmed Ken and Bill greeting each other in celebration on the ground.

Hell, I thought, *piece of cake; we still had over 1,500 feet left.*

Chapter Twenty-six

ROSE

I met my future wife on Lido Beach one beautiful sum- mer day. I remember it was July 3rd because I had been in- vited to a 4th of July party the following day and I didn't have a date. As we sat on the beach talking, I finally summoned up the courage to ask Rose if she might like to go to the party with me and maybe the fireworks display afterward. To my disappointment, her answer was a qualified, "No, I have other plans. But call me after the 4th."

I didn't know then that she really didn't have any plans but was just uncomfortable accepting a date with a total stranger on such short notice.

The next day, I went to the party alone and tried to drown my sorrows. The party was at a home set off by itself out in the country, north of Sarasota.

I arrived at the party in the early afternoon and very quickly had too many drinks too fast. I was really getting smashed, so I wandered out back to get some air. It was a hot day and a bunch of people were in the swimming pool. There was no diving board, but someone had sawed off the top of a palm tree growing near the deep end of the pool. It was about eight feet high and had short boards nailed up the back of the trunk to form a crude ladder. If a person was careful, he could crawl up the trunk, balance on the top, and dive off into the pool. There were no bathing beauties in the pool, so it held no interest for me. Besides, I was too drunk to go swimming; I'd have gone immediately to the bottom. I went past the pool and ended up at a pasture fenced off with barbed wire.

I stood at the fence breathing in big gulps of air, trying to get myself sobered up. It didn't seem to be helping very much. I was standing with my palms outward at waist level, elbows bent, leaning against the top strand of barbed wire. Without warning, I lost my balance and, with my hands acting as a fulcrum, my body somersaulted forward over the fence. I ended up flat on my butt, sitting on the ground with my legs outstretched toward the pasture and my back to the fence. My arms remained stretched up over my head with my hands still holding the strand of barbed wire. It was a perfect stunt that I wouldn't have been able to duplicate if I had been sober.

It all happened so fast, at first I didn't realize exactly what had happened. The sharp sting of pain was the first thing that registered through my alcoholic haze. I looked at my hands with wonder and was surprised to find them bleeding.

How did this happen? I wondered. *Oh, yeah.* I remembered I had been holding onto the top of the barbed wire fence. I had "barbed" my palms all to hell.

I heard a snort and my focus changed from my hands held up before my eyes to beyond. I beheld a cow standing before me. I got up unsteadily and tried to brush off the dirt without getting blood all over myself. I took a few steps toward the animal with an outstretched hand, saying stupidly, "Nice cow, good girl."

It was then that I heard all the commotion from the party side of the fence.

"Mike, Mike! Get out of there! That's El Diablo's pasture!"

Slowly it came to me that they were yelling at me.

So I tripped over a little fence! So what! I thought. *No harm done. What's the big deal?*

By now, everyone at the party had run over to the fence and was yelling at me and pointing at something beyond me.

I smiled at everyone. It was nice that they were so concerned about me but, other than a few cuts, I was fine. Nothing to be worried about.

They seemed to be getting more frantic and agitated but no one came into the pasture to help me. This didn't make any sense. I turned around to see what they were all gesturing at behind me.

It was then that all the pieces of the puzzle fell into place. "El Diablo" would be the name not of a cow, but of a bull. For the first time, I saw the animal in front of me for what it really was. I was looking directly into the crazed and bloodshot eyes of a very large and a very angry purebred bull who was extremely upset that I was in his territory.

Oh, my God! I mouthed the words silently.

The bull was frothing at the mouth and his spittle was drooling down into the cloud of dust he was pawing up with one front hoof. He was swinging his wide and formidable horns wildly, as if he couldn't make up his mind exactly where he was going to gore me. I remember vividly that his horns were black but turned to a pure white near the needlelike points which seemed to sparkle and glint in the sunlight.

I remained perfectly calm. As I saw it, I had two choices: I could back up slowly toward the fence or I could spin around and run like hell.

Wait a minute! A skydiver doesn't run from anybody or anything! It was amazing; I really believed that.

I held up a hand for quiet. Slowly the shouting died out. I locked my gaze with the bull's, lowered my head, and pawed at the ground with one shoe while I made loud snorting noises in a comic parody of the bull's own actions. The bull's eyes widened in surprise. He gave a loud snort and backed up a step. Apparently, nothing had ever dared to challenge him before. He knew he should charge, but he was confused by my antics. I glanced around at the crowd and flashed a smile in victory.

The shouting began again but more pleading this time, "Please, please, Mike, get out of there, he'll kill you!"

I paid no attention and advanced toward El Diablo, stopping to paw and snort as I went. In my mind, I had been transformed into a master matador but I was acting like a bull. It made no sense at all. Meanwhile, the bull and I parried back and forth in the afternoon heat. All the time the crowd was going wild. But to both the bull and I, it had become a matter of pride, and neither of us would back down completely.

Finally, I was satisfied that both the bull and I had fulfilled our macho duty. I stood upright. Slowly and deliberately, I turned my back on the bull. The crowd gasped as I gave them an elaborate bow and, like a great matador, walked slowly back to the safety of the fence and a hero's welcome.

The last I saw of El Diablo, he was happily grazing in his pasture, the entire episode forgotten.

I'm afraid I didn't end the afternoon with such grace. I had a few more drinks before the party began to break up. Even though everybody was leaving, I decided that I had to prove my soberness at the last minute by diving into the swimming pool from the palm tree. I got to the top, lost my balance, and toppled off toward the concrete edge of the pool. Like some Laurel and Hardy comedy, I managed to save myself as I fell with a desperate bear hug around the trunk of the palm tree. It was the type of palm tree that has a rough bark with sharp spines angled upward. I was pinned. The spines were piercing my arms and chest, making it impossible to slide down, and I had no leverage to move up. The last party guest was just driving off and saw me. He hurriedly pulled back into the drive, jumped out of his car, and ran over to help me down. It was very embarrassing.

I managed to drive home without incident. I was too tired and too inebriated to go to the fireworks, but before I collapsed into bed, I pulled myself together enough to call Rose. Somehow I talked her into a breakfast date the following morning.

The next morning, when I picked up Rose, I was a pitiful sight. My hands were badly cut and bandaged up. My arms and chest were lacerated, and numerous palm tree splinters still remained painfully embedded in my arms and chest. My eyes were bloodshot and I felt like hell. I was in no condition to be out in public, much less on a first date. I was one very subdued guy. But I must not have looked as bad as I felt because Rose acted perfectly natural and it seemed as if she was having a wonderful time.

My friend Don Bell was on vacation and had taken a room at the Sheridan Sand Castle Hotel on Lido Beach. He had invited all of the jumpers out for a late breakfast at the pool-side restaurant.

This was to be Rose's first meeting with the rest of the skydivers. Since she was a lovely and cultured young lady, I thought it wise, if I ever wanted to date her again, to expose her to our wild group at a time when they might be a little less crazy than normal. Breakfast would be a perfect opportunity to ease her into the group.

My plan must have worked, because I began dating Rose on a regular basis. Rose began accompanying me every weekend to the drop zone, and it wasn't long before she announced that she wanted to learn how to skydive. I wasn't too keen on the idea. I had taught many other girls how to jump, but I didn't think wanting to have the same interests as your boyfriend was the proper motivation.

I gave Rose every opportunity to back out gracefully, but she was very persistent. Well, if she was determined to learn to jump, I was going to be sure that she was the best trained jump-student in the history of the sport. I trained her relentlessly for weeks. On one windy day when there was no jumping, I even sent her off, dragging behind an inflated chute, to practice wind recoveries. She didn't speak to me for a while, but at least she was prepared for the worst.

Finally I couldn't stall any longer and put her out on her first static-line jump, all the while praying that this wouldn't alienate me from her parents for all time. Rose was a real trooper; a little girl almost lost in all the big heavy skydiving gear. She completed her five required static-line jumps and went for her first solo freefall jump. She did fine and I never once worried that she might not be able to handle it.

Rose completed 12 jumps before her ballet training took precedence. With all the work and sweat she put into dance over a period of years, she just couldn't afford to even sprain an ankle. And a broken leg would have ruined her career.

I always got a kick out of meeting some macho guy who had made a jump or two somewhere and, knowing that I was a skydiver, start talking to me about his bravery. Someone in the group would inevitably turn to Rose and say in a condescending way, "And you, my dear, don't you worry about Mike when he's up in the air skydiving?"

"Oh, no," this beautiful and talented lady would reply. "After I made 12 jumps myself, I never worried about Mike anymore."

Whereupon the guy who had made only two jumps would quietly fade away.

Chapter Twenty-seven

THE WEDDING

O ne of my most memorable jumps was on the day I got married. Since I had been a confirmed bachelor for 34 years, I wanted to do something unusual and spectacular rather than traditional for my new bride and her family. So I secretly planned to skydive on our wedding day into her parents' yard in Jupiter on the east coast of Florida.

The day before, I was in Fort Lauderdale to do a photography job. After the job, my client invited me to his home for dinner. His wife fixed a great meal and after dinner, during the course of conversation over coffee, I mentioned that I was to be married the following day.

"By the way," I asked. "Where can I find a store that has yellow crepe paper?" I had to explain that I was going to skydive into the wedding and I needed the crepe paper to make a wind-drift indicator in order to judge the wind.

Being a woman, my client's wife immediately recognized this to be a typical male stunt: to drift off on the errant winds and be killed, just to avoid getting married! She urgently said, "Finish your coffee, get in your car, and follow us. There's only one store near here and it's about to close. We'll show you where it is so you don't get lost." We made it just in time and they wished me good luck. I wondered if they meant for the jump or the wedding.

Later that night, I was in a cheap motel room rolling a wind-drift indicator and asking myself if I really knew what I was doing. I realized that I needed someone on the ground to coordinate the wedding guests so that everyone would be outside at the time of my jump. Who better to handle intrigue like this but Katherine, Rose's sister? I called her and she was delighted with her assignment. I swore her to secrecy, so all she told Rose the next day was that I would be arriving at the house in a very special way. Since there was so little room to land, Rose never dreamed that I'd attempt to skydive into the area. For some reason, she thought I was going to arrive on horseback.

The next morning was a beautiful Florida April day. It was the day I was to be married and everything seemed to have a dreamlike quality to me. I drove north past West Palm Beach to Indiantown, a small inland town northwest of Jupiter. At this time, Indiantown was the home of one of the best known drop zones in the country. It was owned and run by Paul Poppenhager, who had the most number of jumps of anyone in the world. "Pop" was a neat guy: a pioneer in the sport and a unique individual. He always wore a cowboy hat, and I never saw him without a beer can in one hand, whether he was flying a plane or not.

I went up to Pop and asked him if I could rent a jump plane for my wedding later that day. I half expected him to turn me down, since he ran such a busy drop zone and it would probably cost him money to let the plane go. But he knew who I was from the many times I had attended his meets and also from my jumping with the infamous Delray Aerial Circus. He was also an old friend of Duffy's. Unhesitatingly, he gave me the use of a plane and a pilot and wished me luck. I never knew if he meant luck with my jump or my marriage.

When it was time to go, I changed into a tuxedo and put my jumpsuit on over it. The pilot and I then flew over to Jupiter where I threw my wind streamer over the house. By watching where it landed near the intercoastal waterway, I could see that there was quite a wind from the ocean. My target area was only one house from the beach and since I needed to jump upwind in order to land there, it put my exit point way out over the Atlantic Ocean.

What's the worst thing that could happen? I thought. *I could land in the ocean, drown, and not get married,* I answered myself. "Let's go for it!" I told the pilot.

I knew I could land at the side of the house where there was an empty lot, but, until I was under parachute and closer, I didn't realize how small this area looked from the air. It had power lines on two sides, other homes all around, and a road in front. Since this was before the invention of ram-air parachutes, I was jumping my "round" PC and had no trouble dropping it straight down into the small area, something that would be tough to do with many modern "squares." I made a spectacular stand-up landing a few feet from Rose, who ran up to greet me with a big kiss. As I stripped off my jumpsuit to reveal my tuxedo, I said casually in my best low-voiced imitation of Sean Connery, "Bond, ... James Bond."

I had been rather worried about the reaction of my new father- and mother-in-law to my crazy stunt, but they were delighted. Or at least, they were delighted to have a warm-bodied groom on hand for the big event. How he got there really didn't seem to matter. About that time, the police arrived to see what was going on. If they had come to arrest me, I would have gone peaceably, but my father-in-law-to-be, Preston Rambo, went over and had a friendly talk with them. He told them proudly, "Mike's one of the finest parachutists in Florida. He has over 1,000 jumps!" I don't know if he mentioned that my sister's husband, Marvin Mounts, was a Palm Beach County Judge and had the situation well in hand, but whatever else he told them, the officers went away shaking their heads. Maybe they were wondering who would be crazy enough to skydive into his own wedding!

We all went to a nearby oceanside park where there was a beautiful, shaded forest of Australian pines. There, amid shafts of sunlight filtering through the trees, my brother-in-law, Judge Mounts, performed the wedding ceremony.

The event was a natural for newspaper articles with phrases like: "He really fell for her," "A marriage made in heaven," and "He jumped into the marriage with both feet." Ever since, whenever I get out of line and complain about married life, Rose says, "Well, you always had a choice: you didn't *have* to pull your ripcord!"

Chapter Twenty-eight

NEIL
AND THE GREAT SWAMP JUMP

Rose and I drove in to the drop zone. We had gotten a late start, so we were arriving later than I usually liked. It was almost one o'clock in the afternoon and I wasn't sure that I'd even be able to get on a load, much less make my customary two or three jumps. Normally, if there were a lot of skydivers, the jump plane would be manifested three or four loads in advance.

This was a new place for skydiving. We had no plane or pilot in Englewood at the moment, so someone had told me about this place in Sun City that friends of mine were using as a temporary DZ. It was just five or six miles west of the old DZ we had used years ago opposite the housing development.

I had heard that my old jumper friend, Jim Elmaker, would be flying today; it would be nice to see him again. I didn't know it at the time, but this would be the last time I'd see him at a drop zone. In less than a year I would visit him in a hospital a few days before he died of cancer.

As we drove in, a group of jumpers were landing with their parachutes. One was my old friend Neil Mayer, and I was surprised to see him landing under his reserve. When he recognized me he came over to say "Hi" and I asked him what had happened.

"Aw, I had a bag-lock," he said disgustedly. "I had to cut away my brand new $800 square over the swamp."

I hadn't realized that there was a swamp out here, but that's Florida for you.

"Too bad," I sympathized. "Did you see where it landed?"

"Yeah," he replied. "I think I got a good fix on it after I opened. I'm going to jump into the swamp to find it and hike out. I can't afford a new parachute!" he explained. "Want to join me?" he asked, knowing I was a sucker for adventure.

"What the hell," I said. "I've got nothing better to do on a Sunday afternoon." My wife looked at me with raised eyebrows, but she had long since become accustomed to my spur-of-the-moment exploits.

I got out a machete I always carried in my car and started figuring a way to carry it safely on the jump while Neil packed up his old main he kept as a spare.

"Don't worry, Babe," I said to Rose. "I know exactly what I'm doing. Neil is likely to get lost out there without me along," I said jokingly. "We'll jump in, get his chute, and be back in an hour, hour and a half tops," I assured her.

She went over to say hello to Neil's girlfriend and probably commiserate on how crazy we both were.

On the flight to altitude, Neil and I conferred as we overflew the proposed jump site and agreed to jump into a little open area where the ground looked solid enough to land. We were interested in an accurate landing on this jump, not freefall, so we just hopped and popped at 3,000 feet. We were both flying squares which had 30-mph horizontal speeds, so we knew we'd have to almost stall them in order to sink into the tiny jungle clearing.

Obviously, we wanted to avoid actually hitting a tree and since even landing in the branches of a tree is very dangerous, we had to be extremely careful. If a tree branch snagged your canopy, it could collapse high enough off the ground to kill you, which could really ruin your day.

We still had to hike out with all our gear, so getting even slightly hurt would have been very awkward. A broken leg was unthinkable because it would take a medivac helicopter to get an injured man out of this rugged area.

It was tricky, but both Neil and I made it to the ground with no problems, about 20 yards apart. We field-packed our chutes by daisy-chaining our lines and just stuffing the canopy into the backpacks without folding them. Then we met to agree on a plan of action.

We decided to use the clearing as a staging area. We'd leave our gear there and start a search pattern by circling outward. That way we could split up and double our search efforts but still be able to find each other and our gear when we had to. We knew we were close to Neil's missing canopy and we had no doubt that we'd find it very shortly.

One hour later we met back in the clearing. Neither of us had found a thing. It was very discouraging. We stood around one of our packs talking and trying to figure what else to do. After all this trouble, we certainly didn't want to give up for nothing and hike back to the drop zone empty handed.

As we were talking, Neil looked down and did a double-take. We weren't standing over one of the rigs we had used on our jump after all; it was Neil's lost main! We had half-forgotten that his lost chute had never come out of its bag. It was still packed in its little container lying right at our feet. We let out a whoop and gathered all of our gear for the easy hike out.

As it turned out, the "easy hike out" became the "Gone With The Wind" of survival stories. First let me set the stage: This was Florida. This was July. This was hot. This was insect city. With all of our jump gear, plus Neil's recovered parachute, this was no picnic in the park. It was more like the stroll over the "Bridge on the River Kwai."

We tied our jumpsuits around our waists, hefted our field-packed rigs on our backs like knapsacks, loaded up all the loose stuff like helmets and altimeters, and started walking.

God, was it hot! On a humid Florida day like this, you would sweat just standing still, but with all this exertion, we were sweating freely and attracting lots of bugs.

Landing "out" and having to hike back was no new experience for me. The only thing "new" for me this time was that it wasn't by accident or miscalculation. So, earlier, when I was landing my parachute, I was also taking a direction bearing. That way I knew we had to go due north to reach the drop zone.

Our first obstacle was not just a Florida jungle but a true swamp. We entered a much denser section of trees, which blocked out the sky and made the light gloomy. In front of me, the ground disappeared into thick black swamp water.

I stopped there on the edge of the nasty-looking water and tried to think of any other way to do this. Neil bumped into me from behind and said, "What's wrong?"

I didn't want to tell him what I was thinking. I was thinking about a big alligator silently cruising up behind us as we sloshed through the water, only its primeval nose and eyes showing above the dark water. I didn't want to even think of the poisonous water moccasins that must lurk in here by the hundreds, waiting patiently for survivalists to run their gauntlet.

"What's wrong?" Neil asked again. The insects were driving us crazy. We had to do something even if it were wrong.

"Oh, nothing," I replied as I waded knee-deep into the swamp from hell.

Out on the airstrip the temperature had been in the mid-90s. Here in the swamp, the air was heavy and oppressive and it must have been over 100 degrees. It was beautiful, in an eerie sort of way. There were creeper vines draped from tree to tree. Wild orchids grew randomly, sprouting from trunks and branches. Dead trees tilted over at crazy angles, not quite rotted enough to completely fall. The jagged ends of logs and stumps protruded from the placid water like punji stakes. The evil-looking water was coated with swirls of green and yellow slime. It was impossible to tell how deep the water was ahead, so each step had to be tentative before putting full weight on it.

It was hard to keep our gear held high enough out of the water to keep it dry. I realized if we lost our footing and fell even once, our chutes would become three or four times heavier and we might even have to abandon them. Our arms were occupied with carrying equipment so we couldn't swat the clouds of mosquitoes plaguing us. For some reason, I thought of Humphrey Bogart in "The African Queen."

As hikers and campers know, the life's purpose of a biting fly is to drive people insane. The genetic rule for some reason is only one fly to a person but that *one* must buzz around the head of his selected individual, relentlessly probing for some unprotected place to bite. Even without the painful bite, the incessant buzzing orbiting about your head is infuriating.

Neil and I both acquired our personal fly early on, and life became even more intolerable. But our major problem was something you'd never think of unless you've experienced it. It was mud! With each step into the swamp, our jump boots acquired an additional coating of muck. Soon, taking each step became a monumental weight-lifting exercise. We couldn't go on. It was an agonizing decision but we had to turn back. It took all of our energy to return and get clear of the swamp.

We collapsed on dry ground in waist-high grass and lay there panting.

"We'll have to go around it," I gasped.

Neil was several years younger than me and I'm sure he thought of me at the time as "old," but he was as tired as I was. It was starting to dawn on us both that this was not going to be as easy as it looked from the air. The age difference, along with being a more experienced jumper, seemed to put me in charge of this expedition with Neil's tacit approval. I realized that by assuming responsibility, it was going to be up to me to get us out of this situation, which was starting to become critical as the afternoon waned. I didn't even want to think of having to stay out here after dark.

"OK, let's go," I said after we had somewhat caught our breath. I wanted to get going and get the hell out of there.

We slowly clambered to our feet, gathered our gear, and I led the way to the left of the great swamp. I felt like Frank Buck, for Christ's sake! We took about 20 steps and came up against a wall of vines. We couldn't go any farther.

"Oh, great!" Neil exclaimed. "We're never going to get out of this!"

"Not to worry," I replied. "That's why I brought along the machete."

Neil stood back while I unsheathed the long blade and started swinging. I always kept the blade sharp, but 10 or 15 overhand swings with my full strength produced no noticeable results.

"Christ!" These vines are made of iron!" I muttered as I examined a big blister which had materialized on my hand.

The vines were up to one inch thick and strung from the tops of the surrounding tall pine trees. They hung in inverted arches from tree to tree at ground level to eight feet high, like a giant net blocking our way. There was no way to go under them, they weren't solid enough to climb over, we couldn't go around them, and I had just proven to myself that we couldn't go through them.

My personal fly had returned. Somehow I was sure he was the same one. Neil was starting to get depressed and despondent. It wasn't his fault. He just hadn't ever come up against anything this mindless and foreboding before. I saw that I was going to have to make all the decisions and keep us moving. Neil was a lot stronger than I was, but this was going to be a question of mental determination more than just physical power.

We retraced our steps to the swamp. This time I didn't hesitate but just waded in. I took about five steps and knew it was hopeless. We went back and collapsed in the grass again.

I told Neil that we were going to leave all our gear there and return for it after we cut through the vines. He looked at me as if I were crazy but didn't question my decision. I said that I'd start cutting first. He could rest up and then come and spell me.

It was an impossible task, but, by taking turns, we started to create a path through the indomitable vines. It took us over an hour of back-breaking work but we finally hacked our way through over 20 yards of vegetation.

We were cutting through the last few vines when I noticed that the light was failing. It couldn't be getting dark this early. It was only about 4 p.m. I should have known. It was summer in Florida, which meant a tropical storm swept through every afternoon like clockwork. The whole northern half of the sky was one huge blue-black cloud, and you could see with the naked eye the thunderhead billowing upward like a time-lapse animation, probably at 20- or 30,000 feet.

As we cut the last vine, the wind started to pick up. The air suddenly turned cold, which dried our sweat, and was a welcome relief from the oppressive heat. I knew what was next. A squall-line would be moving through at 30 to 40 miles per hour.

"Let's get our gear and get moving, *now!*" I said with urgency. Heavy rain would be following the wind.

As tired as we were from vine chopping, we ran back, donned our stuff and retraced our steps through the vines, now an easy pathway. I was sure that this was our last obstacle and now we would have a clear shot back to the DZ.

We were in chest-high grass when the first lightning bolt hit. Zzzzzz Ka-rack! It was so close that we heard the sizzle before the earth-shaking thunder-clap deafened us. The flash momentarily blinded us and the hair on our bodies stood up, electrified.

"Hit the ground!" I yelled, but Neil had beat me to it. There was no place to go for shelter. We knew that trees attracted lightning so we were better off staying where we were out in the open.

The Tampa Bay area is the lightning capital of the world. It must have something to do with the configuration of the Gulf of Mexico and the Florida coastline which funnels weather into Tampa Bay and generates the tremendous summer electrical storms.

I figured if we just stayed flat on the ground we wouldn't act as lightning rods. We were lying there hidden in a circle of trampled grass with our gear strewn around us when the rain hit. It started suddenly with huge single drops spaced far apart thundering down on us like tiny meteors, then it turned into a tropical downpour. The squall whipped the tall grass around us, flattening it this way and that with intermittent blasts of wind. Sheets of rain lashed us at impos-sible angles and were frozen in mid-air by strobes of lightning. The roar of the wind and the rain was punctuated by the deafening claps of thunder as lightning bolts hit all around us.

I had seen movies of shipwrecked people adrift in life rafts who held open mouths to catch rain drops from a passing storm. I thought at the time that the scriptwriter must have been really hard up for material. Give me a break. I mean, seriously, how many drops can a person catch in his mouth? But wait! Here I was with my open mouth to the sky trying to quench a raging thirst. Why hadn't I brought a canteen? Hell! For that matter, why hadn't I brought a six-pack of beer on ice!?

The rain slacked off to a drizzle. The squall had passed. Soon the sun would be out again and it would be just as hot as ever. I was trying to enjoy the coolness, but I couldn't help but think of the extra weight of our gear now that everything was all wet.

"Good Lord, Neil, look at this!" I shouted in amazement.

Our hot bodies soaked with cold rain were radiating an aura of white steam at least four feet high. It was the perfect shape of prone bodies extruded upward in a ghostly pale. We lay there and looked at each other, marveling at this weird spectacle. I had never seen anything like it before nor have I ever since. It looked unnervingly like our souls escaping from our bodies and gave us pause to consider if we actually were going to get out of this alive.

The rain had stopped and I knew we had to get moving. The afternoon was getting short. Now that we were past the swamp and the vines, I thought we could really make some distance, but no such luck. What looked like easy hiking through small, stunted trees turned out to be a nightmare.

As we pressed through the little cypress trees, they dumped their rainwater on us and each stubby branch grabbed at our gear and clothes. Our arms and faces were getting scratched, and it was a constant struggle to force our way along.

My personal fly was back. Good — I was worried that he had gotten hurt by the storm. We got into a rhythm of taking a short rest whenever either Neil or I fell down. Neil was starting to drag and I knew I had to fire up his lagging spirit. So, during one rest period, I told him the story of the "pit."

I had done a lot of caving when I was in college at Gainesville, I explained. We had a caving club and we took pride in pushing out from known cave systems into unexplored territory. Warren's Cave was well known by the college crowd as a beer party hangout and was a good training cave for novice spelunkers. But beyond, past the "squeeze," the cave branched out into a major maze of tunnels for miles. Our club had mapped and surveyed a large part of it, but there were still tunnels we knew about that remained blank on our charts.

A friend of mine told me that in one unmapped section, he had come across a pit in the middle of the tunnel floor. He said that he hadn't taken the time to explore it and he described how I could find it. It was several miles further into the cave than even I had gone, so I knew it was a major trip. I filed it away in my brain for future exploration. Being burned out with studying aerospace engineering, it was not long before I decided that I could wait no longer. I had to know what lay in the pit or where it led. The caver's eternal dream is to be the first to discover a whole new cavern. I couldn't even wait to organize an informal exploration party. I was going to do it alone.

"Wasn't that pretty stupid?" asked Neil, interrupting my story. "I thought caving was like scuba diving — dangerous to go alone."

"It was," I answered. "But stop and think — if I were smart, do you think I'd be out here with you right now?"

"You have a point," agreed Neil. "Go on with your story."

Well it was about 11 o'clock in the morning when I left my dormitory room on a day not unlike today. I left a note for my roommate telling him where I was going should I not return in a reasonable amount of time. He would be the only one who would know where I was if anything went wrong. I hoped he would find the note and hadn't gone home for the weekend or something.

I stopped off at the caving club's storeroom and borrowed a long coil of heavy rope which I would need to descend into the pit. I drove out east of Gainesville into the woods to the entrance of Warren's Cave and parked my car out of the way of any partiers that might arrive later. It was almost noon, and no one else was around.

I looped the coil of rope over my right shoulder like a bandolier and got out my caving gear. I checked my helmet light and slipped a fresh spare battery into a knapsack that held other emergency items, such as candles and matches. One thing you didn't want was to be without light several miles deep into the cave. I slipped the headlight battery on my belt and adjusted the hard hat on my head. I was set to go.

Warren's Cave was interesting because it seemed to come to an end about a hundred yards from the entrance. I walked down the ramplike entrance into the yawning mouth of the cave and turned on my headlight. The familiar musty odor of the cave greeted my nostrils like an old friend. I sat on the edge of the ledge and eased into the chimney. Wedging my back against one wall with my feet against the other, I worked my way down about 20 feet to the floor of the main cave. A quick stroll brought me to the end of the corridor and to an almost vertical climb up the rear wall, using natural and man-made handholds in the rock.

At the top of the fairly easy climb was a tunnel about six feet high, leading straight south. The walls were in such a perfect tubelike shape that it was natural to assume that it was formed by the action of an underground river in some prehistoric past. Then about 30 yards back the tunnel ended abruptly.

I always enjoyed guiding a group of new cavers to this point and let them try to figure out where to go next. They never did. Even when I pointed out the entrance to the "squeeze," they thought I was joking until I led the way.

It was quite a trick. This side of the squeeze curved slightly to the south. You entered on your left side so your body could bend at the waist to match the curve of the tunnel as you inched along. It was so tight a fit that you had to hold your helmet, with its attached light, out in front of you with your left hand. The second half of the squeeze curved the opposite way, but halfway between was a tiny chamber just large enough to turn from your left side to your right. The entire length of the squeeze couldn't have been more than 30 feet but it seemed like 300.

It was here that the mind games began. It suddenly dawned on you that, no matter how far you went, how tired you got, or what injuries you sustained, this squeeze was the only way out. If you allowed it to, the whole weight of several hundred feet of rock above you started to exert pressure. Also, somewhere in the back of the cave system there had to be another opening, because the wind always whistled through here and made you swear that there must be a raging storm topside. We always joked that if anyone ever broke a leg past the squeeze, we'd never be able to get them out; we'd have to set up food relays for them until they healed. It was a daunting thought for even the best caver.

Anyway, on this trip I whizzed through the squeeze without a thought. This was barely the start of my trip and I had no time to waste. The back part of this cave system was made up of small crawlways never high enough to stand up in, but at least they were dry, unlike most other Florida caves.

It was a long, tiring, and dirty trip, but following my map part way and my friend's directions the rest, I came upon the pit. It was quite unusual. It took up almost the whole floor of the cave and was about seven feet across, obviously too wide to chimney down with my back against one wall and my feet against the other. I flashed my light into it but I saw nothing but darkness. I was very tired and my mind was starting to play tricks on me. I kept seeing something move just outside my peripheral vision, but I knew it was just my imagination. After a short rest I tied off my rope on a nearby outcrop of rock and tossed the rope into the pit.

Everything up to now was fun and games. Now came the true test: Would I dare go into the pit alone? I'm being melodramatic. Of course I would; that's exactly what I had come all this way to do. I stood on the edge with my back to the pit and tested my rope. It seemed to be holding so I leaned backward into space and started to walk the wall downward. Unexpectedly, about 12 feet down the pit ended. I stood on the bottom and looked around. Nothing! It was simply a shallow empty pit. I had never seen anything like it. What a disappointment! There was nothing left to do but climb back out and start back.

Halfway back I was totally exhausted. I had lost track of time but I knew I had been in the cave for many hours. I was so tired I started taking a rest after crawling for a count of 50. I knew I was back in the charted region of the system, because I was crawling on top of the old survey line which ran along the floor of the tunnel. The survey line was marked every 10 yards with a white ribbon tied to it. As I looked up ahead my headlight picked up the next ribbon and it jumped as my foot kicked the line. My heart gave a leap and I stopped dead in my tracks.

"It's only the ribbon," I said out loud to myself, trying to calm down.

I continued crawling and the same thing happened again. The dark and the silence and the exhaustion were starting to get to me. I had to regain control and stop hallucinating. I was so thirsty, I would have killed for a drink of water. No telling what I'd have done for a beer.

Right then I came up with a plan that has helped me many times since. I convinced myself that waiting at the end of the cave was a beer. No, not just *a* beer ... a *cold* beer. Never mind that I knew logically there was no beer. That didn't matter. All that mattered was that I believed in that magical beer. This thought was going to be my goal, my motivation.

I resumed crawling with renewed vigor. The rest of the trip was agony, but I had no more hallucinations. When I pulled myself up over the edge of the chimney at the mouth of the cave, I couldn't believe I had made it. As I expected, there was no beer, but I knew I had just enough strength left to stand up and walk out of the cave to my car.

When I emerged out of the mouth of the cave I was surprised to find it was night.

God! How long have I been in there? I wondered.

I stumbled in a daze up the slope to the woods and into the middle of some college students having a party around a campfire. Apparently I must have scared them pretty badly, materializing out of the darkness like some apparition, caked from head to toe with dirt, my caving light spotlighting their startled faces. Later they said that they had been there since early afternoon, so they knew that no one had gone into the cave, and now it was something like 10 o'clock at night. I had been in the cave, crawling and climbing, for 10 hours!

And then it happened: an old friend of mine, Corky (whom I hadn't seen since high school and whom I've never seen since), happened to be in the group and recognized me. Without asking, he handed me ... a cold beer!

"End of story," I said. "Let's get moving."

"Wait a minute, wait a minute," Neil said as we stood up. "You aren't really expecting me to think that there will be a cold beer waiting for us, do you?" he asked incredulously.

"Yep," I said.

"You aren't forgetting that this is a dry county and that neither of us have any beer in our cars, are you?" he continued.

"Nope," I said over my shoulder as I forged on ahead. "It really doesn't matter that we both know that there isn't any beer within 30 miles. All we have to do is to believe it and we'll make it back before dark," I explained patiently.

"Well, all right — I'll try," he said unconvincingly.

We got through the scrubby trees and into more open country. It was a lot easier going now but it was getting late and still no end in sight. We didn't talk any more. We just kept plodding along. I was thinking about that cold beer that wasn't there. The light was starting to fade the same as my confidence when we saw a fenceline up ahead.

"Hot damn!" A fence meant a cow pasture, indicating civilization lay somewhere up ahead. We heard a shout. It was the girls. They had driven around and were waiting for us across the fence. We almost cried from relief, we were so happy to see them.

We stumbled up to the fence almost totally exhausted and greeted the girls with joy. As we handed our gear over the barbed wire, Neil gave me a very strange look, for in return, out of nowhere, Rose had handed each of us a cold beer.

Chapter Twenty-nine
THE MALTESE CROSS

I was packing my parachute when I first saw it. Sitting on the ground astride my pack, I stopped stowing my lines for a moment and watched the beautiful blue biplane do a lazy loop in the sky.

Boy, I thought, *what I'd give to make a jump out of that.* I knew it was an idle daydream and resumed my packing.

I had flown to "Topp of Tampa," with my friend Neil Mayer. Topp of Tampa was a small airport about 20 miles north of Tampa on Interstate 275. My friends Cliff and Patty Dobson, who owned "Skydive Tampa Bay", had recently moved their whole drop zone operation here. They had been operating out of a cow pasture just outside the tiny town of Riverview south of Tampa where I had made many jumps in the past. Now, having a paved runway and an actual club-house was definitely a move up, even though the drive was a lot further for me. Like many drop zones, this one now coexisted with a fixed base flight operation on a small but active airport.

Earlier, while we were still in flight halfway to the new drop zone, I had a brilliant idea. Neil was flying, with his girlfriend Cathy in the copilot seat. My wife Rose and I were in the back seat. I told Neil since we were already at altitude and I had my parachute rig in the back, that he ought to overfly the drop zone and let me jump. In the past, we had both jumped from planes with the door on. There was no reason not to do it now. Neil wanted to jump, too, but since neither Rose or Cathy were pilots, he thought they might have a hell of a time landing the plane. When we neared the drop zone, I got my rig out from behind the seat. Putting on a parachute while sitting in a seat was both awkward and unfamiliar. It didn't feel at all comfortable, almost as if I had put it on wrong. I told Cathy to move her seat as far forward as she could to give me room enough to get past her. When we arrived over the DZ, I tilted the back of her seat up against her, forced open the door, and squeezed out. As I got clear of the door and fell out, unexpectedly the door slammed on my foot. With a definite jerk, my foot came out of my sneaker, and, as I fell away from the plane upside down, I looked up at the shrinking plane and saw my shoe lodged in the bottom of the door. For a moment I was rattled, thinking I didn't have all of my equipment. Then, a little sheepishly, I realized that I really didn't need both shoes to land safely, especially jumping with a modern ram-air parachute. When I flew my parachute in to the drop zone unannounced for a stand up landing, I expected a rousing reception from my friends. Instead, everyone just watched curiously as I landed and began to repack my rig. I was a little put out by this lack of attention until one of my friends finally came over to talk to me and I realized what was going on.

"Okay," he said in feigned exasperation, "no one can figure out why you're jumping with only one shoe!" They thought I had come up with some new innovation to skydiving.

What was even funnier was to hear Rose's side of the story after the plane had landed. She was hard pressed to explain her emotions when she saw the bottom of my shoe stuck in the door and didn't know if I was still in it, dangling under the airplane.

I finished packing my chute and had just closed my pack when I saw the blue biplane again. I could see it was a big Stearman as it flew in, landed, and taxied up to the gas pumps. I assumed that unless the pilot stopped expressly for gas, which was unlikely, he must be based here, since there was not much else around except a few hangers. If he was, I knew it would be pointless to ask for a jump, because every jumper within a 20-mile radius must have already solicited him to the point of distraction.

Well, I thought, *even if I don't ask him for a ride, it can't hurt to just walk over and admire the aircraft.* To me, biplanes really epitomized the spirit and essence of aviation.

I felt a little self-conscious walking over in front of the whole drop zone to see the plane. I knew everyone would think I was going over to badger the pilot into a ride, and they probably already knew he'd turn me down if I did. Oh, well, I never gave much thought to what I thought other people thought I thought ... or something like that. I just wanted to see the biplane up close and dream a little.

I had just walked up to the front of the plane when the pilot, in an old-style leather flying hat, climbed out of the back cockpit and jumped down off the wing.

"Hey, Mike!" he cried. "How the hell are you? Do you remember me? Wayne Fuller — I jumped with you guys down in Englewood."

I couldn't believe my eyes. "My, gosh, Wayne, I haven't seen you in years! What are you doing here?"

"Well, when I got out of jumping a few years ago, I missed it so much, I decided to get into flying. Now I'm doing a little aerobatics in this thing," he said proudly, waving at his airplane.

I found out later that this was a gross understatement. Wayne had just become the national aerobatic champion in this style aircraft. He may have been considered new at flying but apparently he was very good.

"Uh, Wayne ... ," I started to say.

He laughed. "I know, you want to jump the biplane. Go get your rig and I'll take you up right now."

I couldn't believe it and probably neither could the rest of the jumpers on the drop zone. I hadn't been over there two seconds and I had talked the pilot into a jump out of the biplane.

How did he do that! they all must have been thinking.

Taking off sitting in the front cockpit, with Wayne flying from the rear, brought back old memories of my flights and jumps out of Dave Allyn's yellow N-3-N. Dave and I made a movie about his classic biplane with him flying while I filmed. When I wasn't shooting from a chase plane, I would mount my gun cameras on the wings and tail of Dave's biplane and run the power cables to off/ on switches in the front cockpit. When Dave got to an altitude for aerobatics, I would duck down into my cockpit to be out of the picture while Dave did loops and rolls. Now, flying in a biplane with Wayne was like reliving old times.

We got to jump altitude all too soon and I climbed out of my cockpit and onto the left wing. Wayne was going to do some more aerobatics after I left, so I remembered to lean back into my cockpit to rehook the seat belt and shoulder straps so they wouldn't flap around.

I strolled casually to the back edge of the wing to check my spot. I saw that I still had lots of time left, so I took a step back and leaned on the edge of Wayne's cockpit to talk to him for a moment, even though we had to shout over the engine noise. The biplane was cruising about half the speed of a normal jump plane and it really tickled me to be so lackadaisical about spotting my exit point.

When I judged we were somewhere over my spot, I said my good-byes to Wayne and walked off the back edge of the wing. It was really a refreshing change to walk off of a plane rather than jump, leap, or otherwise propel myself clear of the aircraft. When I landed in the target area, I was the envy of every jumper on the DZ. Naturally, I made the most of it.

"Biplane? ... Jump? ... Oh, that! It's nothing, just an old jumper friend of mine."

I bumped into Wayne a few times after that at the drop zone and we'd go out afterwards, have a few beers, and talk about old times. He said that if I ever needed a jump plane, he'd be glad to fly down from Topp of Tampa any time. It was not long before I took him up on his kind offer.

A popular Mexican restaurant in Sarasota called El Adobe was owned by a neat lady who was a unique character and known to everyone simply as "Mary." She was the mother of a jumper friend of mine and we had become good friends. Her son, Paul Seery, had moved from Sarasota some time ago, but I still hung out at the El Adobe bar occasionally. Everyone knew me there, so it was a friendly place to go if I wasn't doing anything else.

One evening, I stopped in for a drink and the manager came over to talk to me. We were casual friends, having known each other for many years. Mary wasn't there that evening, so he told me about a surprise birthday party he, along with all of the employees, was planning for her.

"Could you skydive in with her birthday card?" he asked.

"Sure, but not here!" There were just too many hazards and no safe places to land. "How about Island Park down by Marina Jack's?" I knew I could land there, even though it was a little spit of land surrounded by the bay. I had jumped there many times for the city's Fourth of July celebration.

We made all the arrangements, keeping them secret from Mary, of course, and Wayne Fuller agreed to fly me. I thought the biplane would add a nice twist to the exhibition jump.

The day finally arrived, and Rose left me at the airport to meet Wayne while she drove in to Island Park to act as the host to the little surprise gathering at the end of the park. They had lured Mary out there on some pretext or other, and when Wayne and I flew over in his beautiful blue biplane, Rose had no trouble drawing their attention to it. Rose carefully explained to Mary that the pilot had her birthday card and he was going to attempt to land there to deliver it. As unbelievable as that sounded, the biplane was circling and it began to seem almost plausible.

When I jumped, Rose exclaimed, "Oh, my gosh — the pilot's given up on landing the plane and has bailed out." It was pretty funny. For a moment there was a flurry of excitement until they realized that it was all a joke.

In the meantime, before I jumped, I was having a few problems. When I got out on the wing for jump run, I remembered that I hadn't refastened the seat belt. I leaned as far as I could into the front cockpit trying to reach the buckle, but lost my footing and slid headfirst down into the seat with my legs waving up in the air. Wayne must have gotten a good chuckle out of that. By the time I re- gained my position back out on the wing, we had overflown the spot by quite a distance. Instead of losing time by going around again and starting the jump run over, I gave Wayne a signal for a drastic 90-degree turn across the wind line. I said good-bye to Wayne and hurriedly ran off the back edge of the wing. I re- member flipping over in the air to take a photo of the biplane as I fell away and saw the silhouette of Wayne's face as he looked over the side to watch me. That was the last time I was to see Wayne. He died several months later in the small mid-Florida town of Arcadia doing what he loved best, performing aerobatics at an air show.

I landed right on target to present Mary with her birthday card marked "AIRMAIL, SPECIAL DELIVERY" and a bouquet of flowers only slightly crushed by being confined in my jumpsuit. She was thrilled and was really touched by the thoughtfulness of her employees.

Mary told me to stop off at El Adobe later on for a free drink. They would be having an ongoing birthday party there that night. Rose had to go to work teaching a dance class, so I was left alone out in the park. I packed up my rig and took everything back to my car. I was still keyed up from the jump, and, out of habit, I walked over to Marina Jack's for a customary after-jump drink. All of the employees there knew me because one of them, Kenny Rolfe, was a close friend of mine as well as a good jumper and a member of my exhibition skydiving team. When I walked into the lounge there and paused on the head of the stairs, I always felt like Norm on the TV sitcom show, "Cheers." But instead of everyone shouting, "Norm!" they shouted, "Mike!" All except Kenny, that is. He always called me "Mikey" in jest.

They had a good view of Island Park from the lounge but Kenny said that, being inside, he could only see the last part of my jump as I landed. He knew how hard it was to land on the tip end of Island Park. He had jumped with me several times when our team had landed there on the Fourth of July before a crowd of thousands.

I had no more than sat down at a table when Kenny delivered a drink to me. They all knew I always drank rum and Coke so I never had to order like an ordinary customer. I felt great! It was time to unwind, so I had two drinks in a row, back to back. Skydiving always made me thirsty.

It was still early afternoon and I had no other plans except Mary's party later on, so I ordered another drink. I began toying with my two empty glasses on their cocktail napkins while another drink was being brought to me. It was idle bar play, like piling up empty beer cans, except the efficient waiters kept trying to take them away.

The bar was almost empty and while I sipped my third drink, I randomly moved the other glasses on the table like chess pieces. When I finished my third drink and placed the glass in row with the first two, I could see a definite pattern. Starting with one napkin carefully aligned with one corner of the table, I placed all three glasses diagonally on an imaginary line from corner to corner with each of the napkins touching. Yes, I had a definite pattern going here. This gave me a new purpose for drinking. I saw that with only three or four more drinks, I could create a complete diagonal. It seemed like a worthy goal. I held up a hand. I needed a new drink.

When Kenny brought a fresh rum and Coke, he noticed what I was doing and asked, "What're you up to, Mikey? Can't I leave you alone for one minute without you getting into trouble?"

Without even thinking I announced proudly, "I'm going for a diagonal!" as if it were some well-known maneuver in sports. Kenny laughed and went on with his duties. As it got closer to five o'clock, the place began to fill up with more customers. I was beginning to slow down on my drinking. The diagonal thing was just a joke, but by now it was almost completed, so I thought I might as well go for it. One or two more drinks wouldn't hurt me.

Pretty soon I had empty glasses on their respective napkins lined up diagonally all the way across the table. It still wasn't time to go to Mary's, so I thought, *What the hell — I might as well have one more drink to pass the time.*

"Hmmm!" Now, it seemed that the only logical place to put that new empty glass was at the unoccupied corner nearest me, which started another diagonal. Oh, no! Now there was a long empty stretch across the table the other way.

Kenny came back to see how I was doing. "Now what are you up to?"

"I would think it was obvious!" I said. My words were starting to come out slurred but it gave me time to think of a snappy comeback. "I'm going for ... a 'Maltese Cross'!" Where I came up with the "Maltese Cross" expression, I have no idea, but it did have a nice ring to it. Just then, another one of the waiters passed by my table and off-handedly began to pick up a few of my empty glasses.

"What are you doing!" Kenny snapped at him in feigned anger. "Can't you see the man's going for a Maltese Cross?"

"Oh, gosh, I'm sorry!" the guy said with real concern, replacing the glasses. "I didn't realize!" and he hurried off on another errand. Kenny and I laughed.

"Geez! He ought to have known!" we agreed.

To my own disbelief, I actually did complete both diagonals to become the first and, I trust, the only one to complete the famous Maltese Cross in one sitting and still remain conscious. It became a legend at Marina Jack's, at least between Kenny and me.

A couple of days later I asked Kenny how I looked when I left. I was hoping I hadn't made a complete fool of myself like crawling up the stairs or something. He said I looked fine other than walking a little funny. We figured that I must have had at least 16 drinks within a period of about three hours.

But that was just the beginning of my evening.

I was so stewed, I ought to have gone straight home to bed. The problem was that "straight home" took me right past El Adobe. Even in my condition, I knew that the offer of a free drink is an obligation not to be lightly dismissed. I was well versed in the skydiver's code.

Boy, Mary wasn't kidding when she said there'd be an ongoing party! I thought. The place was jumping. I couldn't even find a place to park. I had to drive across the Tamiami Trail to park in Snelling Plaza's parking lot.

A few of the employees of El Adobe had taken their photos of my jump to a quick-print lab and had already gotten them back. In the bar, they were passing them around freely between employees and customers alike. When I walked in, albeit unsteadily, I was an instant celebrity. I couldn't have bought myself a drink even if I had wanted to. The rest of the evening became a blur of happy faces, congratulatory pats on the back, limitless free drinks, and friendly jokes. At one point, I seem to remember bumping into Greg Oliver, an old friend. He had to show me his brand new Corvette he had just bought that morning which was parked just outside. For some reason he wouldn't loan it to me right then so I could try it out. That just goes to show that you just can't figure some people out! He did buy me a drink in consolation, though.

After a few more free rum and Cokes, I judged that I had had enough to drink and disengaged myself. I carefully walked out of the bar to get into my car. One problem ... my car wasn't there. Well, I knew I had driven here. It had to be somewhere, so I walked slowly completely around El Adobe peering at each car in the dark. When I got back to where I had started and still no car, I thought,

"Oh, my God! My car has been stolen!" So I went back into the bar to have a drink to clear my mind and think it over. I was still trying to figure out what to do when I overheard a guy next to me exclaim, "Boy, this place is jammed! I had to park clear across the street!"

Right! The light bulb went on in my brain. I walked across the street and there my car was, right where I had parked it. Now everything would be OK. I could go home, fall into bed, and pass out!

Wrong! When I got home the house was dark and Rose wasn't there. Just as I was wondering where she could be, the phone rang. It was Rose. Her car had just conked out on the way home. It had no lights and she couldn't start it.

"You've got to come get me right now!" she pleaded. "I must have the flu — I feel as if I'm going to faint!"

She was only two miles down the street. What was I going to say, "Sorry, I can't help you at the moment, I'm drunk!"?

"Stay right there," I said. "I'm coming to get you right now." I don't know how, but I got back in the car and started off again.

Luckily, when the car had quit, she had been able to pull half off the road into a driveway. I didn't want to leave the car there overnight so I hooked up some jumper cables while Rose sat in the car, still not feeling well. I managed to get the engine started, but the lights still wouldn't work. On top of everything else, it started to rain.

"OK," I said to Rose. "You drive in front of me in my car since it has headlights and I'll follow as close behind you as I can. Just don't make any sudden stops!"

So we drove slowly home at night in the rain with Rose in the lead car about to faint and me following, drunk and driving with no headlights. It was a mean cop's dream in the making, had we been stopped on the road.

However, without further incident, I was finally able to get home and crawl into bed, which was certainly befitting the first recipient of "The Maltese Cross."

Chapter Thirty
WIDE ANGLE

C ould you put a camera inside your parachute and take a photo looking straight down?" It was John Cloud on the phone. He was an old friend from my high school days.

Did I know how to mount a camera inside a parachute? Boy, did I ever!

"Sure," I said. "No problem. When do you want to do it?"

I made it sound so easy he was a little taken aback. He must have thought that I didn't understand the problems.

"Maybe we ought to meet to talk it over," he replied.

John Cloud, in addition to being a businessman and a pilot, was also a camera buff. He and a local professional photographer, Dick Dickinson, had teamed up to experiment with an extreme wide-angle lens on a remotely controlled motorized Nikon. When we met, they showed me some great slides taken from the top of a sailboat mast, between the flashing lights of a speeding ambulance and a few other unusual camera angles that I had never thought possible.

John explained that the lens was a Nikkor 8mm, one of the best "fisheyes" ever made and worth maybe $2,000. It was on loan from Nikon through their professional services program. But the thing I wanted to see was the remote-control device they were using. It worked on an infrared light principle, and I was amazed at how small and compact both the transmitter and receiver were. *Oh, boy!* I thought. *No more power cables.*

They assumed that I'd have to pack the camera in the chute and they were a little worried about the safety of this very expensive camera system. Including the motorized Nikon body and the remote control, the value must have been $4,000 to $5,000. I assured them that we would not have to pack the camera in with the parachute in order to get the shot. I would only have to rig a pulley inside the parachute and run a line up through it before packing the chute. Then, once I had jumped from the plane and opened the parachute, I could take the camera out of my jumpsuit, hook it onto the end of the line, and hoist it up to take the pictures. This arrangement would also give me the advantage of being able to adjust the height of the camera from just over my head to all the way up inside the parachute.

There was one stipulation that John was adamant about. He wanted the parachute to be one of the old round "cheapo"s that had alternate orange and white panels. I knew what he meant. We used to call them a "candy-stripe." He thought the view from up inside one of these old chutes would be spectacular. Reluctantly, I agreed, and we made plans to meet at the drop zone that very weekend.

The old DZ at Englewood had been closed for many years and the Mission Valley Skydivers dispersed far and wide. A new pilot had arrived in town, Chuck Leonard, and he had started a drop zone east of Sarasota at a place called Ron-Con Ranch. There was a little grass airstrip on this remote property which was about three miles out on the worst dirt road in the county. The road was "washboard city" from start to end, and if you drove over five miles an hour, I guarantee the vibration would loosen the fillings in your teeth. This situation was terrible for a guy like me who liked to arrive at the DZ in a cloud of dust. But I had to admit, the location was a lot more convenient than Zephyrhills or even Englewood.

I had borrowed the required "candy-stripe" from Duffy, who always had a whole roomful of old skydiving gear. At the DZ, Dick and John watched as I rigged the line and pulley in the chute. Once packed up, I was ready to go.

I had been jumping a Para-Commander for many years now, so jumping an old "cheapo" again was going to renew a disagreeable experience, I was sure. Cheapos had practically no forward speed and they dropped out of the sky like a brick. But Dick and John wanted the "candy-stripe" photo, so I tried to act professional and keep my mouth shut.

Even though Chuck was new to the area, he and I had quickly become friends. He had watched me pack the unusual pulley and line system into my chute, and, despite my assurances to Dick and John, he knew the chance I was taking. Even when new and packed perfectly, these antique round chutes had a built-in malfunction rate of about one in 80. When you did anything of an experimental nature to them, they were like an old mule: they'd rather kick or bite you than work. I had acted confident on the ground, but I really had no idea if this thing would open or not, and, without saying anything, Chuck realized this too.

With John and Dick wishing me well (or maybe they were just wishing their camera equipment well), I got in the plane with a couple of student jumpers. After the students did "hop and pops" from 3,500 feet, Chuck flew me to a higher altitude of 7,000 feet. I didn't know it, but this was the beginning of a little ritual between Chuck and me. I would spot and then give the "cut" a little early so I would have time to tell Chuck thanks for the ride and shake his hand before getting out of the plane. For me it was a little comforting gesture. Chuck would be the last person I would see if anything went wrong, and it was nice to have a knowing and sympathetic friend at the controls.

When I got opening shock, it was worse than I had remembered it to be. God! How had we jumped with these old chutes every time? Once I regained my breath, I took out the camera and hooked it onto the line that I had tied off on one riser before packing. I purposefully had not tied the line to my harness so in case of a malfunction, I could cut away cleanly.

The pulley system and the remote control worked perfectly. I hoisted the camera up, took photos from various increments of height over my head, retrieved it, and stowed away the camera with altitude to spare.

Now, after opening at 6,000 feet and concentrating on taking pictures down to 1,500 feet, I looked around for a landing spot. Just as I expected, without paying attention to steering the chute, I was nowhere near the landing field. The drop zone was about a mile away. Instead, I was directly over a large orange grove. I didn't want to be over an orange grove. I like oranges as a fruit, but orange trees are a very hard, nonbending type of tree to land on. It would be very easy to impale oneself on an orange tree branch. I needed forward drive to get past the grove, and this chute didn't have it. I was very slowly approaching the edge of the grove but at the high rate of descent, I didn't think I was going to make it. At the last possible second a little extra wind came from nowhere and I landed with a tremendous thud just a few yards past the grove.

When I got back to the airstrip, John and Dick asked if I was going back up again to try for more pictures. I told them that I thought I had gotten the "candy-stripe" pictures all right but if it was OK with them I'd just as soon try it again the next week with my Para-Commander. No more cheapos, thank you very much. And no more jumping today; I just wanted to get home and ease my body into a hot bath.

By the next week, my body and my enthusiasm were back to normal, and I rigged my Para-Commander with the line and pulley. Dick and John couldn't make it this weekend, so I was on my own.

Chuck and I dropped out students again and enjoyed our flight to altitude. We didn't say much. It was a beautiful Florida summer day. It may have been a little hot on the ground but at altitude it was cool. There was a steady wind and it was a perfect day to jump. Chuck and I solemnly shook hands and out I went.

Everything went perfectly until I stowed the camera and looked around for the field. I saw nothing. There were no airfields, no roads, no homes, no farms, no cows — nothing but raw land. I felt like I was in "The Twilight Zone," for Christ's sake. Where'd everything go? I know we took off somewhere around here. How far could I have drifted?

I was getting very low now and I had to decide on a place to land. I saw a little square field that looked plowed and a small path leading out of it. That would be my landing point since it was the only clue I had as to how to walk out of there. I had a nice soft landing and soon had my chute field-packed for travel.

I put the chute on my back and bundled the camera gear in my jumpsuit for carrying. I was glad I had spotted that path from the air because on the ground it would have been impossible to know which way to go. The sun was directly overhead, so I had no way of telling compass headings. Even as I hiked along the path, I figured I was going the opposite direction from the drop zone, but there was no helping that. The path was the only game in town.

It was brutally hot. The farther I walked, the more frequently I had to stop to rest. At first, I worried about what I would tell a passing motorist if I ever reached a highway. I went over possible dialogues. He'd say, "Hi, where'ya headed?"

I'd say, "I don't know — where am I?"

He'd say, "See ya!" and drive off mumbling, "weirdo!"

Finally, I quit worrying about it because I gave up any hope of ever finding a road. I came to the conclusion that someone, years later, would come across my bleached bones out here and say, "Oh, this must be the remains of the famous 'missing skydiver' I've heard so much about."

It was beginning to feel like the "Great Swamp Jump." That thought made me think of a cold beer. I knew it was an impossibility, but it gave me new vigor and stamina to go on. I knew even if I ever found signs of human habitation, it would take hours to find a ride and drive around the sparse country roads to wherever the airfield was.

After what seemed like hours of hiking in the heat in the wrong direction, I came to a highway. And parked along the highway waiting for me, faithfully, was my wife, Rose. And in my wife's hand was a cold beer!

How had she known where to find me? Easy: Chuck had watched my landing from the plane and, once back on the ground, told Rose where I was bound to emerge. I hadn't been traveling in the wrong direction after all.

The story has an even happier ending. The photos from the Para-Commander turned out to be much better than those from the "candy-stripe." Dick and John were very pleased. We won first-place honors and a $500 cash prize in a local photo contest, the photo was used on a cover of *Parachutist*, the national skydiving magazine, and I sold it for a pictorial in *Outside*, a national sports magazine.

I happened to be traveling on a photo assignment at the time the *Outside* magazine appeared on the newsstands. As I switched planes in Atlanta, I happened to see it in one of the airport shops. It was really a wonderful feeling to realize, at that moment, my photography was on newsstands all over the country. I wanted to rush up to the teenage cashier and proudly exclaim, "Look! I took that picture!"

Chapter Thirty-one
NOT YET

E ven though I'm still enjoying life now, I miss those early days. Most of all, I miss my wild and crazy friends. I joke that all my old buddies are dead, drunk, in jail ... or all three! Maybe that's not entirely true, but those who are left are scattered far and wide, and I've come to realize that what we experienced will never happen again. It was an era that has passed.

I am still jumping, so I'm far from being old and decrepit, but I do have pain every day to remind me of my old skydiving injuries. I don't mind. I wouldn't trade a minute of my skydiving career for physical comfort. The aches and pains serve me as a reminder of what life is all about. It's about friendship; it's about adventure; it's about living every day as if it's your last. And if you do that, then memories are more important than pain.

But no one ought to dwell on the past. Those memories are there as a kind of cushion to get through the hard times and to build upon for the good times still to come.

This story doesn't end here. It may be the end of the book, but it's not the end of the adventure. It's like what the old-timer said when asked if he had lived here all his life. He thought about it a moment and then said slowly, "No ... not yet."

GLOSSARY

Accuracy. An event at a skydiving meet in which contestants attempt to land on a small target in the middle of a pea gravel pit. Before the introduction of ram air parachutes, contestants flew their round parachutes down wind for more accurate canopy control. Even with a target area filled with pea gravel to ease the landings, these high speed accuracy landings usually resulted in many injuries at almost every meet.

Altimeter. An instrument which indicates altitude. In aviation and skydiving, it is usually manually calibrated to show distance above ground level (AGL) as opposed to above sea level (ASL).

Altitude. In aviation, the distance above ground level. However, in general use, such as on maps, it usually indicates the distance above sea level.

Area Safety Officer (ASO). The person appointed by the United States Parachute Association (previously known as the Parachute Club of America) to oversee parachuting safety in a particular region of the United States.

Arri-S. A specific model of 16mm motion picture camera manufactured by Arriflex.

ASO. An abbreviation for "Area Safety Officer," an experienced skydiver appointed by USPA.

Backpack. The container on the back of a skydiving harness which holds the main parachute. This term was more common when reserve parachutes were separate and mounted on the front of the harness before the introduction of the single pack which holds both main and reserve parachutes.

Bag. A cloth or nylon container which holds a folded parachute prior to placing it into the backpack. Also see "sleeve."

Bag-lock. A particular type of high speed parachute malfunction caused when some problem won't allow the parachute to deploy from the bag.

Bail out. An aviation term meaning to make an emergency exit from an aircraft for any reason.

Bail out oxygen bottle. A metal cylinder containing pressurized oxygen small enough to be mounted on a parachute harness. Connected to a mask held in place across the front of a helmet, it is used to provide a few minutes of breathable oxygen to a skydiver or aviator who exits an aircraft above 15,000 feet.

Barrel roll. An aviation term meaning to rotate the aircraft 360 degrees along the axis of the direction of flight.

Base. A skydiving term meaning the group of jumpers which provides a small stable formation at the start of a freefall for the following jumpers to join and build upon. Out of a small aircraft the base might consist of only 2 or 3 jumpers. Using a larger aircraft the base might be as large as 10 to 12 jumpers.

Bends. A term used in SCUBA diving which describes the physiological sickness caused by rapid decompression underwater with the resulting release of nitrogen into the bloodstream. In aviation, the same symptoms result from rapid decompression at high altitudes.

Boiler maker. Also known as in the U.S. Navy as a "depth charge." An alcoholic drink consisting of dropping a shot glass of rum into a glass of draft beer.

Bounce. A skydiving euphemism for a skydiving fatality caused by a high velocity impact with the earth. Usually this type of accident would be caused by the skydiver not deploying either main or reserve parachute and impacting the ground at a speed of 120 mph or faster.

Boyle's law. A natural law discovered by Robert Boyle in 1691 which reveals the relationship between pressure, temperature, and volume when a gas is subjected to compression.

Break off. The act of disengaging from a

freefall formation. This is usually followed by each skydiver performing a 180 degree turn, flying away from the center of the formation, and opening their parachute at a safe distance from each other.

Break-off altitude. The designated altitude above ground at which all skydivers agree to disengage from a freefall formation whether completed or not. This allows enough remaining altitude for each skydiver to move away from each other to safely open their parachute.

Candy stripe. A slang expression for a particular type of round parachute which consisted of an alternating pattern of orange and white vertical panels.

Canopy. The nylon material which constitutes the hemisphere structure of the round parachute or the non-rigid airfoil of the ram air parachute. *Canopy* refers only to the nylon fabric of the parachute, not the lines, pack, or harness.

Canopy relative work (CRW). The specialized activity of parachutists when they intentionally maneuver their parachutes together, make contact, and create formations while descending toward the ground.

Capewell. A heavy duty metal device which allows a quick and easy way to detach a main parachute from the parachute harness. Devised and manufactured for U. S. military parachutes and still in use today, it has been replaced in sport parachuting by a smaller, lighter, cheaper, and simpler device called a "three ring circus" invented by skydiver, Bill Booth. It's major safety feature is the ability to detach (cut away) both risers at the same time using only one hand.

Cardinal Puff. A drinking game originating with World War I pilots. It involves an elaborate series of recitations along with hand movements while drinking a full glass of beer. This game was adopted by early skydivers.

Cheapo. Skydiving slang for the old style military surplus round parachute — so called because it could be purchased "cheap."

Chest strap. The strap on a parachute harness which fastens across the chest connecting the right and left sides of the harness in front.

Chute. Abbreviated form of the word "parachute." It can refer to the whole parachute assembly or only the canopy.

C-mount. A specific type of front plate of a motion picture camera which easily allows different focal length lenses to be exchanged.

Container. The pack which holds a parachute usually packed in a bag or sleeve.

CRW. An abbreviation for "canopy relative work," a specialized parachuting activity involving open parachute formations.

Cuban Air Ministry. The Cuban equivalent of the FAA in the United States.

Cut. To slow the airspeed of an aircraft by decreasing the engine throttle. This is usually done in a jump plane just before parachutists exit the aircraft.

Cut away. The act of detaching the main parachute usually because of a malfunction and before deploying the reserve parachute.

Cutaway. A parachute that has been cut away or detached in the air.

D link. A heavy duty metal connector link in the form of the letter "D."

D ring. In the "barn storming" days of parachuting, this was a slang term for the "ripcord." Later, this became the term for the connector links on the front of the parachute harness below the Capewells onto which the front mounted reserve parachute was attached.

Daisy-chain. A quick and easy way to temporarily stow parachute lines on the ground after a jump so they won't get tangled. One part of "field packing" a parachute so it can be more easily transported and packed later.

DC-3. A specific model of large two engine aircraft popular during World War II as a transport plane. Modified slightly for hauling cargo, it was also known as a C-47. This is a very safe and reliable aircraft and in the 1960s and 70s. it became a favorite skydive airplane for attempting large formations.

Dead Ants. A bar game played by

skydivers. When the words "dead ants" are called out, everyone must hit the floor with both arms and legs up in the air. The last one down has to buy everyone a round of beer.

Dead center. To land on the target disk exactly in the middle.

Decompression chamber. A special metal pressure chamber large enough to hold a number of people for the purpose of simulating high altitudes by pumping out air. These are very expensive to build and operate so they are usually used only for military purposes but are sometimes made available for civilian use.

Decompression sickness. The symptoms, effects, and illness associated with rapid decompression. Commonly called "the bends."

Demo. In skydiving, an abbreviation for "demonstration jump." Synonymous with "exhibition jump."

Deploy. The act of a initiating equipment to perform a certain sequence of events, usually automatically, from some kind of storage configuration into an immediately usable one. An example would be to *deploy* a life raft in high seas.

Depth-charge. A navy drink which consists of dropping a shot glass of rum into a glass of draft beer. Same as a "boiler maker."

Dew point. The exact temperature and pressure at which water vapor in air condenses into a liquid.

Double-L. A specific modification of a round parachute. Two panels were cut out of the back, each in the form of the letter "L." This was only one of many modifications which were used to give a round parachute a forward drive and steerability.

Drop zone (DZ). A military term for a designated area for a parachute drop. In skydiving, it means a permanent place for organized skydiving, usually at an airfield or an airport.

DZ. An abbreviation for "drop zone," a designated skydiving area.

Exhibition jump. A skydive for the en-

tertainment of spectators. Usually these events are someplace other than a drop zone and usually the skydivers are paid.

Exit point. The actual point over ground that skydivers exit the aircraft at the start of a skydive. In order for the skydivers to land on target, the exit point should be over the theoretical "spot" which is determined by the wind conditions. This was much more important before the advent of ram air parachutes since the round parachutes were much less maneuverable.

Eyesight. In terms of guns or cameras, any type of mechanical, optical, or electronic sighting device. See "Newton ring gunsight."

FAA. An abbreviation for the "Federal Aviation Administration," a federal governmental agency that oversees aviation activities.

Federal Aviation Administration (FAA). A department of the federal government which oversees all United States aviation activities.

Final approach. An aviation term which describes the last turn or maneuver of an aircraft before landing on the ground. It denotes the pilot's commitment to land at which point it would be difficult or impossible to abort. In parachuting, the meaning is the same except for the fact that without power, a parachutist has even less opportunity to correct a mistake.

Formation. A parachuting term describing a group of freefalling skydivers.

Freefall. The act of a skydiver falling and maneuvering through the air in the length of time between exiting an aircraft and opening a parachute. Normally a freefall is performed at speeds of between 100 to 200 mph and between altitudes of 15,000 to 2,000 feet.

Gear. Skydiver slang for a parachute and harness including the reserve parachute. Synonymous with "rig."

G-force. An aviation term for "gravity force." One gravity force is the normal pull that Earth's gravity exerts on any given mass. 2gs would be twice that. Anyone who rides on a roller coaster or even an elevator experiences g-forces. As aircraft fly faster and turn sharper, more and more g-forces are exerted on the human body. This is important in flying because high g-forces can cause a pilot to lose consciousness.

Go in. Skydiving slang for a skydiving fatality where no parachute is opened. Synonymous with "bounce."

Golden Knights. The official skydiving team for the United States Army.

Ground rush. The optical effect of the ground rushing up at a skydiver in freefall at an unusually low altitude.

Gun camera. A small 16mm motion picture camera developed during World War II for mounting in the wings of fighter planes to document the results of firing the plane's machine guns. The camera was activated by the plane's machine gun trigger and remained running for a few seconds after the trigger was released. They featured 50 foot or 100 foot film magazines which could easily be removed and replaced by any aviation mechanic unskilled in photography. They were manufactured by Bell & Howell and Fairchild and were designated either N-6 or N-9.

Hand deploy (pilot chute). A new method of deploying a main parachute's pilot chute which begins the parachute's opening sequence. A pilot chute with no metal spring is secured in a small pouch and is connected by a nylon strap to the parachute's bag inside the backpack. This strap is also connected to a metal pin which holds the backpack closed. When the pilot chute is pulled out and thrown by hand by a freefalling skydiver, it pulls the pin, opens the backpack, and deploys the parachute. This replaced the military hardware of a metal ripcord routed through a metal tube to the backpack which, when opened, released the pilot chute activated by a metal spring.

Hand deploy (reserve) A method of deploying a reserve parachute by hand as opposed to the normal deployment via a spring activated pilot chute. This method might be used during a low speed malfunction especially if the reserve was not equipped with a pilot chute.

Hang glider. A generic term for a variety of small, rigid wing, non-powered gliding devices usually steered and flown by the pilot's shifting weight. These are usually launched by foot from a mountain, hill, or cliff.

Harness. A piece of equipment made out of heavy duty nylon webbing to be worn by a person to which something else is attached. In skydiving, both main and reserve parachutes are connected to the harness.

Helmet mount. The design and method of mounting a movie or still camera to a skydiving helmet for the purpose of taking photos in freefall.

Hookup. The act of a freefalling skydiver catching up to other jumpers in a formation and joining them. This usually consists of flying into a slot between two jumpers, taking hold of their wrists, and breaking their grasp, thereby inserting oneself into the formation without losing the continuity of grips between skydivers.

Hop & pop. A slang description of a parachute jump from an aircraft whereupon the jumper opens the parachute immediately after exiting the aircraft with little or no freefall time. This is usually, but not always, performed at a normal opening altitude of between 2,000 to 3,000 feet.

Hyperventilation. The act of over-breathing due to a feeling of a lack of oxygen. This is to be avoided since it can cause dizziness and loss of consciousness even when adequate oxygen is available.

Hypoxia. The physical sickness due to a lack of oxygen. Initial symptoms are blue lips and blue finger nails. If this condition is not corrected, it could lead to unconsciousness and death.

Immelmann. An aviation term for a specific aerial maneuver named after famed World War I German Ace, Max Immelmann. The combat maneuver is a climbing half loop combined with a half roll which results in a reversed direction at a higher altitude.

Jump (noun). A skydive.

Jump (verb). To skydive from an airplane.
Jump run. The final straight flight of a jump aircraft — usually directly up wind over the target — in the final few minutes before the jumpers exit the plane.
Jumper. A person who jumps from a height using a parachute to reach the ground safely. Synonymous with "skydiver" or "parachutist."
Jumpmaster. An experienced (and usually licensed) skydiving instructor in charge of putting a student out of the aircraft on a static line. Even if a static line is not used, the jumpmaster is in charge of lining up the aircraft on jump run and seeing that the student exits the plane at the proper distance and altitude to land safely on the drop zone near the target.
Jumpsuit. A specially designed one piece coverall to be worn over and protect regular clothes from the wear and tear of skydiving activities.
Leg straps. The straps on a parachute harness which connect around each leg of a parachutist and take a large percentage of the opening shock during deployment.
Line. One of many nylon cords which connect the parachute canopy to the skydiver's harness. Synonymous with "shroud line" or "suspension line."
Load. A skydiving term for the group of skydivers which fill a jump aircraft. A Cessna load would be only 3 or 4 jumpers while a load for a larger aircraft such as a DC-3 might be 50 or more skydivers.
Loop. An aviation term meaning a full 360 degree rotation in pitch.
Lower lateral band. The heavy webbing sewn around the bottom of a round parachute which gave the canopy its structural integrity to hold its shape under high stress loads.
Mae West. A type of parachute malfunction. The term applied specifically to a round parachute with a line accidentally over the top causing the canopy to be bra shaped. Jokingly named after Mae West, a movie star of the 1930s known for her voluptuous figure.

Main (parachute). A parachutist's primary parachute used on every jump as opposed to the reserve parachute which is used only in an emergency.
Malfunction. A parachute which has not opened properly creating an emergency situation for the skydiver.
Manifest. A military term for a list. In skydiving, it is a sequential list of plane loads of skydivers made in advance on a first come, first serve basis.
MiG fighter. A Russian manufactured military jet aircraft first used in the Korean War.
MK-13 marine signal flare. A commercially available distress signal flare used primarily by boaters. It has both smoke for day, and a flare for night emergency signaling.
N3N-3 (biplane). An antique biplane originally used by the United States Navy as a training aircraft during World War II. It was designed in 1934 and built on contract for the Navy in 1938 by the Philadelphia Streetcar Company.
Newton ring gunsight. A special optical gunsight used in World War II. It utilized principals first developed by Robert Hooke and Sir Isaac Newton in the 1600s. They discovered that a curved piece of glass in contact with flat piece produces an optical interference pattern of dark rings. Because of their light weight, simple function, and low cost, war surplus Newton ring gunsights became a favorite helmet camera sighting device for early freefall photographers.
Nikon. The Japanese manufacturer of a line of 35 mm still cameras and lenses.
Nikon. A high quality 35mm still camera with interchangeable lenses manufactured by Nikon.
Nikonos. An underwater 35mm still camera manufactured by Nikon.
One hundred eighty degrees (180). To turn half way around, as in, "I did a 180 and tracked away from the formation."
Open. The deployment of a parachute, as in: "I opened at 1200 feet."
Opening altitude. The height at which a

skydiver deploys a parachute or plans to deploy a parachute.

Opening shock. The g-forces experienced by a skydiver as a parachute deploys.

Pack. (noun) A general term for a skydiver's parachute in it's container ready to jump. See "Back pack.," "rig," and "gear."

Pack. (verb) The act of properly folding a parachute for use in skydiving.

Packing area. The area on a drop zone designated for packing parachutes. It may only be a grassy area or it might consist of a packing shed with packing tables.

Parachute. Any number of designs and devices which allow a person to jump from an aircraft and safely land on the ground. These devices are usually made of nylon, pack up small enough to be worn on the back, and have common design features such as suspension lines, a harness, a pilot chute, and a backpack.

Parachute Club of America (PCA). A national organization of skydivers which later became the United States Parachute Association (USPA).

Parachute landing fall (PLF). A method of landing taught to paratroopers and early skydivers which enabled the parachutist to change the momentum of landing from vertical to horizontal and spread the impact forces over various parts of the body.

Parachutist. A person who jumps from a height using a parachute to reach the ground safely. Synonymous with "jumper" and "skydiver."

Parachutist (magazine). The official publication of the United States Parachute Association (USPA).

Para-Commander (PC). A specific type of sport parachute which evolved from the early round parachute. It's unique multitude of drive slots, pulled down apex, and side stabilization panels gave it a unique appearance and a forward speed of about 12 mph. At one time, it was the only type of parachute used by most advanced jumpers. Its demise was caused by the development of the ram air parachute which had much more advanced flight characteristics.

Paratrooper. A military term for a soldier who is trained to parachute from an aircraft into a combat zone. Traditionally, this has been done with the use of static line deployment of round, unsteerable parachutes from large transport planes.

PC. An abbreviation for "Para-Commander," a specific type of round parachute.

PCA. An abbreviation for the "Parachute Club of America," a forerunner of the "United States Parachute Association."

Pea gravel pit. A pit dug in the target area and filled with pea gravel with the specific purpose of cushioning the fall of a parachutist making a competition landing.

Peas. Skydiving slang for "pea gravel" or the "pea gravel pit" target area.

Pilot chute. The small parachute deployed by hand or spring which pulls a parachute out of it's pack and stretches it out in a deployment sequence.

PLF. An abbreviation for "parachute landing fall," a method of absorbing extremely high impact forces while landing under a parachute.

Power curve. An aviation term which refers to a diagram detailing the flight characteristics of lift verses engine power.

Prop wash. The air turbulence caused by a propeller.

Pull. An abbreviation for pulling a ripcord or pulling a throw out pilot chute. Meaning: To open or deploy a parachute. Synonymous with "open."

R & R. A military abbreviation for "rest and recreation."

Ram air parachute. A generic term for a type of parachute. Also referred to as a non-rigid airfoil. This type of parachute holds its airfoil shape by means of air forced into the front vents by the forward motion of the parachute. This is the type of parachute used by virtually all modern sport parachutists as well as military special forces combat teams.

Rapid decompression. The effect of losing compression rapidly. This could be caused by a SCUBA diver surfacing too quickly or a pressurized aircraft losing a window at a high altitude. The physical effects are the same — nitrogen dissolved in the blood stream bubbles out and collects mainly in the joints causing varying degrees of pain and distress. This can result in permanent disability or death if not treated immediately.

Relative work (RW). A skydiving term depicting a group of two or more skydivers attempting to make a formation in freefall. The term originates from the fact that although every skydiver is falling at vertical speeds of over 120 mph, they only have to work with the fairly slow horizontal speeds relative to each other of 10 to 20 mph.

Reserve (parachute). The second or emergency parachute which all parachutists must wear by law for obvious safety reasons. In the United States, this reserve parachute must be repacked every 120 days by a licensed rigger.

Rig. Skydiver slang for a parachute and harness including the reserve parachute. Synonymous with "gear" or "pack."

Rigger. A person, usually licensed, who inspects, repairs, and packs parachutes.

Ripcord. A metal device consisting of a handle and a thin cable ending in a pin which is used to release the closure of a parachute container. Usually, the handle of a ripcord is mounted on the front of a parachute harness and routed through a metal housing to the backpack. On modern parachutes a ripcord is used only for the reserve parachute while the main parachute is activated by a "throw out pilot chute."

Ripstop nylon. A type of nylon woven in a pattern which discourages long rips in the material. This material is used for most parachutes to prevent catastrophic structural failure in the event of an accident causing a tear in the fabric.

Risers. The heavy duty nylon webbing material used to connect the parachute suspension lines with the parachute harness.

Round (parachute). A generic term denoting all types of single surface hemispheric parachutes. Historically, these were the first

parachutes developed.

RW. An abbreviation for "relative work," a term for skydiving formation activity in freefall.

Saddle. The bottom of the old style military parachute harness where the leg straps connected. A parachutist could slide his butt back and actually sit in the saddle rather than hang from his leg straps.

SCUBA. An abbreviation for "self contained underwater breathing apparatus," a device which allows a person to breath air from a tank while swimming under water.

Shroud line. One of many nylon cords which connect the parachute canopy to the skydiver's harness. Synonymous with "line" or "suspension line." This is now an antiquated term referring back to a time when a canopy was called a "shroud."

Skirt. The bottom edge of a round parachute where the suspension lines attach.

Skydive. The act of a person jumping from a height and using a parachute to reach the ground safely. Specifically, the act of freefalling for a distance after leaving an aircraft before opening a parachute. Synonymous with "jump."

Skydiver. A person who jumps from a height using a parachute to reach the ground safely. Specifically, a parachutist who freefalls for a distance after leaving an aircraft before opening a parachute. Synonymous with "jumper" or "parachutist."

Sled (parachute). A specific type of early ram air parachute. One of the first commercially available ram air parachutes based on an original design developed by inventor Dominique Jalbert.

Sleeve. A cloth cover slipped over a folded parachute before it is packed into a backpack. Sleeves were used mostly for round canopies before the advent of ram air parachutes although some Para-Commanders were packed in bags before this. A flap at the mouth of the sleeve held the S-folded stows of suspension lines in loops of rubber bands. The last two stows held the flap closed which insured that all the lines deployed properly before the parachute could come out of the sleeve and open.

Slip stream. The rush of air around an aircraft caused by the propeller and the forward motion of the plane through the air.

Slot. A specific location between two freefalling skydivers into which a third skydiver can enter and make contact within a formation.

Smoke grenade. A signal device producing a thick volume of smoke of various colors usually manufactured for military use. The military M-18 is one widely used for skydiving which, like a hand grenade, utilizes an arming pin, an activation handle, and an explosive timing fuse.

Spot (noun). The imaginary point on the ground over which a skydiver exiting an aircraft may expect to land safely in a designated target area depending on current wind direction and speed.

Spot. (verb). The act of determining the proper exit point for a skydiver to exit an aircraft in order to land safely in a designated area depending on wind speed and direction.

Square (parachute). Skydiving slang for a ram air parachute. Actually, this is a misnomer since ram air parachutes are more rectangular than square.

Stable. This term refers to an arched freefall position which gives the skydiver control over his movements.

Stall. In aviation, the point at which an airfoil in flight ceases to produce lift. Although usually applied to aircraft, this term also pertains to a ram air parachute since it is, in fact, a non-rigid airfoil which exhibits all the flight characteristics of a wing.

Star. A skydiving term for a round formation made up of any number of freefalling skydivers.

Static line. A length of heavy nylon webbing ending in a metal snap which, when attached to the jump plane, opens a student parachute automatically.

Steering line. One of two lines attached to the rear of a parachute which control the chute's ability to turn right or left as well as to increase or decrease its forward speed.

Steering slot. In a round parachute, the hole cut in the rear of the canopy to provide forward drive and steering ability.

Step. A small platform attached on the wheel strut which provides a place for skydivers to step or stand during their exit.

Stow. In skydiving, it is a parachute packing term meaning to contain something. An example would be to stow suspension lines in a rubber band loop or to stow the canopy in its deployment bag.

Streamer. An abbreviation for "wind streamer." Synonymous with "wind drift indicator (WDI).

Streamer (parachute). Skydiving slang to describe a parachute which has been deployed and is out of its sleeve or bag but for some reason has not opened. This would constitute a dangerous high speed malfunction.

Strut. The post on a small aircraft running diagonally from the bottom of the fuselage to the bottom of the wing which adds structural support to the wing.

Suit up. A generic sport term meaning to put on clothing or equipment in preparation for engaging in a particular sport. In skydiving, it means to put on a parachute and any other gear which may or may not include a helmet, goggles, gloves, and a jumpsuit just prior to boarding the jump plane.

Surplus. An abbreviation for "military surplus." A general term originating after World War II when a vast array of military surplus equipment was available on the civilian market including everything from smoke grenades to airplanes.

Suspension line. One of many nylon lines running from the bottom of a canopy to the top of the risers which connects the parachute to the harness. Synonymous with "line" and "shroud line."

Taxi. An aviation term meaning to move an aircraft along the ground under its own power but without lifting off the ground.

T-Bow. An abbreviation for "Thunder-Bow," a triangular style of parachute.

Terminal velocity. The point at which an

object falling through a fluid (such as air) stops accelerating and reaches a constant speed. The terminal velocity for any particular object is a relation between its mass and the cross section it presents to the fluid in the direction of travel. For a typical skydiver in a flat and stable, face-to-earth position, this velocity is approximately 120 mph.

Throw out pilot chute. A foldable pilot chute with no metal spring which is used on most modern parachutes in place of a rip cord assembly. The function of a pilot chute is to open the back pack container and pull out the parachute for deployment. See "pilot chute."

Thunder Bow (T-Bow). A specific type of early triangular parachute developed at the same time as the Para-Commander. It was never very popular because of its irregular deployments and hard landings. Its flight characteristics were never that much better than a Para-Commander's to compensate for its shortcomings.

Toggle. The wooden handle at the end of a steering line of a round parachute. These were replaced in modern ram air parachutes with soft nylon loops.

Track. A skydiving term for a head down, arms back position which enables a freefalling skydiver to move horizontally across the ground at approximately a 45 degree angle. This maneuver is used by jumpers to move away from each other in a big formation at the end of a freefall.

Trim. An aviation term for balancing the aircraft along the nose to tail axis. Most aircraft have a manually adjustable wheel in the cockpit which the pilot can use to accomplish this minor task.

Twill (parachute). A particular type of parachute material used for many of the early reserves. If a rip developed, this material had a tendency to continue to rip causing catastrophic structural failure. It was consequently replaced by parachute manufactures with a special nylon weave called "rip-stop" for obvious reasons.

Unit (parachute). A brand name of a ram air parachute.

USPA. Abbreviation for "United States Parachute Association" a national skydiving organization.

Wave off. The action of a freefalling skydiver before opening a parachute. By waving both arms across each other, a skydiver can alert other jumpers that he is about to pull. This is usually done only if the skydiver has lost track of other jumper's at opening altitude.

WDI. An abbreviation for "wind drift indicator," a simple device for determining wind speed and direction for a skydive.

Wind chill factor. The additional degrees of temperature subtracted from the absolute temperature on a cold day to account for a person's extra loss of heat due to wind conditions.

Wind drift indicator (WDI). A long length of yard-wide yellow crepe paper weighted at one end. When thrown from an airplane over the target at a normal opening altitude, its landing position on the ground determined the proper exit spot up wind of the target for skydivers jumping from an airplane. Synonymous with "wind streamer."

Wind streamer. Same as "wind drift indicator" or "WDI."